Roman Law before the Twelve Tables

Roman Law before the Twelve Tables

An Interdisciplinary Approach

Edited by Sinclair W Bell and
Paul J du Plessis

EDINBURGH
University Press

Edinburgh University Press is one of the leading university presses in the UK. We publish academic books and journals in our selected subject areas across the humanities and social sciences, combining cutting-edge scholarship with high editorial and production values to produce academic works of lasting importance. For more information visit our website: edinburghuniversitypress.com

© editorial matter and organisation Sinclair W Bell and Paul J du Plessis, 2020, 2021
© the chapters their several authors, 2020, 2021

Edinburgh University Press Ltd
The Tun – Holyrood Road
12 (2f) Jackson's Entry
Edinburgh EH8 8PJ

First published in hardback by Edinburgh University Press 2020

Typeset in 10/12 Goudy Old Style by
IDSUK (DataConnection) Ltd

A CIP record for this book is available from the British Library

ISBN 978 1 4744 4396 8 (hardback)
ISBN 978 1 4744 4397 5 (paperback)
ISBN 978 1 4744 4398 2 (webready PDF)
ISBN 978 1 4744 4399 9 (epub)

The right of the contributors to be identifiedasauthorsofthisworkhasbeenassertedin accordance with the Copyright, Designs and Patents Act 1988 and the Copyright and Related Rights Regulations 2003 (SI No. 2498).

Contents

The Contributors — vii

Introduction: The Dawn of Roman Law — 1
Paul J du Plessis and Sinclair W Bell

Part I The Materiality of Roman Law: New Archaeological Discoveries

1. Roman Law in its Italic Context — 9
   James Clackson

2. Central Italian Elite Groups as Aristocratic Houses in the Ninth to Sixth Centuries BCE — 25
   Matthew C Naglak and Nicola Terrenato

3. Authority and Display in Sixth-Century Etruria: The Vicchio Stele — 41
   P Gregory Warden and Adriano Maggiani

Part II Constructing Early Roman Law: Sources and Methods

4. The Twelve Tables and the *leges regiae*: A Problem of Validity — 57
   Carlos Felipe Amunátegui Perelló

5. The *leges regiae* in Livy: Narratological and Stylistic Strategies — 77
   Marco Rocco

6. The *leges regiae* through Tradition, Historicity and Invention: A Comparison of Historico-literary and Jurisprudential Sources — 97
   Rossella Laurendi

7. The Laws of the Kings – A View from a Distance — 111
   Christopher Smith

8. Beyond the *Pomerium*: Expansion and Legislative Authority in Archaic Rome — 133
   Jeremy Armstrong

Part III Roman Law in Historiography and Theory

9. Niebuhr and Bachofen: New Forms of Evidence on Roman History   155
   Luigi Capogrossi Colognesi

10. Finding Melanesia in Ancient Rome: Mauss' Anthropology of *nexum*   171
    Alain Pottage

Index   199

The Contributors

Jeremy Armstrong is a Senior Lecturer in Ancient History at the University of Auckland, New Zealand. He received his BA from the University of New Mexico and his MLitt and PhD from the University of St Andrews. He works primarily on early Roman warfare and is the author of *War and Society in Early Rome: From Warlords to Generals* (2016), as well as editing several volumes on related topics.

Sinclair W Bell is Full Professor of Art History at Northern Illinois University. His research focuses on Etruscan and Roman art and archaeology.

Luigi Capogrossi Colognesi has been Professor of Roman Law from 1980 to 2010 at the University of Rome La Sapienza, where he is now Professor emeritus. His research focuses on the history of Roman property and agrarian history and historiography. His recent books include *Law and Power in the Making of the Roman Commonwealth* (2014) and *La costruzione del diritto privato romano* (2016).

James Clackson is Professor of Comparative Philology at the University of Cambridge and a Fellow and Director of Studies in Classics at Jesus College, Cambridge. He has published widely on the history of the Greek and Latin language and the comparative philology of Indo-European languages.

Paul J du Plessis is Professor of Roman Law at the University of Edinburgh. His research focuses predominantly on the multifaceted and complex set of relationships between law and society in a historical context.

Rossella Laurendi holds a PhD in Roman Law from the Mediterranea University of Reggio Calabria. She is currently Senior Assistant Professor in the Department of Law at the University of Genoa, where she teaches courses in the institutions of Roman law (A–E) and history of Roman law.

Adriano Maggiani is an archaeologist and Etruscologist. He is Professor of Classical Archaeology at the Ca' Foscari University of Venice. His research is concerned with funerary architecture and sculpture, Etruscan religion and epigraphy, and aspects of the art and culture of pre-Roman Ligurians and Venetians.

Matthew C Naglak is a PhD candidate in the Interdepartmental Program in Classical Art and Archaeology at the University of Michigan. His research focuses broadly on the development and use of public space in central Italy from the beginnings of the urbanisation process through the later Republican Period, with particular emphasis on its impact on the physical and social environment.

Carlos Felipe Amunátegui Perelló is a Chilean researcher in Legal History and Comparative law. He is chair professor of Roman law and Legal Theory of the Faculty of Law of the Pontificia Universidad Católica de Chile. He has written six books and more than one hundred articles in scientific journals and book chapters in subjects ranging from Archaic Roman law, Comparative law, Legal Theory and Artificial Intelligence.

Alain Pottage is Professor of Law at the London School of Economics. His work draws on perspectives in history, anthropology, and social theory to explore questions of property and ownership.

Marco Rocco teaches Ancient History at the University of Padua. He has focused his research on political and military institutions and cultures in ancient Rome, in particular the Livian tradition. He has written monographs and essays on the Roman army and the profession of the soldier in the imperial age.

Christopher Smith is Professor of Ancient History at the University of St Andrews and was Director of the British School at Rome from 2009 to 2017. He works predominantly on archaic Rome and Italy. Previous publications include *Early Rome and Latium c.1000 to 500 BC: Economy and Society* (1996) and *The Roman Gens: From Ancient Ideology to Modern Anthropology* (2006).

Nicola Terrenato is the Esther B Van Deman Collegiate Professor of Roman Studies at the University of Michigan. He studied at Rome and Pisa. He specialises in first millennium BCE Italy, in particular early Rome, northern Etruria, and the Roman conquest. He directs the Gabii Project and the Sant'Omobono Project. Other interests include theories of imperialism, field survey, and the history of archaeology. He recently published *Early Roman Expansion* (2019).

P Gregory Warden is President of Franklin University Switzerland, where he is also Professor of Archaeology. He is the Executive Editor of *Etruscan Studies*, a trustee of the Etruscan Foundation, Consulting Scholar at the University of Pennsylvania Museum of Archaeology, and an elected member of the Istituto di Studi Etruschi e Italici. He is the founder and Principal Investigator of the Mugello Valley Archaeological Project.

Introduction

The Dawn of Roman Law

Paul J du Plessis and Sinclair W Bell

1. INTRODUCTION

When the compilers of Justinian's Digest in the sixth century CE reflected on the origins of Roman law as a legal order, they decided that the topic was of such importance that it had to be placed at the very front of the Digest, in book 1 title 2, directly after the introductory title in which central concepts such as 'justice' and 'law' were explained.[1] In compiling this title, they relied on the works of two Roman jurists. The first, the enigmatic Gaius, a jurist of the mid-second century CE who, in a book (now lost) on the Twelve Tables (*lex Duodecim Tabularum*), wrote: 'Since I am aiming to give an interpretation of the ancient laws, I have concluded that I must trace the law of the Roman people from the very beginning of their city. This is not because I like making excessively wordy commentaries, but because I can see that in every subject a perfect job is one whose parts hang together properly.'[2] While there is no doubt some Greek philosophy latent in this statement, it is not the main focus of our discussion here. For us, as for Gaius, it is important to stress that origins matter. No subject can be understood properly without a fundamental appreciation of its history. This fundamental principle is one the Romans understood only too well and, in this time of 'presentism', has become more important than ever.

But the compilers did not rely solely on Gaius' book on the Twelve Tables. We do not know why. Instead, they chose to populate the rest of the title with a long passage from Pomponius' *Enchiridion* (Manual). Much has been written about this account of the history of Roman law, written by a Roman jurist who lived during the reign of Marcus Aurelius.[3] As the only comprehensive narrative concerning the development of Roman law, it has become a cornerstone for subsequent understanding of the nature and contours of the Roman legal order. And although not unproblematic, given the absence of corroborating evidence, it has left an enduring imprint – it is, for example, central to Edward Gibbon's account of Roman law in his seminal *Decline and Fall*.[4]

---

[1] The rubric given to D.1.2 is – *De origine iuris et omnium magistratuum et successione prudentium*.
[2] D. 1, 2, 1, Gai. 1 ad l. XII tab . . . *Facturus legum vetustarum interpretationem necessario prius ab urbis initiis repetendum existimavi, non quia velim verbosos commentarios facere, sed quod in omnibus rebus animadverto id perfectum esse, quod ex omnibus suis partibus constaret: et certe cuiusque rei potissima pars principium est* . . . Translation taken from Watson et al. 1985.
[3] For a very good recent account, see the PhD thesis of Wibier 2014.
[4] Gibbon 1776, chapter 44.

For our purposes, two aspects of this narrative are important. The first is that Pomponius wrote in a narrative style. Much like the Annalists, although not quite in the year-by-year style of Livy or Tacitus, Pomponius' account is one of continuity from the earliest period of Roman history to the end of the Classical Period (roughly the end of the third century CE). The narrative ends here, no doubt deliberately, and gives no account of the three intervening centuries until the start of Justinian's project. Since one of his aims was to restore the glory of Rome, it stands to reason that he chose to focus on the heyday of the Roman Empire rather than its decline. That this style of historical writing gained significant popularity in the eighteenth century under the influence of the Scottish Enlightenment is an interesting related matter, but one which is best left for another book.[5]

The second aspect of this narrative is Pomponius' treatment of the earliest period of Roman legal development. He phrases it thus: '. . . At the outset of our *civitas*, the citizen body decided to conduct its affairs without fixed statute law or determinate legal rights; everything was governed by the kings under their own hand.'[6] After a brief discussion of the so-called 'Royal laws' (*leges regiae*), Pomponius continues: 'Then, when the kings were thrown out under a Tribunician enactment, these statutes fell too, and for a second time, the Roman people set about working with vague ideas of right and with customs of a sort rather than with legislation, and they put up with that for nearly twenty years.'[7] This then leads on to the discussion concerning the enactment of Rome's first popular statute, the Twelve Tables, in c. 450 BCE.

This account of Pomponius has framed much of what modern scholarship accepts as the state of Roman law prior to the enactment of the Twelve Tables. First, the legal order was mainly custom, and secondly, while there may have been Royal 'laws' of a certain type, it was the Twelve Tables that marks the true starting point of Roman legal culture.[8] That the latter is a convenient starting point cannot be denied. After all, recent work on the Twelve Tables and its reconstruction has brought modern scholars much closer to the text than those working in this field at the beginning of the twentieth century.[9]

And yet, the Twelve Tables is not the proper 'start' of Roman legal culture. As most recent scholarship on the matter has shown, it represents not a beginning, but rather a transition from one phase to the next.[10] The interesting question

---

[5] Comprehensively treated in various chapters by Kelley 1997.
[6] D. 1, 2, 2, 1 Pomp. l. s. enchirid. *Et quidem initio civitatis nostrae populus sine lege certa, sine iure certo primum agere instituit omniaque manu a regibus gubernabantur* (translation taken from Watson et al. 1985).
[7] D. 1, 2, 2, 3 Pomp. l. s. enchirid. *Exactis deinde regibus lege tribunicia omnes leges hae exoleverunt iterumque coepit populus Romanus incerto magis iure et consuetudine aliqua uti quam per latam legem, idque prope viginti annis passus est.* (translation taken from Watson et al. 1985).
[8] See, for example, Carandini 2011.
[9] See, for example, the reconstruction in Crawford 1996.
[10] The overarching conclusion reached by the author in the edited volume Cursi 2018.

following on from this is whether it is possible to say anything of substance about Roman law before the enactment of the Twelve Tables. As is well known to scholars of early Roman society, the dearth of written sources severely hampers matters. In addition, as scholars of law and anthropology will attest, custom tends not to leave the same traces in the records as written law. These two factors combined has led one prominent scholar of Roman law to comment that '... it would be easier to climb the north face of the Eiger wearing a tracksuit than to say anything meaningful about early Roman law'.[11]

This may be true, but *Wissenschaft* cannot progress without returning to the original sources and scrutinising them anew through modern eyes, as well as taking stock of the latest discoveries by archaeologists and epigraphers. To that end, the group of scholars included in this volume were specifically selected to revisit the 'origin narratives' of Roman law because of their prior work on early Roman law. In addition, archaeologists and anthropologists were included in the conversation to overcome some of the main problems caused by the lack of contemporary written records. To that end, a workshop took place at the University of Edinburgh, School of Law, on 6–8 December 2017, which was generously funded by the School of Law, The Society for the Promotion of Classical Studies, and Northern Illinois University, including both its College of Law and the College of Visual and Performing Arts.[12] This book is the product of that workshop. The aim of this chapter is to outline the book's contents, to highlight the authors' central conclusions and points of cross-disciplinary interaction, and to map out directions for further work in this vein.

2. GENERAL THEMES

Edited collections stand or fall by the strength of their coherence and the extent to which the individual contributions coalesce into a unified whole. To assist the reader in traversing the individual contributions, we have grouped them under three headings, namely 'The Materiality of Roman Law: New Archaeological Discoveries', 'Constructing Early Roman Law: Sources and Methods', and 'Roman Law in Historiography and Theory'. These three headings provide an endoskeleton for the volume.

In the first section, 'The Materiality of Roman Law', new fieldwork forms the core of the three chapters. Clackson focuses on new epigraphic discoveries containing 'legal' texts in regional languages predating Latin in order to assess whether there was a 'communality of inscriptional habits' among these groups and to what extent Greek law had an impact on the formation of Roman law. As he notes, 'even a very brief examination of the etymology of some Latin legal terminology supports a view that different tributaries fed into the stream of Roman

---

[11] A statement attributed to the German Romanist, Professor Dr Alfons Bürge.
[12] The editors gratefully acknowledge the support of these institutions.

law, and that as these waters merged they gave rise to something new and different' (p. 9). Naglak and Terrenato's chapter focuses on recent findings from Gabii and interprets this evidence in light of Levi-Strauss' 'house model'. This permits them to draw larger conclusions concerning the relationship between the 'house model', 'house societies', and state formation, and thereby to clarify the social conditions in Latium that promoted the creation and codification of Roman law. The last chapter in this section, by Warden and Maggiani, focuses on a new discovery known as the Vicchio Stele, which is inscribed in Etruscan with one of the three longest religious texts to date. Theirs is a detailed account of the content of this new inscription and the religious significance of the text as well as its location, where they hold it 'stood as a symbol of power, authority, and elite hegemony'. In summary, the first section of this collection focuses on three important aspects of early Roman law: namely the interplay between orality (custom) and written law; the formation of the early Roman state and its internal organisation around the 'house model'; and, finally, the common 'epigraphic habit' of various groups on the Italian mainland and beyond as well as the extent to which written laws, epigraphically attested, functioned as symbols of power and authority.

The second section of the volume, 'Constructing Early Roman Law', is devoted to the two great 'sources of law' of this period known to modern scholars, namely the *leges regiae* and the Twelve Tables. The first three contributions, by Amunátegui Perelló, Rocco, and Laurendi, form a triad and should ideally be read together. Collectively, they are concerned with the narratives surrounding the creation of these two bodies of law (Amunátegui Perelló), Livy's aims – in a narratological sense – when weaving information about the creation of these bodies of law into his narratives about early Roman law, as well as the extent to which the literary and jurisprudential sources for these two bodies of law should be reinterpreted in light of recent archaeological discoveries to assess the veracity of various claims surrounding the nature of Roman kingship and their legal powers. The final two contributions in this section, by Smith and Armstrong, take an external perspective on these bodies of law. Smith eloquently re-examines the sources and raises fundamental questions about processes of urbanisation as well as the nature of early Roman kingship, while Armstrong focuses on the limits of the community through the concept of the *Pomerium* and the reach of early law beyond this limit. Collectively, the chapters in this section demonstrate the main complexities when dealing with early Roman law: namely, the nature of the sources and their interpretation. As the authors demonstrate, these sources cannot be understood without taking a broad and interdisciplinary approach in which law, archaeology, anthropology, and philology are united in conversation.

The final section of this volume, 'Roman law in Historiography and Theory', contains two thought-provoking chapters on matters of context. Capogrossi Colognesi, by examining the lives of Bachofen and Niebuhr – two of the Great

German jurists of the late nineteenth/early twentieth centuries, whose work had a profound impact on modern scholarly knowledge of early Roman law – shows the sheer extent to which modern scholarship remains latently influenced by the assumptions of these scholars. Pottage, in a wide-ranging discussion of the early history of anthropology through the lens of Mauss' *The Gift* as applied to the knotty question about the legal nature of *nexum*, demonstrates the importance of interdisciplinarity when tackling this period. Seen together, these chapters demonstrate the value of historiographical perspectives as well as the far-reaching impact that discussions of Roman law have had in other fields.

3. FURTHER WORK

For much of the early part of the twentieth century, works such as Henry Maine's *Ancient Law* dominated Roman legal scholarship.[13] The merest glance at contemporary textbooks on Roman law shows that the spectre of Maine remains alive and well.[14] Supporters of the evolutionary model of legal development, proposed by Maine and his followers, argued that legal systems evolve from primitive to sophisticated through various stages of development. This idea, first mooted in Enlightenment scholarship of the eighteenth century, provided a ready and seductive, if ultimately flawed, framework for classification also of contemporary legal systems.[15] It also gave rise, towards the middle of the twentieth century, to a flurry of literature about 'primitive law', the rationale being that certain basic patterns or structures could be identified within these legal systems.[16] While the debate about 'primitive' law has died down, much still remains to be said about the origins of the Roman legal order.

Law is a product of the human intellect. It shares communalities with other written expressions of the Roman mind, such as poetry and prose, and is therefore worthy of detailed scholarly study. What sets law apart from other forms of literature, however, is its real-world effects. And since no legal system has ever sprung from the head of Zeus fully formed, it is important to study the origins of this legal order quite carefully in order to uncover the implicit assumptions and structures of thought upon which it was founded. As one of the most enduring and successful legacies of the Roman mind, Roman law remains a fascinating cultural artefact.[17] And as the field is currently undergoing an unprecedented revival, the origins of Roman law have become more important than ever. It is at this salutary moment that we hope this collection will not only engage in existing debates but also spur new questions and provoke future inquiry.

---

[13] Maine 1861.
[14] Kaser 1971.
[15] Westbrook 2010.
[16] Diamond 1971.
[17] Kehoe and McGinn 2017.

Works Cited

Carandini, A, 2011. *Rome: Day One*. Princeton, NJ: Princeton University Press.
Crawford, M H, 1996. *Roman Statutes*. London: Institute of Classical Studies, School of Advanced Study, University of London.
Cursi, M F, 2018. *XII tabulae: testo e commento*. Naples: Edizioni Scientifiche Italiane.
Diamond, A S, 1971. *Primitive Law, Past and Present*. London: Methuen & Co.
Gibbon, E, 1776. *The History of the Decline and Fall of the Roman Empire*. Dublin: William Hallhead.
Kaser, M, 1971. *Das römische Privatrecht. 1, 1*. Munich: Beck.
Kehoe, D P and T A J McGinn, 2017. *Ancient Law, Ancient Society*. Ann Arbor: University of Michigan Press.
Kelley, D R, 1997. *The Writing of History and the Study of Law*. Aldershot: Variorum.
Maine, H S, 1861. *Ancient Law*. London: John Murray.
Watson, A et al., 1985. *The Digest of Justinian. Vols 1–4*. Philadelphia: University of Pennsylvania Press.
Westbrook, R, 2010. 'The Early History of Law: A Theoretical Essay.' *Zeitschrift der Savigny-Stiftung fur Rechtsgeschichte* 127.1: 1–13.
Wibier, M H, 2014. *Interpretandi Scientia: An Intellectual History of Roman Jurisprudence in the Early Empire*. Unpublished PhD dissertation, The University of St Andrews. http://hdl.handle.net/10023/6368 (accessed 20 February 2019).

Part I

The Materiality of Roman Law: New Archaeological Discoveries

Chapter 1

Roman Law in its Italic Context

James Clackson

1. INTRODUCTION

Where does Roman law come from? There are several possible answers to this question. First, it is possible that Roman law is an outgrowth of an oral tradition of law shared with other Indo-European languages.[1] Second, Roman law might reflect legal traditions that developed in Italy over centuries of interaction between local communities; a parallel situation is envisaged to explain the Roman onomastic system, which appears to be the product of a cultural *koiné* between the peoples of central Italy in the first half of the first millennium BCE.[2] A third possible source of Roman law is the influence from other cultures in the ancient Mediterranean: several ancient Near Eastern cultures had developed sophisticated law-codes already in the second millennium BCE; Greek and Phoenician traders and colonists may well have spread legal traditions and law-codes into the western Mediterranean. The Romans themselves, as is well known, gave various accounts which stressed their debt to Greek law, including the story that Numa had gained his legal learning from Pythagoras,[3] and another that three commissioners responsible for the Roman law of the Twelve Tables were sent by the Senate to copy Solon's laws at Athens and those of other Greek states.[4]

These three possible origins do not necessarily stand in opposition to each other, and there may very well be no single source of Roman law. Whatever the original impetus for legal institutions or practices in Rome was, the Romans adapted these to their own purposes. Indeed, even a very brief examination of the etymology of some Latin legal terminology supports a view that different tributaries fed into the stream of Roman law, and that as these waters merged they gave rise to something new and different. Some Latin words relating to legal concepts and practices are inherited from the vocabulary of the parent language, known as Proto-Indo-European: for example, *ius* 'justice' and *iustus* 'just', words which have parallels in Indo-Aryan and Celtic languages;[5] some words appear

---

[1] Benveniste 1969; Watkins 1994a, 1994b.
[2] Clackson and Horrocks 2007, 42–5.
[3] Liv. 1.18.
[4] Liv. 3.31.
[5] See Ernout and Meillet 1959, s.v. and de Vaan 2008, s.v. for the etymology of these and subsequent words discussed in this paragraph.

to be shared among the Indo-European languages of Italy, but not further afield in the Indo-European language family, such as *lex* 'law' and derivatives;[6] and there are other words which show shared semantic ranges across Indo-European and non-Indo-European languages, such as the terms relating to slavery, and the concept of the *familia*;[7] finally, a few legal terms are borrowed from Greek, for example, *poena* 'penalty'.[8] Moreover, these terms, whatever their origin, are found combined with each other from our earliest textual evidence; there is no sense that the 'Italic' words form a coherent group against, for example, 'Mediterranean' words.

When dealing with discrete elements such as words, it is possible to isolate separate elements and identify their origin through etymology. When specific laws or examples of legal phrasing come into consideration, however, it is much more difficult to tease apart the strands that combine to form Roman law. In order to illustrate this problem, I shall use the example of a very simple text, among the shortest Latin Republican legal texts that survive, which is inscribed on a bronze tablet from Lavinium and dated to the third century BCE.

CIL 1² 2847 = ILLRP 509
Cerere(m) auliquoquibus | Vespernam por(r)o
'(One must propitiate) Ceres with stewed entrails, Vesperna with a leek.'[9]

This is clearly a *lex sacra*, setting down appropriate offerings to two deities. It is in the simplest possible form, with no verb expressed and case forms distinguishing the divinity (inflected as accusative) from the offering (ablative). Texts of this type are also found across Italy written in other languages than Latin, and comparable structures occur in Greek sacred laws.[10] Let us consider two examples from Italy. First, a stone inscription from Vestine territory, Aveia 1,[11] in which the words denoting the offerings (*aunom* and *hiretum*) are expressed in the accusative case, and the name of the deity (*atrno*) in the dative case (as is usual in Greek texts).

---

[6] See Untermann 2000, s.v. *lixs*.

[7] See Rix 1994 for detailed discussion of the development of terms for slavery in the languages of ancient Italy, including Etruscan.

[8] I do not know of any Latin legal term that is directly borrowed from a Semitic or other ancient Near Eastern language family; those Semitic terms that are found in Latin, such as *arrabo* 'deposit' (also attested in shorter versions *arra*, *rabo*) have entered the language via Greek.

[9] For this interpretation and restoration, see *AÉpigr* 1976. 110; I have translated with the verb 'propitiate' since Latin *pio* is found with the accusative of the deity and ablative of the offering.

[10] See, for example, Carbon and Clackson 2016 for a recently discovered Greek sacred law written on bronze which uses this elliptical structure, for example line 19 τōρακλει οϝιν ορεν[α 'To Heracles, a male sheep'. The deities in this text are all in the dative, but the offering is sometimes expressed in the nominative, sometimes in the accusative. Other Greek texts listing prescribed offerings show similar patterns; none of them (to my knowledge) gives the deity's name in the accusative.

[11] In this, and all subsequent references to Italic or Sabellian inscriptions (i.e. Oscan, Umbrian, South Picene, Marrucinian, Sabine, Oenotrian, and other) inscriptions, I use the sigla of Crawford et al. 2011.

mesene | flusare | poimunen | atrno || aunom | hiretum
'In the month of Floralis, in (the precinct of) Pomona, to Aternus (one sacrifices) a lamb (and) a ram.'

An early third-century Oscan text, Vibo 2, provides our second example. It is written in Greek letters on bronze:

διουϝει ϝερσορει ταυρομ
'to Zeus Tropaios (one sacrifices) a bull.'

In this text, as in Aveia 1, the name of the deity is in the dative case, the offering in the accusative.[12]

This sort of legal text could therefore have arisen under Greek influence, but it could equally well be an example of shared inheritance from Proto-Indo-European or areal convergence between Latin and the other ancient languages of Italy. In favour of the inheritance/areal-diffusion theory, it can be observed that the Latin inscriptional texts reproduce a pattern that seems to be formulaic in the language of prayer. In Latin and Umbrian it is possible to make an offering to a god just by using the name of the god (or the pronoun 'you') in one case form and the name of the offering in another, with the omission of any explicit verb meaning 'offer' or 'propitiate'.[13] This pattern was highlighted by Calvert Watkins, who dubbed this type of phrase an 'elliptical offering formula'.[14] A Latin example from literary sources is given in the words to be uttered at the sacrifice of a pig to Mars in Cato (*Agr.* 141.4):

te hoc porco piaculo
'(I propitiate) thee (*accusative*) with this piglet (*ablative*) as offering.'[15]

The syntax of CIL 1² 2847, with the deities in the accusative and offerings in the ablative, appears to follow the syntax of the inherited prayer formula, but the practice of inscribing the text on bronze, and displaying it in the context of a sanctuary, is a Greek practice, which has been adopted elsewhere in Italy. In this case, it is possible to see the Latin inscription as the result of two different traditions merging to give a hybrid *lex sacra*. The comparable material from the Italic languages helps to identify more clearly the debt to Greek models, since two of the texts, Aveia 1 and Vibo 2, follow the normal Greek syntax of such texts exactly.

---

[12] For the date of Vibo 2, see Zair 2016, 180. For another non-Latin law of this type, note the 'Sabine' text Marruuium 1, written on stone, showing a different syntactic structure, with apparently nominatives both of the deities and the offering.

[13] It is possible, but far from certain, that Etruscan prayers are present on the *liber linteus* and that they are formed in an analogous way, see Rix 1991, especially 343–45.

[14] Watkins 1995, 214–28. Watkins (1995, 218) noted that a similar pattern occurs in Sanskrit, although he thought that the similar phrasing of the Latin and Umbrian was the result of areal diffusion rather than an Indo-European inheritance.

[15] Note that *piaculo* is not a verb form here, but the ablative of *piaculum* in apposition to *porco*, see TLL s.v. *piaculum* 10.1.2070.52–4 and also s.v. *piaculo*.

Only by taking the Lavinium text together with other Italic texts do we arrive at a full understanding of this text-type in ancient Italy.

In the rest of this paper I shall gather the examples of inscribed laws from elsewhere in Italy in order to shed further light on the question of the origins of Roman law. The use of inscribed texts can, to some extent, help to separate out what is owed to the inherited element of Roman law and what is borrowed. Speakers of Proto-Indo-European did not know writing, and it is impossible to attribute practices of inscribing laws to them. The inclusion of non-Indo-European traditions in the discussion further helps to isolate what is inherited or developed within the Indo-European languages in Italy from what is not. An increase in material evidence will furthermore give us a better handle on Roman law. In the sixth and fifth centuries BCE, Rome was just one of many small city-states in Italy, and we have very little contemporary evidence about its legal system beyond the fragmentary and short inscription on the *Lapis Niger*. Furthermore, by examining the later traditions of law in the rest of Italy, we can judge the evidence we have from literary and other sources in Rome against unbiased and largely 'uncontaminated' parallel traditions.

The longer texts in languages other than Latin or Greek from the Italian peninsula, such as the Oscan *Tabula Bantina* or the Umbrian *Tabulae Iguvinae*, are generally well known. These are not the only texts to have survived from antiquity that can be classed as 'legal', and there are a number of shorter or fragmentary texts that can help to build a complete picture of legal practices in Italy in the first millennium BCE across different cultures. There is no recent collection of all legal texts, and so before considering what we can find out from these texts I shall gather material from the most recent corpora and publications. For all of the languages discussed below there are some areas where our understanding is deficient, and often the decision as to whether a text is 'legal' or not is dependent on the judgement of the researcher. Moreover, what can be counted as 'legal' is also not definitely fixed. I have tried to err on the side of pragmatic inclusivity here, including texts that may be termed 'sacred laws' (*leges sacrae*),[16] but excluding simple injunctions made by private individuals, building inscriptions, dedications, and other inscriptions made by or for public officials. I shall present this material in two ways: firstly assessing the evidence in terms of the language it is written in, and then secondly grouping texts from different language families together over time to examine the evolution of the practice of writing down laws and the style of their phrasing.

2. EVIDENCE BY LANGUAGE GROUP

2.1 Sabellian

First, let us consider the texts in the Sabellian languages, Indo-European varieties which are closely related to Latin, starting from the north and working southwards. I have already mentioned the Iguvine Tables, seven large bronze tablets recording

---

[16] Although I have decided not to include the Oscan *iúvilas* inscriptions, which appear in a funerary context, see Crawford et al. 2011, 27–9.

Umbrian rituals and regulations. The earlier tablets, probably dating from the third century BCE, are written in Umbrian script, and the later ones, which may be as late as the first century BCE, have Umbrian written in the Latin alphabet. The texts written in the Latin alphabet sometimes repeat rituals described earlier but give more detail, including the prayers used by the priests. There is one other possible legal text from the Umbrian-speaking area, Tadinum 2, which is a fragment of a large limestone stela, dated to before 300 BCE, on which it is possible to read just two words: *tarina*[, plausibly the beginning of a word denoting the citizens of Tadinum, and *eitupes*, which is very likely to be the local counterpart to the verb *eitipes* on the Iguvine Tables, and hence given the meaning 'they decreed'. If these reconstructions are correct, then we may be faced with an Umbrian decree with the equivalent closing verb as *censuere* 'they decreed' found on Latin *senatusconsulta*.

Our knowledge of the Sabellian languages in the centre of Italy, the area south of Umbria and north of Campania and Samnium, is hampered by a relative paucity of texts; those that survive bear testament to changing populations and language use in the area over the last five centuries BCE. Roman authors spoke of the Sabines as the original inhabitants of a large part of this area, but there are only very few inscriptions that can be definitely categorised as written in the Sabine language. Around twenty large stone stelae from the fifth and fourth centuries BCE survive, written in a script and language now known as South Picene.[17] Many of the South Picene inscriptions are fragmentary, and others are obscure, but what can be read indicates, together with the stelae's archaeological contexts (where known), that they were intended as burial markers. In later periods some important legal texts are found in this area. The Rapino Bronze (Teate Marrucinorum 2, now lost) is a third-century text with twelve lines apparently containing sacrificial regulations ending with a prohibition. The text starts with an invocation to the gods (compare the Greek practice of beginning legal documents with the invocation θεοί) and declares itself to be a *lixs* (= Latin *lex*) for the *totai maroucai* 'the Marrucinian people'. The Velitrae bronze ([Velitrae 1]), another third-century sacred law from central Italy,[18] mentions the name of the two magistrates (*meddices*) who set up the text, and gives regulations relating to a sacred area. From the second century BCE there are two other short *leges sacrae* from the central area: the first, from Sabine territory, Aveia 1 (discussed earlier), just lists the month, place, name of deity and sacrificial victims; the second, also on stone, names the gods in the nominative followed by 'a favourable sacrifice' (Marruuium 1).

The Sabellian language most widely spoken in southern Italy was Oscan, and I shall first consider the *leges sacrae* in this language. One of the most celebrated of these is the Agnone Tablet (Teruentum 34), a second-century bronze text inscribed on both sides which gives the names of deities for whom altars are to be set up. There is one shorter *lex sacra* from the Oscan-speaking area, a three-word-long third-century bronze from Vibo Valentina (Vibo 2), detailing that a bull is to be

---

[17] Crawford et al. 2011, 10–13 gives a brief overview of the South Picene texts, and tentatively identifies their makers with the *Sabini* of Roman authors.
[18] Its exact provenance, although long thought to be Velitrae, is not certain.

sacrificed to Jupiter (discussed above). The Oscan area makes up for its comparative lack of *leges sacrae* by providing the most important collection of other legal texts in bronze in any language other than Latin and Greek from Italy. The Tabula Bantina (Bantia 1) is widely known as the longest and best example of Oscan law, even though it seems clear that, while not a direct translation of a Roman original, it does incorporate Oscan renderings of Latin phraseology.[19] Earlier bronze tablets from the south include Buxentum 1, a third-century law written on both sides of a bronze tablet, for which the most recent interpretation is that it deals with the law of theft, instigating a principle of searching familiar from Greek law and the Twelve Tables.[20] There are three other fragments, or possible fragments, of law: the second-century Histonum 2, which mentions women;[21] the third-century bronze tablet Campania or Samnium 1, of which all that is recognisable is names, and which could equally well be a dedication plaque; and the very fragmentary Histonum 3, on which it is possible to ascertain that the name of a magistrate occurred on the top line of the document, but nothing more certain can be read.

Finally, from the south of Italy there are two large stone stelae. The so-called Cippus Abellinus (Abella 1) records an agreement between the communities of Abella and Nola about rights relating to a temple which lay on their mutual boundary. The Tortora stela (Blanda 1), found in Tortora in what is now Calabria, is one of the earliest legal documents from Italy, dating from the late sixth century. It is written in the Achaean Greek alphabet in an early variety of Sabellian, sometimes called Oenotrian, a dialect that seems not to be the direct ancestor of the Oscan later spoken in this area. The Tortora stela is written along the length of a stone stela; one side is not inscribed, and two lines of writing appear on the top surface of the stone. The order of writing, discernible from the direction in which the letters face, is best described as 'broken boustrophedon.' The non-boustrophedon lines appear to indicate new paragraphs. Exactly the same technique of 'broken boustrophedon' is apparently used on the *Lapis Niger* and a sixth-century Greek stela with civic regulations from Chios, which also shows the script running the length on two of three inscribed sides of the stela.[22] Although the text from Tortora is not completely comprehensible, it has universally been taken to be a legal text. Arguments in favour of this from the language of the text are as follows:[23]

1) The use of what is apparently a third-plural past tense verb αματεσ, similar to the verb *amatens* (of uncertain meaning) occurring on the Rapino Bronze. A problem with this theory is that the Tortora stela would then show both the innovative third-person plural ending *–ens* (here written –ες) and the older third-person ending –οδ. All other Sabellian languages opt for one of the two

---

[19] See Decorte 2016a for a recent survey.
[20] McDonald and Zair 2013.
[21] Crawford 2007.
[22] The Chian stela is no. 8 in Meiggs and Lewis 1969. The similarity between the layout of these three texts is pointed out by Crawford 2011, 155.
[23] See also the discussion in McDonald 2015, 188–92.

endings, rather than using both. Accordingly it seems likely that αματεσ is not in fact a verb at all, and the similarity between it and the Marrunicinan *amatens* is coincidental.

2) A sequence νε πισ τακιοσqτοδ which appears to be similar to other injunctions in ancient laws from Italy, such as *ne quis uiolatod* from a Latin law (*CIL* 1² 366).[24] Unfortunately, there is no agreement about the interpretation of the sequence τακιοσqτοδ, nor what the base verb could be.[25]

3) The institutional term τοϝτια, a derived adjective from the noun for 'people' or 'community'.

The strength of a legal interpretation for the Tortora text is the combination of the textual evidence with the similarity in layout to the *Lapis Niger*, and its affinity with roughly contemporary *leges sacrae* from Greece.[26] However, it should be noted that the eighteen roughly contemporary South Picene stelae share similar layouts: broken boustrophedon with text running the length of the stone. Furthermore, some of the South Picene texts also feature words or phrases which might not be out of place on a legal text, such as the word for 'community' (**toúta,** Interamnia Praetuttiorum 1, Interamnia Praetuttiorum 3, Cures 2), a word possibly related to the Latin word *multa* 'fine' (**molk[1]a,** Superaequum 1) and a clause headed **suai / pis** 'if anyone' (Asculum Picenum 3). All of these South Picene inscriptions, however, are funerary, rather than legal. The South Picene stelae serve as a reminder of the possible misattribution of fragmentary or partially comprehensible inscriptions to the category of 'legal', and urge caution in the interpretation of the Tortora stela.

2.2 Etruscan

Turning to the Etruscan corpus, we find a number of possible legal texts, but few of which have a certain interpretation. In the most recent edition of the Etruscan text corpus, texts are listed in the category 'juristic'.[27] Over half of these texts (twenty-nine in total) are boundary markers, and contain little to interest the legal scholar.[28] A further four are written on the walls of tombs or on urns, and appear to be instructions for offerings or injunctions against

---

[24] See Poccetti 2009, 196 for further examples.

[25] For suggestions, see Poccetti and Lazzarini 2001, 178–9 and Martzloff 2007, 183.

[26] On the Greek parallels, see Poccetti and Lazzarini 2001, 26. On the classification of the Tortora text, see further McDonald 2015, 188–92.

[27] See Meiser 2014, 48. Juristic texts are indicated by the number 8 in the reference, immediately following the two-letter code for provenance, as Ta 8.1 or Co 8.4. A possible addition to the list is a fifth-century bronze plaque from Marzobotto, published at Govi 2014, too late to make it into Meiser's edition. The Marzobotto text, however, includes the word *hecce*, normally taken to mean 'built', making it unlikely that this is a legal document. All Etruscan texts referred to are given their sigla as they appear in Meiser 2014.

[28] I judge the following to be boundary stones from their context or from the occurrence of the word *tular*: AS 8.1, AS 8.2, Cl 8.4, Cl 8.5, Pe 8.1, Pe 8.2, Pe 8.3, Pe 8.5, Pe 8.6, Pe 8.7, Pe 8.8, Pe 8.9, Co 8.1, Co 8.2, Fa 8.1-6, Sp 8.1, Af 8.1-8.

despoiling the tomb.[29] There are eight texts on bronze, of which two, Ta 8.1 and Co 8.4 (the Cortona Tablet), are lengthy enough to merit discussion below; the others are too short, or their context too limited to allow any clear idea of their original meaning.[30] Eight texts survive written on stone, but again only three of these will be discussed below, the others being mostly very short or fragmentary.[31]

Two further Etruscan texts should be included with our assessment of Etruscan legal texts now known, and an initial consideration of these two will help set the parameters for the other texts. The documents in question are the *liber linteus*, or linen book, containing around 240 lines of text written in the second or first centuries BCE; and the Capua Tile, a fifth-century BCE roof-tile with thirty lines of text. These two texts are probably the best understood of the longer Etruscan texts, and there is general scholarly agreement about their purpose and interpretation. The *liber linteus*, which owes its survival to its later function as a mummy wrapping, is the longest surviving Etruscan text, showing similarities in its vocabulary and structure with the Capua tile. Both texts are ritual calendars, giving instructions for the operations of festivals and sacrifices throughout the year; in the Capua Tile ten months are represented, but the *liber linteus* only gives the months from June to September. However, the *liber linteus* expands the detail of the rituals greatly in comparison with the Capua Tile, perhaps also giving the ritual prayers uttered by the priest during the ceremonies.[32] Both texts make use of formulae that include verbal forms with an inflectional ending *–ri* added to a verbal root. For example, consider II 8 on the Capua Tile, which starts the beginning of the second section, dealing with the second month of the Etruscan year, April:[33]

ioveitule ilucve apirase leθamsul ilucu cuiesχu perpri

Here *ioveitule* may signify a location; *ilucve apirase* almost certainly indicates the date (probably 'the ides of April'); *leθamsul ilucu cuiesχu* is the name of some sort of festival of the god Leθams; and *perpri* is a verb, possibly meaning 'make a sacrifice' or similar, with inflection marker *–ri*. Compare this sequence with a section heading in the *liber linteus*, VIII 3:

celi. huθis. zaθrumis. flerχva. neθunsl sucri. θezeric

---

[29] Cr 8.3, Ta 8.2, Ta 8.3, Vs 8.1.

[30] Vt 8.2 is written on both sides, but is too fragmentary to make sense of; Vs 8.2 and Pe 8.10 have only two words; Cl 8.1, Cl 8.2 and Cl 8.3 only seem to record names.

[31] Texts not further discussed are Cr 8.2, a tufa cippus of the late seventh century with four lines of text on two sides, but incomplete (see further Colonna 2005); Vs 8.3 a tufa block reading *θval melθlumes*; Vs 8.4 a tufa block with five letters; Cl 8.6 a fragmentary block with the middle of three lines; and Co 8.4, a cippus with two words inscribed.

[32] This explanation, for which see Rix 1991, is influenced by the fact that the later Iguvine Tables include a representation of the spoken prayers absent from the earlier versions.

[33] For further discussion of these forms and texts, see Wylin 2000, 87–90.

Here *celi. huθis. zaθrumis* indicates the date (24 September), *flerχva. neθunsl* indicates some sort of sacrifice to the god Neptune (*Neθuns*), and *sucri* and *θezeri* are two verbs in *–ri* joined by the connective particle *–c*.

These sequences mirror Greek festive calendars, which also signify dates, locations, and festivals, with instructions for the sacrificial animal or other details included.[34] Greek sacred laws, where they have verbs, use the infinitive or imperative or sometimes the optative mood;[35] the Etruscan form in *–ri* has been termed a 'necessitative'.[36]

Work on these longer Etruscan texts has consequently shed light on the shorter documents which may have legal content. Note, for example, Cr 8.1, a seven-line text written on a sandstone block from the late fifth century from Caere. There are no recognisable dates or personal names on the texts, but five 'necessitative' verbal forms ending in *–ri*. The final line also contains the Etruscan negative particle *ei* (without a *–ri* following).[37] It thus looks likely that this text is legal, since it cannot be funerary or a building instruction. Unfortunately, in the words of Facchetti, 'nondimeno esso resta, nel complesso, assolutamente incomprensibile'.[38]

Unfortunately, the other Etruscan longer legal texts do not feature many forms in *–ri*, although they do occur (*fusleri* on the Perugia cippus (Pe 8.4), *seθasri* on Ta 8.3). The use of *ei* to mark prohibitions is also found at the end of Ta 8.1, a third-century text on bronze, which starts by naming the magistrate in whose term of office the text was drawn up.[39] Other legal texts give details of who wrote them or how they were written.[40] The final section of the Capua Tile is now mostly illegible, but it is possible to read the verb *ziχunce* 'he/she/they wrote' at the ends of the last two lines. The Perugia Cippus (Pe 8.4) also ends with details of the writing of the text: *iχ ca ceχa ziχuχe* 'thus this writing was written'. The Cortona Tablet (Co 8.3) is a second-century bronze text which contains details of a land agreement, including the names of guarantors, which was probably housed in a (?private) archive. This tablet contains what looks like a formulaic phrase *cên zic ziχuχe* 'this writing was written' (line 18), which is followed by a name. This phrase is not at the end of the whole text, but appears to follow the main text of the agreement, and is followed by the list of guarantors or witnesses. For the reference within the laws to their own written status, compare the end of the Iguvine Tables, or the *senatusconsultum de Bacchanalibus*, CIL 1²

---

[34] Cristofani 1995,110–12 gives Greek parallels, to which others can be added; see the recent archaic law from Arcadia, published at Carbon and Clackson 2016.
[35] McDonald 2015, 174.
[36] Rix 1983, following Pfiffig 1969, 42–3.
[37] The Etruscan particle *ei* is presumed to be a negative particle owing to its appearance in the formula *ei min(i)/(pi) capi* (and variants), best explained as meaning 'don't take me' (Agostiniani 1984). The formula is attested at Cm 2.13, Cm. 2.46, Vc 2.3, Pa 2.1, Li 2.24.
[38] Facchetti 2000a, 103.
[39] See Fachetti 2000a, 89–94 and Wylin 2000, 254–62 for discussion of this text.
[40] The Etruscan root *ziχ* (sometimes spelt *zic*) is confidently ascribed the meaning 'write' owing to the representation of the Etruscan name *Zicu* by Latin *Scribonius* on a bilingual text (Cl 1.320).

581. There is one further longer Etruscan text which appears to be legal: Vt 8.1, a cippus from the end of the last millennium BCE, which starts with a name but the rest is obscure.[41]

2.3 Other Italic Languages

From the other languages attested in inscriptions in Italy, the evidence is even more difficult to interpret. An inscription from Mendolito in Sicily, written on a large stone block apparently on the wall of a public building, appears to mention a community (τουτο-) and some sort of public institution which is also known in Oscan (ϝερεγαιεσ).[42] For the Messapic language there is nothing that can securely be termed a legal text. There is one bronze tablet fragment from the third century,[43] and a number of roughly contemporary stone cippi and stelae from the third century which do not appear to be funerary,[44] although further interpretation is uncertain. There are no legal texts preserved among the Faliscan or Venetic documents. The last text from Italy which might be judged to be legal is a sandstone stela from the area around Novilara (the exact provenance is unknown) in what is now Le Marche, in an undeciphered language which has sometimes been called North Picene. Its only claim to be a legal text is that it contains the word *polem* twice, perhaps reminiscent of the Greek πόλις. Unfortunately, it seems very possible that this text is a modern forgery, as are undoubtedly two of the other three so-called North Picene documents.[45]

3. CHRONOLOGICAL SCOPE OF THE EVIDENCE

Let us now take stock of the legal documents we have from Italy in terms of date. From before 400 BCE there are, I reckon, four surviving important legal texts from Italy, three on stone: the *Lapis Niger*, the Tortora Stela, and the Etruscan Cippus Cr 8.1 and the Etruscan sacred calendar inscribed on terracotta (the Capua Tile). As noted above, the Tortora Stela and *Lapis Niger* use boustrophedon order in their presentation of the text, and they both share the convention of breaking this order to mark a new paragraph, a framing device which is also found on a sixth-century stela from Ionia.[46] The Capua Tile also uses 'broken boustrophedon', beginning each new section with text reading from right to left; sections are

---

[41] See Wylin 2000, 262–5, who also includes a photograph of this text.
[42] For the Mendolito inscription, see Agostiniani 1992. For the problem of the meaning of the word *vereia* and its cognates, see Crawford et al. 2011, 24–6.
[43] 19 Cae in De Simone and Marchesini 2002. The fragment has six lines and no word breaks. On line 5 it may be possible to restore the divine name *apro]ditan*.
[44] These are (following the sigla of De Simone and Marchesini 2002): 3 Car, which appears to begin k]laohi zis; 10 Ruv, which has the divine name *damatura* in line 1; 11 Ur; 22 Ur, where side B begins klaohi] zis; 4 Uz; 9 Uz.
[45] See Agostiniani 2003.
[46] See note 22 supra.

further marked by the use of horizontal lines (which are easier to draw on wet clay than carve on stone stelae). The Cippus from Caere, Cr 8.1, does not use boustrophedon at all, and boustrophedon order is not found in later texts. It is worth further noting here that boustrophedon is not found in Phoenician documents from the west; the Nora stela from Sardinia, which dates from the ninth century, has all lines written right to left. The maintenance of boustrophedon as late as the sixth century seems to be peculiar to Greek and Italian documents.[47] As for other aspects of the layout of texts, only the Caere Cippus and the *Lapis Niger* use word-dividers. A final noteworthy feature of these early texts is the apparent presence at the end of the Capua Tile of the identity of the scribe. The next surviving text to include any 'meta-text' – that is, information on how the text came to be written and erected – is the early stone stela from Tadinum in Umbria, which appears to name the body which had the authority for the creation of a law or decree. After this date, it is not unusual to find the identity of the magistrate or other institution responsible for enacting the law. Roman and Sabellian laws inscribed on bronze do not normally identify the engraver, but the long Greek legal text from Heraclea (IG 16 645, on two bronze tables, dated to around 350 BCE) does include the scribe's name at the end of the first table.

From the beginning of the third century there are an increasing number of surviving bronze legal texts from Italy, and the use of bronze is widespread in both religious and community laws.[48] Many, but not all, of these bronze texts use word-dividers. The exceptions are Buxentum 1 (Oscan), Vibo 2 (Oscan, although this does use slightly larger spaces to separate off words), Teate Marrucinorum 2 (Marrucinian, word-dividers do occur but are not consistent), Campania or Samnium 1 (Oscan, very fragmentary); word-dividers are also sometimes missed in the Etruscan Cortona Tablet. Many of these documents bear nail holes or other devices for attachment such as a chain, which suggests that they were displayed in public,[49] but some, such as the Cortona Tablet, which has a 'handle' to facilitate its removal for consultation, may have been stored in archives.

Although the evidence from the early period is very sparse, there do seem to be shared practices of writing down laws in the period from 700 to 200 BCE, and commonalities with Greek laws over the same period suggest that these practices were largely taken over from Greece. Most striking is the use of the broken boustrophedon, and its subsequent abandonment in favour of a regular writing direction (left to right in the case of Latin, right to left in the other Indo-European languages and Etruscan). Although metal was used for dedication texts, the

---

[47] Note that boustrophedon is also used on non-legal documents from Italy in the fifth century, such as the South Picene stelae discussed above.

[48] As well as in other documents. Note the recent discovery of an Etruscan bronze plaque from fifth-century Marzobotto, as published in Govi 2014.

[49] Note that the Agnone Tablet (Teruentum 34) was found wedged between rocks, and may only have been taken out and read or consulted at certain occasions in the festival cycle (see commentary at Crawford et al. 2011).

earliest evidence for laws written on bronze is from the south of Italy. Crawford is of the view that in Rome the practice of legal texts in bronze only starts in the second century, when inscribed texts were sent out to colonies (as is clearly the case with the *senatusconsultum de Bacchanalibus*),[50] but there is clear evidence for the use of metal for inscriptions much earlier elsewhere in Italy (note, for example, Vibo 2 discussed earlier). Texts inscribed on bronze are more likely to have word-dividers than not. Neither Roman inscribed laws nor the Iguvine Tables identify the scribe who wrote them, but some Etruscan legal texts seem to have given the names of their scribes, as is found in Greek laws (for example, the Tabulae Heracleenses). The inscribers of Roman statutes on bronze generally strive not to write a single word breaking over two lines, but the same scruples are not found in inscribed Oscan laws.[51]

4. CONCLUSIONS

In the language and structure of legal documents there seem to be similarities across the different language groups, and although these may reflect Greek models, the evidence is much less clear-cut. First, many texts in Indo-European languages make use of future imperatives, cognates to Latin imperatives in –*to* (written –*tod* in early Latin documents). Although these future imperatives are found in laws in Oscan (including the Tabula Bantina), Latin (including the Twelve Tables), the Velitrae Bronze and possibly the Tortora stela, they are neither obligatory nor universal in legal documents. The Rapino Bronze, for example, a self-declared *lixs*, does not use future imperatives, but instead employs subjunctives in order to indicate what is required.[52] In Latin texts, 'future imperatives' come to be seen as quintessential markers of legalese in the late Republic,[53] but in earlier periods they also occur in non-legal documents, for example in conversational Latin as recorded in Plautus. The *Lapis Niger*, almost certainly our earliest Latin legal text, has no clear –*to(d)* imperative surviving, but subjunctive forms do occur. Consequently, the existence of possible future imperatives in the South Picene stelae does not necessarily indicate anything about the legislative practice in archaic Italy.[54] This feature is an inheritance from Indo-European, and its presence in early laws is a natural outgrowth of its inherited meaning; a future imperative is neither a necessary nor sufficient ingredient in a legal text. Indeed, the range of different ways of issuing commands in laws of ancient Italy is in accord with a freedom of practice in Greek law, where various different strategies are used to indicate commands and prohibitions.[55] In Etruscan, the suffix –*ri* seems to have

---

[50] Crawford 2011, 154.
[51] See Crawford 2007 on Histonum 2 and the Tabula Bantina.
[52] Poccetti 2009 gives a full survey of the use of future imperatives.
[53] See most recently Decorte 2016b, 809.
[54] *pace* Crawford et al. 2011, 13.
[55] McDonald 2015, 174.

marked out legal obligations, although it is not widely used with the negative particle *ei*, where a different form of the verb is usually employed.[56] Given our current knowledge of Etruscan, we cannot be sure that other means of issuing commands were not also employed.

It is consequently difficult to use the future imperative forms found in many ancient laws of Italy as the 'smoking gun' that proves beyond doubt that there was a shared Italic legal practice, rather than possibly independent developments or adaptions of Greek models. The casuistic style of much Latin law, shown by the reliance on structures using conditional or relative clauses, of the *si quis* 'if anyone . . .' or *qui* 'who . . .' type, looks to be evident in at least some of the other legal traditions in Italy.[57] Greek law is one possible origin of both of these styles, but they are also found in other legal traditions, both within and outside the Indo-European language family.

We are now in a better position to look at the origin of Roman law in the context of the other laws of Italy. While we cannot conclude with any certainty that there was a common period of development of 'Italic Law', or deny any contribution from prehistoric Proto-Indo-European law, the commonalities of inscriptional habits and practices across the Italian peninsula are noteworthy, not just by the appearance and growing popularity of certain document types (large stone stelae, bronze law tables) at certain historical times, but also the spread of certain elements of legal texts, such as the inclusion of the names of the responsible magistrates in some documents, or the use of final prohibitions at the end of laws forbidding tampering with the object itself. There is evidently diversity between different language traditions, as shown by the prevalence of giving the name of the scribe in Etruscan documents but apparently not in Latin or Sabellian ones. Despite this, the pervasive influence of Greek law on the laws of ancient Italy should be apparent from these examples. The peoples of ancient Italy adapted Greek models continually throughout their history.

Works Cited

Agostiniani, L, 1984. 'La sequenza *eiminipicapi* e la negazione in etrusco.' *Archivio Glottologico Italiano* 69:84–117.

———, 1992. 'Les parlers indigènes de la Sicilie pré-grecque.' *LALIES. Actes des sessions de linguistique e de littérature* 11:125–57.

———, 2003. 'Le iscrizioni di Novilara.' In *I Piceni e l'Italia medio-adriatica. Atti del XXII convegno di studi etruschi ed italici. Ascoli Piceno, Teramo, Ancona 9–13 aprile 2000* 115–25. Atti di Convegni, Istituto Nazionale di Studi Etruschi e Italici 22. Pisa: Istituti Editoriali e Poligrafici Internazionali.

---

[56] Agostiniani (1984, 109) gave several possible examples of *ei* followed by a verb with *-ri*, but these either follow *ein*, which may not mean the same thing, or are now read differently. The only remaining example known to me is Ta 8.3 *ei: muχ: ara: an: ei: seθasri*, where the sense of *seθasri* is unclear.

[57] Again, our present knowledge of Etruscan does not make it possible to identify a clear example of this structure.

Benveniste, É, 1969. *Le vocabulaire des institutions indo-européennes*. 2 vols. Paris: Minuit.
Carbon, J-M and J Clackson, 2016. 'Arms and the Boy: On the New Festival Calendar from Arkadia.' *Kernos* 29:119–58.
Clackson, J and G Horrocks, 2007. *The Blackwell History of the Latin Language*. Malden, MA and Oxford: Blackwell.
Colonna, G, 2005. 'Il cippo di Tragliatella.' *StEtr* 71:83–109.
Crawford, M, 2007. 'A Hitherto Unrecognized Fragment of an Oscan *Lex*.' In *Studi per Giovanni Nicosia*, edited by E Nicosia, vol. 3:45–7. Milan: Giuffrè.
——, 2011. 'From Ionia to the Twelve Tables.' In *Römische Jurisprudenz. Dogmatik, Überlieferung, Rezeption: Festschrift für Detlef Liebs zum 75. Geburtstag*, edited by K Muscheler, 153–9. Berlin: Duncker & Humblot.
Crawford, M et al., 2011. *Imagines Italicae*. BICS Supplement 110. 3 vols. London: Institute of Classical Studies.
De Simone, C and S Marchesini, 2002. *Monumenta linguae messapicae*. 2 vols. Wiesbaden: Reichert.
Decorte, R, 2016a. '*Sine dolo malo*. The Influence and Impact of Latin Legalese on the Oscan Law of the *Tabula Bantina*.' *Mnemosyne* 69:276–91.
——, 2016b. '*Sic habeto*. The Functions of *–to* Imperatives in Legal Latin and Beyond.' In *Latinitatis Rationes. Descriptive and Historical Accounts for the Latin Language*, edited by P Poccetti, 801–19. Berlin and Boston: de Gruyter.
de Vaan, M, 2008. *Etymological Dictionary of Latin*. Leiden: Brill.
Ernout, A and A Meillet, 1959. *Dictionnaire étymologique de la langue latine*. 4th edn. Paris: Klincksieck.
Facchetti, G M, 2000a. *Frammenti di diritto private etrusco*. Florence: Olschki.
——, 2000b. *L'Enigma svelato della lingua etrusca*. Rome: Newton Compton.
Govi, E, 2014. 'Una nuova iscrizione dal tempio urbano di Tinia a Marzabotto.' *StEtr* 77:109–47.
Lazzarini, M L and P Poccetti, 2001. 'L'iscrizione paleoitalica da Tortora.' In *Il mondo enotrio tra VI e V secolo a.C. Atti dei seminari napoletani (1996–1998)*, edited by M Bugno and C Masseria, 1–213. Naples: Loffredo.
Martzloff, V, 2007. 'Latin *pollinctor*, grec λίπ(α), picénien VEPSES. Phraséologie et élaboration poétique.' In *Procédés synchroniques de la langue poétique en grec et en latin*, edited by A Blanc and E Dupraz, 171–89. Brussels: Safran.
McDonald, K, 2015. *Oscan in Southern Italy and Sicily. Evaluating Language Contact in a Fragmentary Corpus*. Cambridge: Cambridge University Press.
McDonald, K and N Zair, 2013. 'Oscan ϝουρουστ and the Roccagloriosa Law Tablet.' *Incontri Linguistici* 35:31–45.
Meiggs, R and D Lewis, 1969. *A Selection of Greek Historical Inscriptions to the End of the Fifth Century* B.C. Oxford: Oxford University Press.
Meiser, G, 2014. *Etruskische Texte (auf Grundlage der Erstausgabe von Helmut Rix)*. Studien zur historisch-vergleichenden Sprachwissenschaft 4. New edn. Hamburg: Baar.

Pfiffig, A J, 1969. *Die etruskische Sprache. Versuch einer Gesamtdarstellung.* Graz: Akademische Druck- und Verlagsanstalt.

Poccetti, P, 2009. 'Lineamenti di tradizioni "non romane" di testi normative.' In *L'umbro e le altre lingue dell'Italia mediana antica. Atti del I convegno internazionale sugli antichi umbri, Gubbio, 20–22 settembre 2001*, edited by A Ancillotti and A Calderini, 165–248. Perugia: Jama.

Rix, H, 1983. 'La scrittura e la lingua.' In *Gli Etruschi. Una nuova immagine*, edited by M Cristofani, 199–227. Florence: Giunti.

———, 1991. 'Etrusco *un, une, unuc* "te, tibi, vos" e le preghiere dei rituali paralleli nel *liber linteus.*' *ArchCl* 43:665–91.

———, 1994. *Die Termini der Unfreiheit in des Sprachen Alt-Italiens.* Forschungen zur antiken Sklaverei 25. Stuttgart: Steiner.

Untermann, J, 2000. *Wörterbuch des Oskisch-Umbrischen.* Heidelberg: Winter.

Watkins, C, 1994a. 'Studies in Indo-European Legal Language, Institutions and Mythology.' In *Selected Writings. Vol. 2. Culture and Poetics*, edited by L Oliver, 422–55. Innsbruck: Institut für Sprachwissenschaft. Originally published in G Cardona, H M Hoenigswald and A Senn, eds, *Indo-European and Indo-Europeans.* Philadelphia: University of Pennsylvania Press, 1970.

———, 1994b. '"In the Interstices of Procedure": Indo-European Legal Language and Comparative Law.' In *Selected Writings. Vol. 2. Culture and Poetics*, edited by L Oliver, 718–27. Innsbruck: Institut für Sprachwissenschaft. Originally published in W Meid, ed., *Studien zum indogermanischen Wortschatz.* Innsbruck: Institut für Sprachwissenschaft, 1987.

———, 1995. *How to Kill a Dragon: Aspects of Indo-European Poetics.* New York and Oxford: Oxford University Press.

Wylin, K, 2000. *Il verbo etrusco. Ricerca morfosintattica delle forme usate in funzione verbale.* Rome: 'L'Erma' di Bretschneider.

Zair, N, 2016. *Oscan in the Greek Alphabet.* Cambridge: Cambridge University Press.

Chapter 2

Central Italian Elite Groups as Aristocratic Houses in the Ninth to Sixth Centuries BCE

Matthew C Naglak and Nicola Terrenato

1. INTRODUCTION

Early Roman laws like those expressed in the Twelve Tables did not come forth *ex novo* in the middle of the fifth century BCE; instead, it is far more likely that they formalised and regulated customary practices that had already been accruing for decades, if not centuries. Arguably, this process was intertwined with the emergence of urbanisation and state organisation at the sites that would later become the major cities of the western coast of central Italy. Investigating the groups who established these settlements and their customary interactions with one another can therefore prove beneficial for understanding how and why early Roman law developed the way it did. Due to the lack of surviving literary sources from this period (the ninth to sixth centuries BCE generally), evidence must largely be derived from the realm of archaeology.[1]

Although a significant amount of good-quality new archaeological data is now available for most of Italy, it is not intrinsically suited to proving that specific events did or did not happen; rather, it can lend itself, when adequately handled, to the kind of broad structural treatments that can clarify important connections and the deep workings of the forces involved in these processes.[2] Unfortunately, archaeological data has been used sparingly when attempting to understand the origins and development of social groups on the Italian peninsula, with the debate instead centred on the impact of generalised internal and external triggers to urbanisation.[3] For studies of this period to move forward, new heuristic models must be utilised that are able to bring together and take advantage of all types of available evidence, whether textual, epigraphic, or archaeological. As a further benefit, such an approach would reconnect early Rome and Latium with recent developments in the larger discipline of social and state formation studies around the world, offering the opportunity for a greater amount of cross-cultural comparison and hypothesis formulation beyond the standard problematic comparison with the Greek *genos*.[4]

---

[1] See also the chapters by Clackson, Smith, and Warden in this volume for discussions of the potential and limits of the archaeological evidence.
[2] An approach already suggested in Momigliano 1963; Grandazzi 1991.
[3] Overview in Fulminante 2014, 7–34.
[4] Smith 2006, 140; Naglak and Terrenato 2019.

Archaeological discoveries in the last few decades have driven a re-evaluation of the social and state formation processes taking place in central Italy during the transition to urban life in the late Iron Age by offering an alternative to the endless dissection of historians like Livy and Dionysius of Halicarnassus. This information has led to a plethora of new theories and models focused on how the relationships between individuals and groups may have developed as a part of the growing urban environments of Latium, where settlements have clustered in the landscape in an entirely new way.[5] This movement should be seen as a positive development for historical studies in the region in general, which have, for the most part, been stuck in a rut in debates over the validity of this source or that, or in trying to pick out the kernels of truth in the mythological stories of early Rome. Archaeological evidence allows us to approach the problem from a different vantage point, moving from the late Bronze and early Iron ages forward to the better understood Republican Period, complementing the standard use of later documents to push backwards into the past. In this way, we may hope for a better understanding of the changes in social organisation taking place during the urbanisation process in central Italy, where groups are more intimately connected than ever before and are slowly adjusting from an economic and military focus to a more social and political function with the rise of the state.

One model slowly coming into vogue among archaeologists in the Mediterranean basin is that of a Lévi-Straussian 'House society'. Widely applied in ethnographic circles since its original formulation in *La Voie des Masques*,[6] it has only more recently caught on among archaeological scholars, having reached the world of classical archaeology last of all.[7] This fact is somewhat surprising considering the material nature of a House, the remains of which often survive well in the archaeological record when all other traces have disappeared. These material remains are exactly what tie an abstract model to a specific place and time, allowing a consideration of the bonds of kinship of those who left them behind. With a deeper understanding of the social situation at the multifocal settlements which would become the major cities of Latium, it is possible to consider more closely the effects that the development of the state may have had on these types of relationships, some of which were eventually codified into Roman law.

The aim of this paper is not to present in full the theory behind Lévi-Strauss' House society model.[8] Instead, after briefly introducing the concept, our goal is to consider what types of evidence are more or less useful in identifying House societies in Latium and Etruria. Although studies focused on this region are admittedly rare in comparison to places like Minoan Crete or Neolithic Asia Minor,[9] we argue that, with the proper kinds of evidence taken into consideration, a House model should be seen as widely applicable in Latium. Indeed, it offers a lens through

---

[5] Terrenato 2011; Pacciarelli 2017.
[6] Lévi-Strauss 1975.
[7] Latest of all, Carsten and Hugh-Jones 1995; Joyce and Gillespie 2000; Beck 2007.
[8] Discussed in Gillespie 2000; Gillespie 2007.
[9] Driessen 2010, 2012; Düring 2007.

which many aspects of life both in this period and in the later Republican times may be viewed with interesting repercussions. We close with a reflection on some of the possible implications of the model with respect to the emergence of state and legal structures in the region, hypothesising how certain well-known facets of urban life may have originated during this period.

2. A HOUSE SOCIETY MODEL

In *La Voie des Masques*, Lévi-Strauss briefly defined a House as a:

> Personne morale détentrice d'un domaine composé à la fois de biens matériels et immatériels, qui se perpétue par la transmission de son nom, de sa fortune et de ses titres en ligne réelle ou fictive, tenue pour légitime à la seule condition que cette continuité puisse s'exprimer dans le langage de la parenté ou de l'alliance, et, le plus souvent, des deux ensembles.

> moral person, keeper of a domain composed altogether of material and immaterial property, which perpetuates itself by the transmission of its name, of its fortune and of its titles in a real or fictive line held as legitimate on the sole condition that this continuity can express itself in the language of kinship or of alliance, and, most often, of both together.[10]

A few facets of the House jump out as particularly useful for archaeologists and archaeological studies.[11] The system is centred on the continuation and distribution of capital through time, whether it be social and ritual (immaterial possessions) or economic (material possessions). One of these immaterial possessions is a 'name', a concept well recognised in the later *gentilicial* social group of the Republican Period.[12] Importantly, there is the focus on 'a real or fictive line' based around 'kinship or of alliance'. This ability to transcend standard text-based prosopographical studies is a major benefit of the model as a whole, allowing us to look farther into the past and consider the ways in which individuals and groups may have expressed and legitimised different degrees of relatedness through fictive kinship techniques along with the standard blood kinship relationships.[13]

What types of evidence, then, are useful for the identification of a House society? The existence of the social group through multiple generations centred on a physical occupation structure and the ownership of property that is passed down through time, perhaps along with a name, are two places to start. Notably, this should include certain rights and obligations, tied up with the moral personhood of the House, which go beyond individuals and are rather maintained by the social structure as a whole.[14] In this vein, two vital axioms should be recognised,

---

[10] Lévi-Strauss 1975, 47; translation from Gillespie 2007, 32.
[11] Discussed more extensively in Naglak and Terrenato 2019.
[12] Smith 2006, 17–20.
[13] For more on the difficulties involved in purely prosopographical analyses, see Hölkeskamp 2010.
[14] Fiorentini 1988.

concepts which have sometimes been forgotten in the desire to apply the House model to a wide variety of societies and situations. The first, only apparently obvious, is that a physical house structure is not equivalent to a social House.[15] It is difficult to find a group which does not repeatedly utilise some sort of physical shelter in its daily existence, ranging from the tents of hunter-gatherers to the subdivisions of middle-class Western culture. These two examples, however, should certainly not be viewed as House societies. The house of a House society is more than a physical structure; it plays a symbolic role in tying a group together across generations while simultaneously grounding them in the physical and cultural landscape in which they live and work. In this way, the house becomes not just a material structure utilised time and again but also one full of symbolic meaning obtained both through its permanence and its relationship with other types of material and immaterial wealth.

Although more difficult, the symbolic nature of the house structure can often be identified in the archaeological record through its association with the bones of the dead, heirloom artefacts, and origin narratives.[16] As with the physical architectural house, each category ties into the material and immaterial wealth, which may be passed down from generation to generation. The bones of the dead, and the ancestor worship which often attends them, offer a tangible social connection to the individuals of past House iterations, while heirlooms can perform a similar function with respect to material goods. Both can take advantage of oral traditions which pass on stories of earlier periods of the House's existence in the larger physical and cultural landscape. When multiple forms of this kind of evidence come together, it can suggest to the archaeologist that a House may indeed be present.

This leads us to the second axiom: a House alone does not make a House society. The connections within and between Houses, and the heterarchies and hierarchies which naturally form from these connections, create the foundation of the society as a whole and are indispensable to the identification and understanding of the social structure. This is a fact that is often missed when House society models are being considered. What is the scope of a singular House, and where are the other Houses which belong to the same 'society'? How do these groups interact with one another, and how may we identify the results of these interactions archaeologically? Such questions remain important yet are often understudied in the desire to focus in on the physical structure of a house for the identification of such a group. It is to be hoped that more intensive excavation of settlement sites like that of Gabii outside Rome will assist in answering these types of questions, complementing a continued focus on late Republican textual accounts or the 'great houses' of Etruria.[17] Nevertheless, there is already much to suggest the application of the model to Latium and possibly Etruria may prove useful.

[15] See Gillespie 2007 for a more extended discussion.
[16] Beck 2007.
[17] Torelli 1981, 83–8.

3. EVIDENCE FOR HOUSE SOCIETIES IN LATIUM AND ETRURIA

As summarised by A González-Ruibal and M Ruiz-Gálvez,[18] the House society model has been applied across the Mediterranean from Çatalhöyük to Sardinia. It is here, however, where the archaeologist must take pause in order to consider exactly what types of archaeological evidence are useful in each region and time period, ensuring that one is able to recognise both Houses and the larger society of which they are a part. Without this type of scholarly awareness, with a specific consideration of the axioms described above, it is possible that the over-application of the term can cause it to become useless for cross-cultural comparisons.

While a detailed look at the evidence used for the identification of a House society in each time period in the Mediterranean would prove beneficial, such an effort is far beyond the scope of this volume. Instead, let us turn here to our main point of interest, Latium at the end of the Iron Age, and what kinds of evidence may or may not prove useful for identifying a House society there. A first point of order is the distinction between Etruria and Latium[19] for, while similar processes may be taking place in both regions, the nature of the evidence is quite different. Unfortunately, the main sources of information generally utilised to talk about Houses in Latium have so far been Etruscan in origin. The elaborate and monumental tomb architecture of Etruria,[20] which often takes the form of domestic space and banqueting halls, as well as the famous Etruscan sarcophagi depicting both males and females, used to suggest that the woman's line of descent remained prominent, have both been utilised to suggest that various aspects of a House society may be present from the seventh century onward.[21] Evidence of this kind is not available for Latium. On the other hand, the presence of hut urns does cross the regional divide, suggesting that further study may be useful when Latium is considered. Hut urns do indeed suggest the symbolic importance of the physical house structure and are a valuable piece of evidence for the identification of a House society, even if the question of how much they reflect the reality of a house's structure or decoration remains debated.[22]

On the settlement scale, the evidence presented by González-Ruibal and Ruiz-Gálvez even for Etruria is much weaker. The emergence of nucleated settlements is only briefly mentioned, a topic which is instead highly relevant for a discussion of interactions between Houses;[23] instead, discussion is centred on the large sites such as Poggio Civitate in Murlo or Acquarossa, which have been called 'great

---

[18] González-Ruibal and Ruiz-Gálvez 2016.
[19] A point noted in a recent look at the application of the model to the early Roman *gens*; Smith 2019.
[20] Naso 2017.
[21] González-Ruibal and Ruiz-Gálvez 2016, 423–7.
[22] Potts 2015, 20.
[23] González-Ruibal and Ruiz-Gálvez 2016, 420.

houses' due to their size and luxuries.[24] While certain aspects of Murlo, for example, may be associated with a House (including its possible terracottas of ancestors, possible trade or economic features, possible areas of social and ritual power, depictions of the *lituus* as a possible heirloom of power), the larger social implications of the designation have yet to be addressed. Externally, with whom is this House closely interacting and what are the results of this interaction? Internally, what evidence is there for social stratification or differentiation within the social structure? While the available evidence is certainly not disqualifying, these issues of inter- and intra-House relationships have yet to be considered and may be difficult to analyse using evidence from isolated locations like Murlo or elite house-tombs. This type of evidence may perhaps tell us something about the physical house structure, but informs us little about the bonds that form the basis of the society itself, much less how or why it developed. Rather, we suggest that further consideration of settlement-level archaeology on sites such as Tarquinia or Veii would prove useful in shoring up the argument for this region. The recognition of multifocal settlement patterns on these plateaus strongly suggests a formation process in which multiple small, elite-led communities converge on the same plateau.[25] Considering how these groups worked together in their unique localities may prove a far more useful avenue for continued research in this area.

Excavation within the walls of the Etruscan town of Vetulonia has already proven the benefits of this type of settlement-level excavation. The discovery of a deposit of over 120 bronze helmets near the walls of the city offers evidence for private armies and the military nature of powerful Houses. Although severely damaged, the single-word inscription *haspnas*, an Etruscan family name, was discovered on at least fifty-six of the helmets. This has been interpreted as an indication that the helmets were the property of this family and as such were indicative of a more kinship-based military unit.[26] From the shape of the helmets as well as the morphology of the word form, the deposit has been dated to the first half of the fifth century BCE; while later than the period under question here, this may reflect a practice passed down for centuries in the region. More evidence comes from the literary and epigraphic record (for instance, an archaic inscription from Satricum),[27] leading some scholars to see these groups as temporary warbands operating under the leadership of a House leader.[28] Indeed, it has been recently argued that even the structure of the mid-Republican Roman army was not so radically different from that of the private armies of the state-formation period. In a recent and thorough study, the manipular army has been described as being like an aggregation of 'Rome's early warbands'.[29]

[24] Turfa and Steinmayer Jr 2002.
[25] Pacciarelli 2017.
[26] Rich 2017; Maras 2018.
[27] Di Fazio 2017.
[28] Rawlings 1999.
[29] Armstrong 2016, 267.

Returning to Latium, the settlement-level evidence used to discuss Houses is somewhat less substantial due to a lack of extensive stratigraphic excavation in the region. Instead, antiquarian elements such as the hut of Romulus have been used to suggest 'the symbolic primacy of the house in central Italy'.[30] While the perpetual reconstruction of this physical hut structure certainly says something about Romans during the Republican Period and the importance they placed on their own origins, its strength as an indicator of a House society in Latium during the Iron Age is minimal at best. The use of textual evidence is perhaps more egregious, with a suggestion that Cicero and Livy can be reliably used to argue that the maternal line during the time of the kings in Latium was actively considered and involved in how power was passed from generation to generation. This textual evidence, written centuries after the events it purports to relate, is unlikely to reflect the reality of the eighth century and is more interestingly used to consider the role of women in the passing of power in the late Republic and early Imperial periods. A better approach to this subject may be through epigraphic analysis, which from an early date may suggest the importance of both the maternal and paternal lines of a family.[31] Even so, the question of inter-House relationships is left unexplored through this kind of evidence alone.

What then can we say about Latium during this period? Two approaches suggest fruitful avenues for future study. On the more textual and historical side, a move away from focusing on the myths of early kings to a consideration of the existing social system during the early Republican Period would prove both valuable and more judicious. The epigraphic analysis mentioned above is a good first step in this direction. A second useful source of evidence are the Twelve Tables themselves, a document which theoretically codified practices in Rome during the middle of the fifth century BCE. A section discussed recently by Smith in his reconsideration of the Roman clan jumps out as immediately pertinent:[32]

> V.3 As he has disposed by will concerning his familia (?) or goods (?), or guardianship, so is there to be source of rights.
> V.4 If he dies intestate, to whom there be no *suus heres*, the nearest agnate is to have the familia (?) and goods (?).
> V.5 If there be no agnate, the gentiles are to have the familia(?) and goods (?).

This passage immediately focuses in on the economic function of the early Roman *gens* through the passing down of material possessions through a line of kinship. There is a clear concern with property and estate preservation and reproduction so that goods would not move outside of the kinship group even when there was no direct claimant. This kind of evidence seems to suggest that by approximately 450 BCE the *gens* was already well-established and intimately

---

[30] González-Ruibal and Ruiz-Gálvez 2016, 426.
[31] Bartoloni and Pitzalis 2011.
[32] Smith 2019.

connected with testamentary law and inheritance, aspects that a House would also be associated with prior to the development of the state. This economic focus thus appears to be a surviving trait from the earlier social system, still present even as the primary role of the *gens* was changing as state power was expanding.

While one may argue that the Twelve Tables are based on textual sources dating centuries after the moment it was codified, recent archaeological studies like those of Osteria dell'Osa and Gabii in Latium allow us to identify more directly the social structures and relationships of Houses in the Iron Age. The specifics of these sites have been discussed extensively elsewhere,[33] so here we will simply review the importance they hold to a consideration of the House in Latium. With respect to the establishment and continual existence of physical house structures, it is possible to recognise the continual use and renovation of houses over a period of hundreds of years within the hut cluster of Area D at Gabii, suggesting their importance as established locales in the landscape.[34] The symbolic importance of these structures is enhanced through the presence of the infant burials oriented in conjunction with them, tying the bones of the dead to the physical house. Possible heirlooms and group-specific items have been identified within the tombs, suggestive of a consistent group memory of the past. Finally, the proximity and similarity between the grave goods at Gabii and Osteria dell'Osa give a glimpse into possible origin narratives and ways in which the past might be claimed for future social capital.[35]

Importantly, Gabii allows us to begin to consider the social system of a House society through both intra- and inter-House relationships in ways that are impossible at sites like Murlo. The distribution of hut clusters across the site, as originally recognised by M Guaitoli,[36] may be indicative of a spatial hierarchy between Houses. We are also able to see intra-House hierarchy through the burials, with different grave goods and burial types perhaps reflecting different roles within a House system. The infant burials at Gabii may allow us to begin to hypothesise about both inter- and intra-house ties, as argued by M Naglak and S Cohen in their look at the role the burials may play as mediators of House identity.[37] While this analysis is obviously preliminary, and more excavation of other hut clusters is necessary both at Gabii and elsewhere to confirm the hypothesis, the initial results appear promising and open up new avenues for considering the social system during this pivotal period in Latin history.

The hierarchical structure implied by the infant burials in the city seems to be reflected at the nearby necropolis of Osteria dell'Osa during the same period, with an elite inhumation burial surrounded by burials containing lesser numbers of

---

[33] Bietti Sestieri 2005; Naglak and Terrenato 2019; Mogetta and Cohen 2018.
[34] Evans et al. 2019.
[35] Cohen forthcoming.
[36] Guaitoli 1981.
[37] Naglak and Cohen forthcoming.

grave goods.[38] Osteria dell'Osa lies just to the west of Gabii, approximately 200 m from the volcanic lake of Castiglione. In total over 600 graves were excavated on the site, with by far the majority dating in the ninth and eighth centuries BCE. In one section, an isolated group is set off from the rest, with the majority of the burials dating to the middle of the eighth century and later. Approximately fifty-six burials are found in this group, and an internal division within the group into two or three subgroups appears to be present.[39] Males and females are relatively equally represented within the group and within each subgroup as a whole. Very few children are present, with only four burials of sub-adults less than twelve years of age discovered. In several cases, the superimposition of new burials on top of old ones is attested, suggesting some sort of relationship between the individuals. There is a high number of grave offerings, but with little differentiation apparent according to gender, role, or status, with two major exceptions. On the one hand, there are six burials that seem to lack any type of grave goods at all. On the other hand, at the centre of the entire grouping appears the inhumation of an old man with a bronze javelin head. Next to him are the remains of a cremated younger woman of uncertain relationship. At this point in time in Latium, cremation was an unusual burial method, and this is the latest example of such a burial found in the necropolis. The biological connections between individuals within this group are uncertain, but the fact that some form of relatedness must exist is clear.

Previous scholarship has doubted the usefulness of the mortuary evidence from Osteria dell'Osa for considering social organisation during this period.[40] With the new excavations at Gabii, however, the question arises: is this group connected in some way with the hut clusters situated at the future site of Gabii or, at minimum, representative of a certain kind of social grouping present during the Iron Age period in Latium? In considering the first question, a direct biological connection between the mortuary remains is impossible to confirm without further osteological and DNA study. However, the time of these burials lines up well with the early phases of the hut clusters at the site half a kilometre away. Meanwhile, by this time the majority of earlier settlements in the surrounding region have already coalesced at the future site. Further, the lack of sub-adults on the necropolis (in accordance with the lack of adults at Gabii) also seems to point in this direction, as does the presence of similar types of rich grave goods at each location.

Taking a step back, this mortuary group suggests a certain type of social organisation. On a most basic level, there is approximately equal representation of males and females, evidence for superposition, and apparent stratification between individuals through grave goods. There also seem to be central figures around which the others are organised. The excavator of Osteria dell'Osa saw the mortuary remains as an archaeological correlate of the early stage of a Latin *gens*, with the central individuals as aristocratic members of *gentes* and those with less or no

---

[38] Bietti Sestieri 1992b.
[39] Bietti Sestieri 1992a, 199–203.
[40] Smith 2006, 147–9.

grave goods early *clientes*.[41] We would argue instead that this evidence points more usefully to a House group, avoiding the conflation with a specific type of social entity which may not be appropriate to this early period.[42] While further analysis is needed, what we may be seeing here is the burial ground for one of the Houses situated at Gabii, one which had maintained its (real or fictive) connections with the past through the continual use of Osteria dell'Osa when all other groups had moved elsewhere.

4. CONCLUSIONS

Having discussed the new findings at Gabii within the context of the theoretical framework provided by the House society model, it is time to draw some general conclusions about the urbanisation process. Needless to say, a very considerable amount of central Italian archaeological evidence has been recruited in recent decades as evidence for the nature of the process. A lot of it falls in the category of unwise use of archaeological evidence for historical purposes, mainly because of the very specific and event-oriented type of remains in question. There have been many examples of dangerously far-fetched connections between individual archaeological features and textual elements. In both realms it is far more advisable to look for broader patterns that are widely attested and use them to infer even broader structural elements of the urbanisation process, rather than attempting an *histoire événementielle* that is doomed to be unconvincing.[43]

The observation of the leopard-spot occupation pattern offers a good model in that it has been verified independently at a number of sites, so it cannot be dismissed as a local anomaly.[44] Coming as it does from survey archaeology, its reliability is not perfect at all sites, with issues of surface visibility certainly having an impact on the patterns detected. The phenomenon is however too macroscopic to be all (or even mostly) an artefact of these collection biases. The complex at Gabii that we have just illustrated is the first of these habitation clusters to be extensively excavated. Its contribution is to show that, from its very beginning, at least this unit contained an elite House, together with lesser participants in the cohabitation. The presence of infant burials plays a key role in drawing this conclusion, since the huts composing the leopard spot in and of themselves would not indicate social status. As a further hypothesis, it may be advanced that the elites in question were responsible for the relocation of the habitation group to the site of the future city, since elites are attested in the area since the tenth century and it seems highly unlikely that the ones at Gabii Area D became elites after moving there.

[41] Bietti Sestieri 1992a, 241.
[42] See Naglak and Terrenato 2019 for further discussion.
[43] Full discussion in Terrenato 2019, 34–42.
[44] Pacciarelli 2001.

If the convergence of Late Bronze Age village communities onto the urbanisation sites was indeed promoted by Houses,[45] this would be further confirmation that cities in central Italy had a multifocal formation process. Rather than having grown from a single community, they would have originally been composed of tens of elite-led nuclei that lived separately from each other on the same plateau. They would have converged there from some of the Final Bronze Age hilltop villages, in a move that does not seem to have been dictated by an overarching political structure. The new multifocal community appears to be a relatively levelled landscape of power, in which no one hut cluster is obviously dominant over the others.[46] So far, for the initial phase of the ninth century no communal cult places or public spaces have been identified. Even fortifications are minimal or absent,[47] despite the fact that communal defence must have been one of the main functional reasons for the coalescence of these centres in the first place. While the relationships between these entities are not easy for us to reconstruct on a purely archaeological basis, there is another line of evidence that can be combined to produce interesting results.

Perhaps the only other main archaeological indicator that has representativeness and meaning enough to be a part of this discussion is the definition of a burial-free zone in the early life of these emerging urban centres. It has been known for a while that at Rome adult burial was initially concentrated in the valleys between the hills (the area later corresponding to the so-called Sepulcretum near the Sacra Via, the Forum of Caesar, and the Roman Forum). After a specific moment during the late ninth century BCE, however, further interment was apparently banned and only allowed on the Esquiline, where it would remain predominant for most of the pagan life of the city. After the shift, only infant burials would instead be deposited within the settled area.[48] Comparable trends are now discernible, if on a less pronounced distance, at other budding urban sites, such as at Satricum or Veii.[49] In those cases, the graveyards are slowly pushed away from the area where the leopard spots are merging together. In other words, these communities must have agreed on a notional line inside of which it was forbidden to bury their adult dead.

It would be hard to overstate what a radical change the ban on new burials must have marked in the social life of these settlements, and especially for the Houses in them. The connection with the House ancestors was (and would always remain) a key element of the mentality of these aristocratic groups. Producing a spatial discontinuity between generations (since the existing burials obviously had to remain in their original location), it represented a difficult junction for social actors that were constantly trying to reaffirm their prestige and legitimacy. It is

---

[45] An indication in this sense seems to be coming from another excavation area at Gabii; Banducci and Gallone forthcoming.
[46] Terrenato and Motta 2006.
[47] Fontaine and Helas 2016.
[48] Bettelli 1997.
[49] Tol 2012.

therefore unlikely that the move was undertaken lightly or that it was simply a spontaneous trend. It can only be imagined as an actual regulation that was formally stipulated and enforced. Considering that there would have been little legal precedent for an unpopular restriction of this kind, it is highly probable that it would have been underpinned by some sort of religious taboo, perhaps extending the range of existing smaller ones, and was codified as a law only later.[50]

Whatever the specifics of the process might have been, there can be little doubt that the ban is the earliest indication visible to us of true collective action on the part of emerging communities. This important act of self-regulation, if not law-giving, would have required a major effort of coordination that would have been negated if even just one of the leopard spots continued in the old funerary tradition. It must have been a compromise grudgingly accepted by the Houses as a result of mediation and negotiation. In this sense, it stands at the head of a long line of delicate political interactions in central Italy aimed at producing balanced constitutional frameworks that made the interaction among houses less conflictual and more isonomic. The revolutionary concept was introduced of a rule that impinged directly on what was customarily understood to be within the jurisdiction of each House.[51] Much of the legislation that characterised Roman society would follow in this original wake and would progressively erode and curtail the traditional prerogatives of the aristocrats, without ever eliminating them entirely.

An important question is why a ban on new burials would be introduced as a founding element of every urban community we know in the region. Going back to a crucial insight articulated by Fustel de Coulanges,[52] it must be considered that the creation of a visible tomb marker of an important (and presumably deified) ancestor was a powerful way for a House to stake a symbolic territorial claim. Each new burial added next to it would only renew and reinforce that claim. Such a strategy had been the norm since the late Bronze Age and it must have been like second nature to the conurbated Houses at that point. Stopping this century-old custom would take away a key ingredient for factional strife, demilitarising, so to speak, the domain of the future city and creating a more neutral space in which Houses could interact. If a new (and level) political arena was to emerge slowly, these larger-than-life (and larger-than-death) ancestors had to be put out to pasture, at least in their most materially striking manifestation, their tombs and the rituals that went with them. Regardless of the reason, this step should be seen as a foundational turning point in the slow process of urban evolution in central Italy.

The definition of the line of burial exclusion must have been a highly pregnant decision, which many cities maintained for their entire existence. It was a process that apparently went hand in hand with defence considerations. Virtually everywhere, the chosen line coincided with that of the earliest circuit of fortifications,

---

[50] As attested by the provision in the Twelve Tables.
[51] It should be noted that since burial was an elite privilege at this time, the new rule would only make a practical difference for the aristocrats in the community.
[52] Fustel de Coulanges 1864; see also Zifferero 1991.

which were however built centuries later. At some sites, like the cities of South Etruria, there were natural boundaries that made the selection rather simple. Plateaus with steep edges were obvious choices, for instance at Tarquinia or at Veii. Other geographic settings, like the volcanic slope of Gabii, offered more room for different options, while a uniquely diverse site like Rome's could be delimited in a number of different ways.[53] In any case, the Houses everywhere agreed that the same line should be used for fortification and for burial exclusion. The association of these two apparently unrelated functions is revealing. The space that the community would defend was the one that had been cleared of symbolic private encroachment, which therefore defined the coalescing polity itself. The mutual defence that was one of the key functional reasons why the clustering happened in the first place could only be understood as a true common good once the most blatant House symbols were removed. It would be tempting to juxtapose with all this the prohibition against bearing weapons that the same line would be attested to have at Rome later on.[54]

In conclusion, the evidence reviewed here provides a fascinating, if conjectural, case of the origination of concerted action and shared regulation. Houses that traditionally had complete control over their fate gradually had to learn to pool some (but never all!) of their authority, to be able to take some key decisions that affected everyone. The tension between aristocratic privilege and increasing public jurisdiction would continue to characterise the political life of these polities for many centuries. The gradual introduction of legislation must therefore be understood to have been embedded within a context of customary practices progressively impacted by new rules that cohabitating elites gingerly agreed upon. Far from having the omnipotence that political theorists since Hobbes have tended to attribute them, early states were intrinsically fragile entities that initially existed only at the pleasure of the Houses that chose to be within their boundaries. Any behavioural restrictions, such as the one banning adult burial within the city, would have to be introduced by means of a negotiation between those that truly held the power, rather than imposed by an absolute ruler. On this somewhat precarious basis were founded the Italian city-states that would go on to constitute the Roman Empire. With all its political and legal sophistication, the largest and most durable superpower the Mediterranean ever saw never completely shed some of the traits of instability that characterised it from the very beginning.

Works Cited

Armstrong, J, 2016. *War and Society in Early Rome: From Warlords to Generals*. Cambridge: Cambridge University Press.

Banducci, L and A Gallone, eds, forthcoming. *An Imperial Graveyard and a Quarry from Gabii*. Ann Arbor: University of Michigan Press.

---

[53] Indeed, Rome is the only attested site at which eighth-century tombs are located inside (if only marginally) the sixth- century wall circuit; Gjerstad 1953.

[54] Drogula 2007.

Bartoloni, G and F Pitzalis, 2011. 'Mogli e madri nella nascente aristocrazia tirrenica.' In *Dalla nascita alla morte: antropologia e archeologia a confronto. Atti dell'Incontro Internazionale di studi in onore di Claude Lévi-Strauss*, edited by V Nizzo, 137–60. Rome: ESS.

Beck, R A, ed., 2007. *The Durable House: House Society Models in Archaeology*. First edn. Center for Archaeological Investigations Occasional Paper no. 35. Carbondale, IL: Southern Illinois University.

Bettelli, M, 1997. *Roma, la città prima della città: i tempi di una nascita. La cronologia delle sepolture ad inumazione di Roma e del Lazio nella prima età del ferro*. Rome: 'L'Erma' di Bretschneider.

Bietti Sestieri, A M, 1992a. *The Iron Age Community of Osteria dell'Osa. A Study of Socio-political Development in Central Tyrrhenian Italy*. New Studies in Archaeology. Cambridge: Cambridge University Press.

———, 2005. 'A Reconstruction of Historical Processes in Bronze and Early Iron Age Italy based on Recent Archaeological Research.' In *Papers in Italian Archaeology VI: Communities and Settlements from the Neolithic to the Early Medieval Period*, edited by P A R Attema, A Nijboer and A Zifferero, vol. 2:9–24. BAR International Series 1452. Oxford: Archaeopress.

———, ed., 1992b. *La necropoli laziale di Osteria dell'Osa*. Soprintendenza archeologica di Roma 1. Rome: Quasar.

Cohen, S, forthcoming. 'Catalogue of the Tombs and their Finds.' In *Elite Infant Burial Practices and Urbanization Processes at Gabii, Italy: The Area D Tombs and their Contents*, edited by M Mogetta. JRA Supplementary Series. Portsmouth, RI: Journal of Roman Archaeology.

Carsten, J and S Hugh-Jones, eds, 1995. *About the House: Lévi-Strauss and Beyond*. Cambridge: Cambridge University Press.

Di Fazio, M, 2017. 'Figures of Memory. Aulus Vibenna, Valerius Poplicola and Mezentius between History and Legend.' In Omnium Annalium Monumenta: *Historical Writing and Historical Evidence in Republican Rome*, edited by K. Sandberg and C J Smith, 322–50. Leiden: Brill.

Driessen, J, 2010. 'Spirit of Place: Minoan Houses as Major Actors.' In *Political Economies of the Aegean Bronze Age*, edited by D J Pullen, 35–65. Oxford: Oxbow.

———, 2012. 'A Matrilocal House Society in Pre- and Protopalatial Crete?' In *Back to the Beginning: Reassessing Social and Political Complexity on Crete during the Early and Middle Bronze Age*, edited by I Schoep, J Driessen, and P Tomkins, 358–83 Oxford: Oxbow.

Drogula, F K, 2007. 'Imperium, Potestas, and the Pomerium in the Roman Republic.' *Historia* 56.4:419–52.

Düring, B S, 2007. 'The Articulation of Houses at Neolithic Çatalhöyük, Turkey.' In *The Durable House: House Society Models in Archaeology*, edited by R A Beck, 130–53. Center for Archaeological Investigations Occasional Paper no. 35. Carbondale, IL: Southern Illinois University.

Evans, J M, J T Samuels, L Motta, M Naglak, and M D'Acri, 2019. 'An Iron Age Settlement at Gabii: An Interim Report of the Gabii Project Excavations in Area D, 2012–2015.' *Etruscan Studies* 70(4):1–33.

Fiorentini, M, 1988. *Ricerche sui culti gentilizi.* Pubblicazioni dell'Istituto di diritto romano e dei diritti dell'Oriente mediterraneo 69. Rome: La Sapienza.

Fontaine, P and S Helas, eds, 2016. *Le fortificazioni arcaiche del Latium vetus e dell'Etruria meridionale (IX–VI sec. a.C.): stratigrafia, cronologia e urbanizzazione.* Artes 7. Brussels: Institut Historique Belge de Rome.

Fulminante, F, 2014. *The Urbanisation of Rome and Latium Vetus: From the Bronze Age to the Archaic Era.* Cambridge: Cambridge University Press.

Fustel de Coulanges, N-D, 1864. *La cité antique. Étude sur le culte, le droit, les institutions de la Grèce et de Rome.* Paris: Hachette.

Gillespie, S D, 2000. 'Lévi-Strauss: *Maison* and *Société à Maisons*.' In *Beyond Kinship: Social and Material Reproduction in House Societies*, edited by R A Joyce and S D Gillespie, 22–52. Philadelphia: University of Pennsylvania Press.

———, 2007. 'When Is a House?' In *The Durable House: House Society Models in Archaeology*, edited by R A Beck, 25–50. Center for Archaeological Investigations Occasional Paper no. 35. Carbondale, IL: Southern Illinois University.

Gjerstad, E, 1953. *Early Rome.* Lund: C W K Gleerup.

González-Ruibal, A and M Ruiz-Gálvez, 2016. 'House Societies in the Ancient Mediterranean (2000–500 BC).' *Journal of World Prehistory* 29.4:383–437.

Grandazzi, A, 1991. *La fondation de Rome.* Paris: Belles Lettres.

Guaitoli, M, 1981. 'Gabii. Osservazioni sulle fasi di sviluppo dell'abitato.' In *Ricognizione archeologica: Nuove ricerche nel Lazio,* 23–57. Quaderni dell'Istituto di topografia antica della Università di Roma 9. Florence: Olschki.

Hölkeskamp, K-J, 2010. *Reconstructing the Roman Republic: An Ancient Political Culture and Modern Research.* Princeton, NJ: Princeton University Press.

Joyce, R A and S D Gillespie, eds, 2000. *Beyond Kinship: Social and Material Reproduction in House Societies.* Philadelphia: University of Pennsylvania Press.

Lévi-Strauss, C, 1975. *La voie des masques.* Paris: Skira.

Maras, D F, 2018. 'Kings and Tablemates. The Political Role of Comrade Associations in Archaic Rome and Etruria.' In *Beiträge zur Sozialgeschichte der Etrusker, Akten der internationalen Tagung (Wien, 8.-10.6.2016)*, edited by L Aigner Foresti and P Amann, 91–108. Phersu. Etrusko-italische Studien 1. Vienna: Holzhausen.

Mogetta, M and S Cohen, 2018. 'Infant and Child Burial Practices from an Élite Domestic Compound at Early Iron Age and Orientalising Gabii.' In *From Invisible to Visible. New Data and Methods for the Archaeology of Infant and Child Burials in Pre-Roman Italy*, edited by J Tabolli, 47–58. Uppsala: Åstrom

Momigliano, A, 1963. 'An Interim Report on the Origins of Rome.' *JRS* 53:95–121.

Naglak, M and S Cohen, forthcoming. 'Infant Burials as Mediators of House Identity at Iron Age Gabii.' In *Elite Infant Burial Practices and Urbanization Processes at Gabii, Italy: The Area D Tombs and their Contents*, edited by M Mogetta. Berlin: Topoi Press.

Naglak, M and N Terrenato, 2019. 'A House Society in Iron Age Latium? Kinship and State Formation in the Context of New Discoveries at Gabii.' In *La società gentilizia nell'Italia antica tra realtà e mito storiografico*, edited by M Di Fazio and S Paltineri, 99–119. Bari: Edipuglia.

Naso, A, 2017. 'Death and Burial.' In *Etruscology*, edited by A Naso, 317–39. Berlin: De Gruyter.

Pacciarelli, M, 2001. *Dal villaggio alla città: la svolta protourbana del 1000 a.C. nell'Italia tirrenica*, Grandi contesti e problemi della protostoria italiana; 4. Florence: All'insegna del giglio.

———, 2017. 'Society, 10th cent.–730 BCE.' In *Etruscology*, edited by A Naso, 2:759–72. 2 vols. Berlin: De Gruyter.

Potts, C R, 2015. *Religious Architecture in Latium and Etruria, c. 900–500 BC*. Oxford Monographs on Classical Archaeology. Oxford: Oxford University Press.

Rawlings, L, 1999. 'Condottieri and Clansmen. Early Italian Raiding, Warfare and the State.' In *Organised Crime in Antiquity*, edited by K Hopwood, 97–127. London: Duckworth.

Rich, J, 2017. 'Warlords and the Roman Republic.' In *War, Warlords, and Interstate Relations in the Ancient Mediterranean*, edited by T Ñaco del Hoyo and F López Sánchez, 266–94. Leiden: Brill.

Smith, C J, 2006. *The Roman Clan*. Cambridge: Cambridge University Press.

———, 2019. 'Revisiting the Roman Clan.' In *La società gentilizia nell'Italia antica tra realtà e mito storiografico*, edited by M Di Fazio and S Paltineri. Bari: Edipuglia.

Terrenato, N, 2011. 'The Versatile Clans. The Nature of Power in Early Rome.' In *State Formation in Italy and Greece: Questioning the Neoevolutionist Paradigm*, edited by N Terrenato and D C Haggis, 231–44. Oxford: Oxbow.

———, 2019. *The Early Roman Expansion into Italy*. Cambridge: Cambridge University Press.

Terrenato, N and L Motta, 2006. 'The Origins of the State *Par Excellence*. Power and Society in Iron Age Rome.' In *Celtes et Gaulois, l'Archéologie face à l'Histoire, 4: les mutations de la fin de l'âge du Fer*, edited by C C Haselgrove and V Guichard, 225–34. Glux-en-Glenne: Bibracte.

Tol, G W, 2012. *A Fragmented History: A Methodological and Artefactual Approach to the Study of Ancient Settlement in the Territories of Satricum and Antium*. Groningen Archaeological Studies 18. Eelde: Barkhuis.

Torelli, M, 1981. *Storia degli Etruschi*. Bari and Rome: Laterza.

Turfa, J M and A G Steinmayer Jr, 2002. 'Interpreting Early Etruscan Structures. The Question of Murlo.' *PBSR* 70:1–28.

Zifferero, A, 1991. 'Forme di possesso della terra e tumuli orientalizzanti nell'Italia centrale tirrenica.' In *Papers of the Fourth Conference of Italic Archaeology: The Archaeology of Power*, edited by E Herring, R Whitehouse and J Wilkins, vol. 1:145–51. London: Accordia.

Chapter 3

Authority and Display in Sixth-Century Etruria: The Vicchio Stele

P Gregory Warden and Adriano Maggiani

1. INTRODUCTION

The discovery of an inscribed stele (Figure 3.1) at the sanctuary of Poggio Colla (Vicchio, FI) provides new information about the sanctuary and its cults and raises important questions about literacy and elite authority at the northern edge of Etruria in the Archaic Period. The stele was unearthed in 2015, during the twenty-first and final season of excavation at the sanctuary of Poggio Colla. That final season was focused on the architecture of the acropolis sanctuary.[1] The stele was found in a secure archaeological context, carefully placed in the front podium of a temple constructed around 500 BCE. The date of the temple provides a *terminus ante quem*; thus the monument was displayed in the earliest phase of occupation at the site, Phase 0, and during the sixth century BCE.

2. THE SANCTUARY

Poggio Colla was a hilltop sanctuary, situated at a dominant position, the junction of the broad Mugello basin and the Sieve River valley.[2] The site controls an important route, connecting the Apennine passes and the plains of Etruria Padana with the region of Fiesole, thus providing access to and from two major areas of the Italian peninsula. The sanctuary was surrounded by extensive settlement and production areas, only a few of which have been excavated. They range from early date, Orientalising (seventh century BCE) production areas for ceramics and stone on the North-West Slope, to a Hellenistic complex for ceramic production in the Podere Funghi[3] about a kilometre from the acropolis. The site flourished from at

---

[1] Excavations were conducted under the auspices of the Mugello Valley Archaeological Project (MVAP), a consortium of universities that includes Southern Methodist University, Franklin and Marshall College, Franklin University Switzerland, The University of Texas, the University of Pennsylvania Museum, the Open University (UK), and the University of Florence. We are grateful to the Soprintendenza Archeologia, Belle Arti, e Paesaggio per l'area metropolitana di Firenze e le province di Pistoia e Prato (SABAP), Dr Andrea Pessina, Soprintendente, and Dr Susanna Sarti, Archaeological Inspector for the Mugello.
[2] Warden et al. 1999; Thomas 2001; Warden et al. 2005; Fedeli and Warden 2006; Warden 2007; Warden 2009a.
[3] Thomas 2000a.

Figure 3.1 Vicchio Stele, discovered at the sanctuary of Poggio Colla (Vicchio, FI), where it was interred c. 500 BCE. Source: Mugello Valley Archaeological Project (reproduced with permission).

least the seventh century through the second century BCE, but human presence is attested even earlier, from the Holocene through the Neolithic and Middle Bronze Age, suggesting that Poggio Colla's importance as a cult centre may pre-date the Etruscan Period.[4]

The acropolis sanctuary has at least four major phases of construction. The first (Phase 0), a pre-monumental phase (seventh and sixth centuries BCE), is a characteristic 'hut village' of the type well known in Etruria and Iron Age Italy (Phase 0).[5] There is evidence of timber-framed oval structures, only one of which has been identified and excavated, on the south flank of the terrace (PC 21) in an area undisturbed by later construction. Evidence of occasionally preserved postholes elsewhere on the terrace suggests the existence of other structures of this type.

The sanctuary had a long life, remaining an important ritual and economic centre through most of the Etruscan Period. The major alteration, Phase 1, came at the end of the sixth century when the entire acropolis underwent major renovation. The plateau was terraced to the north with earthen fill that included large amounts of debris from Phase 0; the heavily burnt soil includes

---

[4] A coring survey of a larger area has been conducted: Van der Graaff 2010.
[5] We continue to follow the established terminology in order to avoid confusion with earlier reports that identified three major phases of construction. The 'hut' phase is currently termed Phase 0. This report is only concerned with Phases 0 and 1: the 'hut' phase and the period of construction of the late Archaic temple (Phase 1). The destruction of the temple did result in the construction of a second temple/courtyard complex (Phase 2), and a subsequent courtyard with altar (Phase 3). For the temple: Thomas 2016. Both later structures (Phases 2–3) have a significantly different orientation from the Phase 1 temple.

large quantities of ceramics. The bucchero includes drinking shapes, suggesting that these ceramics may have been associated with banqueting in the early phase of sanctuary activity.[6]

The Phase 1 terracing activities were intended to accommodate a monumental structure. Extensive restructuring of this type on the northern edge of the plateau suggests that the exact placement of the temple in this area was important, for it would have been much easier to place the temple farther to the south where there is more space and abundant bedrock to support a monumental structure. The new structure is a temple approximately oriented on a north–south axis.[7] The foundations consist of large and well-finished blocks, sometimes up to two metres in length. Six Tuscan column bases and numerous podium blocks with characteristic Tuscan half-round mouldings are all that remain of the superstructure, apart from some scattered tiles and two tattered antefixes. These and the ceramic evidence from the north terraces provide the crucial evidence that dates the temple, and thus the final interment of the Vicchio stele, to c. 500 BCE. Of possible pertinence to the placement of the stele in the temple foundations is the handling of the temple remains after it was subsequently destroyed. After that destruction, when the sanctuary was rebuilt (Phase 2) in all elements of the superstructure, both podium blocks and column bases were moved and placed elsewhere, often turned upside down and in one case used to seal off what seems to be the most sacred aspect of the sanctuary, an underground fissure, discussed below. Their placement and handling seem connected to rituals associated with the trauma of the destruction of the Phase 1 temple.[8]

The sanctuary underwent other changes throughout its long history, and the late Archaic monumental temple was replaced by two courtyard complexes. The complicated history and stratigraphy of the sanctuary will be discussed elsewhere and do not have any particular pertinence to the stele, save that the ritual actions evident in later phases could be relevant if the interment of the stele was a deliberate ritual action. In any case, the reconstruction of the Phase 1 temple, which has been studied and will be published by Michael Thomas, presents challenges. Only the footings of the eastern flank of the temple are preserved, but there may be evidence for the columniation: a series of large blocks are placed at regular intervals and may have supported the large Tuscan bases. What is clearer is that the temple would have had a large podium in front made up of large sandstone ashlars similar to those used for the foundations of the temple proper. This section of the podium foundation was cleared in 2015 (PC Trench 48) and produced a large sandstone slab, curved at one end. It was the Vicchio stele.

---

[6] The ceramics and their context, as well as the Phase 0 occupation, are being studied and will be published by Phil Perkins. Some of these, along with other remains from the site, are on display in the Dicomano Museum, for which see Cappuccini et al. 2009.
[7] For a preliminary presentation of the architecture, see Thomas 2016.
[8] Warden 2010 and 2012a with previous bibliography.

Figure 3.2 Inscribed letters and signs on the lateral edges of the Vicchio Stele.
Source: Mugello Valley Archaeological Project (reproduced with permission).

3. THE STELE

When first discovered, the stele bore no discernible traces of decoration, but its shape did recall funerary monuments known from the Volterra-Fiesole area. Further examination revealed traces of inscribed letters and signs on the lateral edges (Figure 3.2). Light cleaning with water also revealed that both edges were inscribed. With the assistance of the Soprintendenza,[9] the stele was taken to the Centro di Restauro in Florence. It was cleaned in 2015 and 2016, and preliminary reports were published in 2016.[10] Now fully cleaned,[11] it awaits a decision about its eventual place of exhibition.

The stele is made of local sandstone, measuring 1.2 metres in height.[12] The upper part is well finished and inscribed; a lower section has an unfinished, rougher texture that would have been inserted in the ground. The upper part is rounded, and the edges are bevelled, presumably to receive the longest of the inscriptions. This inscription might have run along the top edge as well, but the top edge is now heavily abraded and deliberately scarred. One face, referred to here as the front of the stele, is well finished and inscribed. There is no evidence of decoration, but there is a small hole in the centre of the upper portion of the inscribed face as well as rectangular cuts (mortices?) on the sides.[13] After the Vicchio stele was

---

[9] We are extremely grateful to Dr Susanna Sarti and the Soprintendenza for immediate support of removal of the stele, its transport to Florence, and the subsequent conservation efforts. Sarti and Nocentini 2015.

[10] Maggiani 2016b; Warden 2016a and 2016b.

[11] The cleaning and conservation were ably handled by Stefano Sarri of the Centro di Restauro. We wish to acknowledge the support of Dr Andrea Pessina, Superintendent, SABAP, for providing immediate support for the conservation process.

[12] Maximum preserved length: 1.20 m. Max. preserved width: 0.64 m. Max. preserved thickness: 0.20 m.

[13] The stele might have been held upright by a wooden armature, hence the four mortices.

carefully cleaned,[14] it was documented with photogrammetry and then laser scanned in order to produce a digital model. Further analysis is required, as multispectral analysis could reveal traces of pigment or paint.[15] The stone itself is being analysed in Florence. Inscriptions are being studied by Adriano Maggiani and Rex Wallace, and full monographic publication of the monument is planned.

Upright stone markers or stelai are common in north Etruscan funerary contexts, and very often the stone slab evokes the human body through context, size, or decoration. For instance, large undecorated stones surround the monumental San Jacopo tumulus at Pisa;[16] they are inscribed with the names of family members who thus stand sentinel around the monument of the ancestor. To the north, at Bologna, funerary stelai are common from the Villanovan through the Classical periods, and some resemble the Vicchio stele closely in shape.[17] Even more apropos are the so-called Fiesole Stones, the *pietre fiesolane*,[18] found throughout the Val di Sieve, agro Fiorentino, and lower Arno Valley. The Vicchio stele is similar in shape to the stele of Larth Ninies in the Casa Buonarotti, which is slightly larger at 1.38 metres in height.[19] Another close parallel in shape and usage (inscribed and undecorated) is the stele of Laru Arianas from Panzano.[20] Many of the *pietre fiesolane* in fact evoke the human figure by placing human figures prominently on their faces – humans whose elite status is evoked through specific attributes. Larth Ninies, for instance, holds a spear and an intricately realised adze. Others might hold a lituus[21] or another type of weapon. Women are imaged as well as men.[22] Thus it is likely that the Vicchio stele, when placed upright in the sanctuary, would have evoked a human body; it is anthropomorphic, part of a long tradition in North Etruria of stone markers that in the funerary realm represent the individual, as well as the individual's status or rank. What is extraordinary about the Vicchio stele is that it is not funerary. It is from an entirely different context, yet one that is religious in nature and controlled by elite religious authority. Given the tradition of anthropomorphic stone markers in northern Etruria, the monument's visual authority possibly would have resulted in part from this evocation of an elite human presence.

The archaeological context of the stele is important for its interpretation and understanding. The stele is one of the three longest religious texts found to date,[23] the earliest, and the only one from a secure archaeological context. Key elements of this context are that the stele is indubitably in a secondary context in the

---

[14] Warden 2016b, fig. 4.
[15] For the digital documentation: Nocentini 2016; Nocentini and Warden 2017; Aterini et al. 2017.
[16] Floriani and Bruni 2006, 206.
[17] Certosa Tomb 215: Steiner forthcoming/2019, n. 14.
[18] For the latest discussion: Perazzi et al. 2016.
[19] Perazzi et al. 2016, 88 cat. no. 1.
[20] Maggiani 2016b, 76, fig. 3.
[21] The Frascole stele: Perazzi et al. 2016, 113 cat. no. 28.
[22] Most famously on the Londa stele: Perazzi et al. 2016, 90 cat. no. 3.
[23] The others are the *liber linteus* (Zagreb mummy) and the Capua tile; see Maggiani 2016a.

foundations of the Phase 1 temple. These foundations were cut into the north terrace fill that based on ceramic evidence provides a *terminus post quem* of the third quarter of the seventh century BCE. The Phase 1 temple can be dated to 500–480 BCE, thus providing a *terminus ante quem*. The stele would have been displayed in the sanctuary in its pre-monumental phase in the final quarter of the sixth century BCE. The timber-framed oval structures of the Phase 1 hut village are probably contemporary with the display of the stele.

The stele was an integral part of the sanctuary in its earliest phase, and it is part of a long series of ritual contexts that have been unearthed at Poggio Colla. The history of the sanctuary is characterised by a remarkable series of ritual deposits, one of which may even postdate the actual destruction of the sanctuary c. 178 BCE.[24] Some of these are foundation deposits; others votive dedications; and still others connected to rites of purification or expiation. These contexts have been discussed in detail elsewhere.[25] They are characterised by specific ritual actions: fragmentation, reversal, and directionality, as well as the reuse of structural elements of the Phase 1 temple in later phases. Every single architectural element of the temple was moved from its original location and in many cases interred upside down. The action of turning elements (ceramics as well as architectural elements) upside down when consigning (or returning?) them to the earth is widely attested at Poggio Colla. Some of these later contexts would have been visible, for instance a series of Phase 1 podium blocks and a large Tuscan column base that are moved and adapted to form an altar platform (Area PC6) on the north-east part of the acropolis. It has been argued that the reuse of these blocks in a way constituted a ritual process that mimicked human burial: that the temple was in fact regarded as a body. The destruction of the temple and its subsequent associated trauma necessitated ritual actions by members of the community that evoked rituals associated with human burial, lending the temple itself a kind of metaphorical animation and corporeality.[26]

The reuse and display of temple parts thus constituted both a termination and a promulgation of memory. The temple is laid to rest, put back into the earth, but its elements are displayed and in fact reborn as part of later structures that memorialise the temple. Is this what was done with the stele? Significantly it was laid to rest face up, with the inscriptions facing the sky. Would it have been visible?[27] Would the bevelled edges have been visible? Its incorporation in the temple must have had significance. One of the unanswered questions is that the face of the stele has a central hole, quite obviously purposely drilled into the surface.

---

[24] Thomas 2012. The destruction of the sanctuary and surrounding settlement is dated by both historical (Thomas 2012) and numismatic (Thomas 2008b) evidence.

[25] The most recent summary can be found in Warden 2012b. The nature of the contexts and the connection of material culture to identity was discussed by Warden 2013. See also Warden 2015.

[26] Warden 2012a, 88–110.

[27] I am grateful to Phil Perkins for suggesting this possibility. The display of sections of earlier temples or altars in later structures is known elsewhere, for instance at Sant'Omobono.

The hole is too shallow to hold any kind of attachment when the stone was vertical, but it could have had a purpose if the stele functioned as a table. Might the stele have been placed in the temple foundations, remained visible, served as a memorial or as a memory, for continuity, or even been used ritually? That the stele was placed in the podium, traditionally the place of ritual interactions and performance, rather than under the temple, may be significant. Another question that may not ever be answered is whether the precise spot, on the eastern flank of the podium, had any significance given the importance of 'directionality' in ritual practice at this site. What is certain is that in Etruscan ritual practice the podium is the place of performance, interaction, and display.[28] The podium, with the scaenographic temple as a backdrop, is the place where the presiding elite, the magistrate/priest, would perform or oversee ritual, and also a place where elite objects[29] are viewed as they are used in ritual, and possibly a place where such objects might have been displayed.

The practice of reuse of architectural elements (as well as of 'reversal', or the turning of the objects upside down) may be connected to the possible chthonic character of the cult. The most important example of this practice at Poggio Colla is the 'Fissure Deposit', where a moulded podium block of the temple was deliberately broken – the chisel marks are clearly evident at either end – and turned upside down to ritually seal an underground fissure that was the centre of ritual activity at the sanctuary. Next to the block were deposited a thin gold ring and a textile decorated with gold threads that must have belonged to an elite or sacred textile. This context is particularly important in relation to the evidence of the stele, for the chthonic character of the cult at Poggio Colla, along with the discovery of the remarkable birth scene on a bucchero vase,[30] along with dedications by women,[31] and strong evidence for female agency at the site,[32] had already led excavators to suspect that the primary deity of the sanctuary might be Uni.

4. THE INSCRIPTIONS

The Vicchio stele has a very long series of inscriptions, possibly the longest Etruscan lapidary inscription to date. It is made of a type of sandstone that is fine grained but easily degraded; it offers difficulties for the reading of long sequences of letters. A good part of the text may therefore be irrevocably lost, but the entire text may have been two hundred letters in length. From a palaeographic point of view, the closest parallels are with a small group of stone inscriptions from Fiesole, recently recognised and attributed to a local epigraphic workshop. The Panzano

---

[28] For detailed discussion, see Warden 2012a.
[29] For objects as communicators of elite authority at Poggio Colla: Steiner and Neils 2018; Steiner forthcoming/2019.
[30] Perkins 2012.
[31] Castor 2009.
[32] Meyers 2010 and 2013; Meyers and Steiner 2015.

stele is a particularly convincing parallel because of the form of the object, as well as the form of the letters, and especially the interpunctuation of three superimposed dots. It is datable from 525 to 510 BCE, and thus approximately contemporary with the Vicchio stele.[33]

The stele is a palimpsest. It was inscribed four times, twice on the edges and twice on the face, as follows:

Text 1: The pseudo-boustrophedic text on the bevelled edges of the stele may have run over the top, thus two extremely long lines. The upper part of the stele has been deliberately defaced, so much of the text may be lost. The text is still being studied, but certain words that can be identified with certainty (*esχaχa*) or with some confidence (*akaśha* or *zina*××) indicate that the text refers to specific dedications at the sanctuary.

Text 2: Top front. Several letters can be identified, but the specifics remain elusive.

Text 3: The text on the front lower left was published by Maggiani as follows:[34]

   (vacat) tinaś: θ(?)anuri: unial(?)
   ẹ ỵ ị: zal
   ame (akil??)

An approximate translation might thus be:
'Of Tinia (for Tinia) in the xxxx of Uni/xxxx(objects) two / must (akil ?) be

Text 4: Upper left edge. A small section of Text 1 on the upper left edge was effaced/erased and a new text was superimposed. It is not presently readable.

While the details are still being worked out, it is clear that the texts are sacred in nature and late Archaic in date. The identification of the names of Tinia and Uni in Text 3 and the possibility that Uni is the titular divinity of at least one part of the sanctuary fits the evidence for ritual discussed above. Testimony for Tinia and Uni closely connected at a site accords well with the new evidence from Marzabotto where temples to these two divinities have been found side by side.[35] A superimposition of the cult of Tinia in the place of (*θanuri*) Uni is intriguing given the suggestion that the cult of Tinia, attested at nearby Monte Giovi, might have been transported to another sanctuary in the Mugello, possibly Poggio Colla.[36]

The stele is clearly an extraordinary monument, an *unicum*, and a number of questions come immediately to the fore, some specific to the object in question, others broader and connected to our understanding of the region in the Archaic Period and after. Why was it inscribed a number of times? Why was part of it erased and reinscribed? Why was the top of the stele deliberately and systematically defaced? Was the stele used in more than one way? How and by

---

[33] Maggiani 2016b, 221.
[34] Maggiani 2016b, 223.
[35] For which, most recently, see Govi 2018.
[36] Cappuccini 2017, 193 n. 32.

whom would it have been read? What does it tell us about literacy and authority at an Etruscan sanctuary in northern Etruria?

There is evidence for literacy in the area around Fiesole,[37] and there is also other evidence at the sanctuary of Poggio Colla. Short inscriptions on ceramics have been found, but most important is the evidence of the 'Inscription Deposit', a purification context given that bones of a sacrificed piglet were included. It also included elements that must have been displayed in the late Archaic temple, probably placed here after the traumatic destruction of the temple.[38] One of the objects included in this deposit, a pyramidal sandstone base, inscribed with the name of its dedicator, provides evidence for literacy and elite authority at the site.[39]

The deposition of the stele marked a moment of great import in the life of the sanctuary and for the community connected to it. The deposition of the Vicchio stele, a monument that articulated the religious authority of the place, was an act of political consequence and religious significance, and subsequently an entirely new and even greater symbol of authority arose on the acropolis of Poggio Colla. The new temple would have been easily visible across the Mugello, a notable visual symbol to anyone crossing over the Apennines, entering Etruria from the north. Could the stele of Vicchio have served a similar purpose?

As we have seen, the stele was displayed in the sanctuary in the later stages of the sixth century. At that point, the hilltop would have been covered by oval huts and worship would have centred on the sacred fissure. Perhaps the fissure was covered by a structure at that point, or perhaps a hut next to it might have served as a locus of worship, a possible early temple. Nothing of the sort, however, has been preserved. It is not unreasonable, however, to surmise that the stele stood somewhere in the vicinity of the fissure, thus placed not far from where it eventually came to be deposited at the end of the century. Even in its earliest phase Poggio Colla seems to have been an important place, a 'santuario di confine' that marked the upper reaches of Etruria, a place of deep cultural interaction. The seventh- and sixth-century bucchero is of exceptional quality, imported from as far south as the major urban centres of southern Etruria. Bronze figurines that were displayed in the temple, and Archaic bronzes that eventually found their way into the deposits of later date, attest to the wealth of the site. The sanctuary was an important economic engine that drove the local economy.

At the same time, its location connected it, via the Sieve and the Arno, to the important centres to the south, Fiesole, Arezzo, Volterra, and the Senese. The sanctuary was connected to Marzabotto and Bologna via the nearby Apennine passes and thus to the vast and sweeping plains of Etruria Padana. Poggio

---

[37] Maggiani 2016c. For more general issues on Etruscan literacy and religion: Maggiani 2016a.
[38] For a full description of the contents and ritual involved: Warden 2009b.
[39] First published by Camporeale 2012. For a different interpretation, see Colonna 2015.

Colla was more than a mere 'santuario di confine'. It was a liminal site of some importance, a place that connected the Etruscans with their neighbours to the north, the Liguri, the Veneti, and the Celts. The area of the Mugello and the Apennine passes was a place of intense regional interaction, not unlike southernmost Etruria which in this regard is better documented.[40] Rather than being a barrier, the mountains may have connected various regions and peoples.[41] This was certainly the case in the fourth and third centuries BCE when Gauls and Ligurians were present south of the Apennines, and when major centres such as Marzabotto and Gonfienti were abandoned. The material culture of smaller centres such as Monterenzio attests to the arrival on Celts from the north, and the presence of both Celts and Ligurians is well documented in the historical sources.[42] Etruscan interaction with Italic populations of northern Italy is also attested in the many votive deposits from both the Apennines and Emilia-Romagna even as early as the sixth century BCE,[43] and Poggio Colla, given its strategic location and proximity to major urban centres northern and southern, would have been at the centre of this rich multiethnic landscape.

The Vicchio stele is a surprising monument. Why do we not have something like it farther to the south, in central or southern Etruria? Why is there a need to document elite religious practice at this particular sanctuary? The answer may be that it is precisely at a liminal site like Poggio Colla,[44] a place frequented by diverse populations, that religious authority and elite power need to be clearly and specifically articulated and displayed. If these inscriptions do indeed document religious practice, if they prescribe and proscribe through example, and if they are indeed a *lex sacra* or *lex arae*, as they seem to be, then they may have been set into stone here, for one and all to see, because Poggio Colla is a place that was not just visited by Etruscans. It is a place where peoples of other cultures came to worship or to trade. Here the Vicchio stele stood as a symbol of power, authority, and elite hegemony.[45] The stele communicated both as an inter-elite document, asserting and reasserting the authority of the ruling elites (or supplanting that authority if the 'erasures' are intentional), and communicating the authority of both the human elites and the ruling divinities to all viewers and segments of society. In the Etruscan theocratic landscape where secular and religious authority were often

---

[40] For instance by Rajala and Tikkanen 2018.
[41] Currently being researched by Phil Perkins. I am grateful to Prof. Perkins for sharing his research with me. A preliminary report was presented at a conference in Cambridge: http://www3.arch.cam.ac.uk/iron_age/2013/
[42] For recent discussion of Ligurian presence in the area as well as the historical sources: Thomas 2012, 32–6.
[43] Romualdi 1987; Miari 2000.
[44] I am grateful to the participants of the Edinburgh conference, particularly Christopher Smith, for articulating and helping define some of the considerations that led to this particular line of argumentation.
[45] For a thought-provoking theoretical summary of early writing in Etruria and its connections to authority: Smith 2018.

interchangeable, the stele is testament to the authority of divinity interpreted through human action, as expressed in writing at a time when the written word would have served as both text and image.

As law, the stele could have been consulted and interpreted by the literate few, but its authority would have been easily understood even without being read. It is as powerful a symbol as the imposing temple that arose in its place in the next century, a temple whose own authority rested on the foundation, physical and symbolic, of the Vicchio stele.

Works Cited

Aterini, B, A Nocentini, and P G Warden, 2017. 'Digital Technologies for the Documentation, Analysis, and Dissemination of the Etruscan "Stele di Vicchio".' In *New Activities for Cultural Heritage*, edited by M Ceccarelli et al., 158–65. New York: Springer.

Camporeale, G, 2012. 'Ager Faesulanus, Poggio Colla.' *Rivista di Epigrafia Etrusca*, SE 75:187–8.

Cappuccini, L, C Ducci, S Gori, and L Paoli, 2009. *Museo Archeologico Comprensoriale del Mugello e Val di Sieve*. Florence: Aska.

Cappuccini, L, ed. 2017. *Monte Giovi. 'Fulmini e saette:' da luogo di culto a foretezza d'altura nel territorio di Fiesole etrusca*. Florence: All'Insegna del Giglio.

Castor, A, 2009. 'An Early Hellenistic Jewelry Hoard from Poggio Colla.' MAAR 54:245–62.

Colonna, G, 2015. 'Ager Faesulanus. Poggio Colla (Vicchio). Rivista di Epigrafia Etrusca.' *Studi Etruschi* 78:223–4.

Fedeli, L and P G Warden, 2006. 'Recenti scavi a Poggio Colla (Vicchio).' *Notiziario della Soprintendenza per i Beni Archeologici della Toscana* 2:334–7.

Floriani, P and S Bruni, 2006. *La tomba del Principe. Il tumulo etrusco di via San Jacopo*. Pisa: ETS.

Govi, E, 2017. 'La dimensione del sacro nella città di *Kainua*-Marzabotto.' In *La città etrusca e il sacro. Santuari e istituzioni politiche*, edited by E Govi, 145–79. Bologna: Bononia University Press.

Maggiani, A, 2016a. 'Epigrafia e religione.' In *Gli Etruschi maestri di scrittura. Catalogo della mostra, Museo dell'Accademia Etrusca di Cortona*, edited by L Agostiniani and M L Arancio, 96–105. Cortona: Silvana.

———, 2016b. 'The Vicchio Stele: The Inscription.' *EtrSt* 19.2:220–24.

———, 2016c. 'La scrittura a Fiesole in età arcaica.' In *L'ombra degli etruschi. Simboli di un popolo tra pianura e collina*, edited by P Perazzi, G Poggesi, and S Sarti, 73–81. Florence: Edifir.

Meyers, G E, 2010. 'Weaving as Worship: Women and Ritual at the Etruscan Site of Poggio Colla (Vicchio).' Paper presented at the 111th Annual Meeting of the Archaeological Institute of America, Anaheim.

———, 2013. 'Women and the Production of Ceremonial Textiles: A Reevaluation of Ceramic Textile Tools in Etrusco-Italic Sanctuaries.' *AJA* 117:247–74.

Meyers, G E and A Steiner, 2015. 'Women in the Sanctuary: New Evidence for Female Participation in Ritual at the North Etruscan Sanctuary of Poggio Colla.' Paper presented at the 116th Annual Meeting of the Archaeological Institute of America, New Orleans.

Miari, M, 2000. *Stipi votive dedll'Etruria padana*. Rome: Giorgio Bretschneider.

Nocentini, A, 2016. *La stele etrusca di Vicchio, metodologie di rilieveper un'iscrizione da svelare*. Testo di Dottorato di Ricerca, Università degli Studi di Firenze, Dipartimento di Architettura DIDA.

Nocentini, A and P G Warden, 2017. 'Il santuario di Poggio Colla: dalla ricerrca archeologica all rappresentazione digitale, testimonianze per il rituale etrusco.' In *Territori e Frontiere della Rappresentazione*, edited by A Di Lucco et al., 1025–32. Rome: Gangemi International.

Nocentini, A, S Sarti, and P G Warden, 2018. *Acque Sacre. Culto etrusco sull'Appennino toscano*. Florence: Consiglio Regionale della Toscana.

Perazzi, P, G Poggesi, and S Sarti, 2016. *L'ombra degli etruschi. Simboli di un popolo tra pianura e collina*. Florence: Edifir.

Perkins, P, 2012. 'The Bucchero Childbirth Stamp on a Late Orientalizing Period Shard from Poggio Colla,' *EtrSt* 15: 146–201.

Rajala, U and K W Tikkanen, 2018. 'Multicultural Interaction, Colonial Boundaries and Changing Group Identities: Contextualizing Inscriptions, Languages and Alphabets.' In *The Archaeology of Death: Proceedings of the Seventh Conference of Italian Archaeology held at the National University of Ireland, Galway, April 16–18, 2016*, edited by E Herring and E O'Donoghue, 107–27. Papers in Italian Archaeology VII. Oxford: Archaeopress.

Romualdi, A, 1987. 'La piccola plastica votiva e i luoghi di culto della Romagna nel periodo arcaico e classico.' In *La formazione della città in Emilia Romagna*, edited by G Bermond Montanari, 284–306. Bologna: Nuova Alfa.

Sarti, S and A Nocentini, 2015. 'Vicchio (FI). Il recupero di una stele etrusca iscritta.' *Notiziario della Soprintendenza per i Beni Archeologici della Toscana* 11:107–9.

Smith, C, 2018. 'Recent Approaches to Early Writing.' In *The Archaeology of Death: Proceedings of the Seventh Conference of Italian Archaeology held at the National University of Ireland, Galway, April 16–18, 2016*, edited by E Herring and E O'Donoghue, 30–6. Papers in Italian Archaeology VII. Oxford: Archaeopress.

Steiner, A, forthcoming/2019. 'Communicating Elite Authority: Red-figure Pottery in Ritual Contexts at Poggio Colla.' In *Griechische Vasen als Kommunikationsmedium*, edited by C Lang-Auinger and E Trinkl. CVA Österreich Beiheft 3. Vienna: Austrian Academy of Sciences.

Steiner, A and J Neils, 2018. 'An Imported Attic Kylix from the Sanctuary at Poggio Colla.' *EISt* 1.1:1–48.

Thomas, M L, 2000a. 'The Technology of Daily Life in a Hellenistic Etruscan Settlement.' *EtrSt* 7:107–8.

———, 2000b. 'An Imitative Unsealed Semis from Northern Etruria.' *American Journal of Numismatics* 12:113–18.

———, 2001. 'Excavations at Poggio Colla (Vicchio di Mugello): A Report of the 2000–2002 Seasons.' *EtrSt* 8:119–30.

———, 2012. 'One Hundred *Victoriati* from the Sanctuary at Poggio Colla (Vicchio di Mugello): Ritual Contexts and Roman Expansion.' *EtrSt* 15:19–93.

———, 2016. 'New Evidence for the Early Phases of the Temple at Poggio Colla (Vicchio di Mugello).' Lecture delivered at the 117th Annual Meeting of the Archaeological Institute of America, San Francisco.

Van der Graaff, I, R Vander Poppen, and T Nales, 2010. 'The Advantages and Limitations of Coring Survey: An Initial Assessment of the Poggio Colla Coring Project.' In *TRAC 2009: Proceedings of the Nineteenth Annual Theoretical Roman Archaeology Conference*, edited by A Moore, G Taylor, E Harris, P Girdwood and L Shipley, 53–65. Oxford: Oxbow Books.

Warden, P G, M L Thomas, and J Galloway, 1999. 'Excavations at the Etruscan Settlement of Poggio Colla: The 1995–1998 Seasons.' *JRA* 12:231–46.

Warden, P G, M L Thomas, A Steiner, and G Meyers, 2005. 'The Etruscan Settlement of Poggio Colla (1998–2004 excavations).' *JRA* 18:252–66.

Warden, P G, 2007. 'Vicchio (FI). Poggio Colla. Campagna di scavo 2006.' *Notiziario della Soprintendenza per i Beni Archeologici della Toscana* 3:38–40.

———, 2009a. 'Vicchio (FI). Recenti scavi (2008) a Poggio Colla.' *Notiziario della Soprintendenza per i Beni Archeologici della Toscana* 4:402–5.

———, 2009b. 'Remains of the Ritual at the Sanctuary of Poggio Colla.' In *Votives, Places, and Rituals in Etruscan Religion. Studies in Honor of Jean MacIntosh Turfa*, edited by M Gleba and H Becker, 121–7. Religions in the Graeco-Roman World 166. Leiden: Brill.

———, 2010. 'The Temple is a Living Thing: Fragmentation, Enchainment, and the Reversal of Ritual at the Acropolis Sanctuary of Poggio Colla.' In *The Archaeology of Sanctuaries and Ritual in Etruria*, edited by N de Grummond and I Edlund-Berry, 55–67. Portsmouth, RI: Journal of Roman Archaeology.

———, 2012a. 'Monumental Embodiment: Somatic Symbolism and the Tuscan Temple.' In *Monumentality in Etruscan and Early Roman Architecture: Ideology and Innovation*, edited by M L Thomas and G Meyers, 82–110. Austin: The University of Texas Press.

———, 2012b. 'Giving the Gods their Due: Ritual Evidence from Poggio Colla' (with an appendix by A Trentacoste). In *Francesco Nicosia. L'archeologo e il soprintendente. Scritti in memoria*, edited by G Camporeale et al., 249–57. Notiziario della Soprintendenza per i Beni Archeologici della Toscana Supplemento 1 al n. 8/12. Florence: All'Insegna del Giglio.

———, 2013. 'Etruscans at the (Northern) Edge: The Sanctuary of Poggio Colla (FI).' Paper presented at the conference on 'Frontiers of the European Iron Age', Magdalene College and the McDonald Institute, Cambridge, 20–22 September 2013.

———, 2015. 'Recent Discoveries at the Sanctuary and Settlement of Poggio Colla (Vicchio di Mugello).' Paper presented at the conference 'Dalla Valdelsa al Conero. Ricerche di archeologia e topografia storica in ricordo di Giuliano De Marinis', Colle di Val d'Elsa, San Gimignano, and Poggibonsi, 27–29 November 2015.

———, 2016a. 'The Vicchio Stele and Its Context.' *EtrSt* 19.2:208–19.

———, 2016b. 'Una scoperta recente: la stele iscitta del santuario etrusco di Poggio Colla (Vicchio).' In *L'ombra degli etruschi. Simboli di un popolo tra pianura e collina*, edited by P Perazzi, G Poggesi, and S Sarti, 83–5. Florence: Edifir.

Part II

Constructing Early Roman Law: Sources and Methods

Chapter 4

The Twelve Tables and the *leges regiae*: A Problem of Validity

*Carlos Felipe Amunátegui Perelló**

1. INTRODUCTION

In modern legal systems rules of law are, generally speaking, created through legislation and broadly understood custom. Legal scholars usually envisage the laws of the Twelve Tables as the first such body of legal rules in Roman law and, therefore, as an antecessor, of sorts, to all legislated law.[1] According to the *communis opinio*, the mid-fifth century BCE represented a turning point where legislation would either be invented or imported into Roman culture, with the Twelve Tables being hailed as a model. Thus, all reports of earlier legislation were written off as later annalistic inventions which retrospectively projected the situation of subsequent centuries onto the previous, formative era,[2] which should be considered as part of the customary order, rather than the legal one.[3] This last part of the argument is rather perplexing: for sometimes it recognises the very existence of rules of law in the Roman legal order, but instead of interpreting them as legal norms, it casts them out from the legal order on account of their alleged customary nature.[4]

While attributing the Twelve Tables a privileged status as Rome's first statutes at the very origin of Western legal tradition might serve to buttress Roman legal scholars' pride in the material they study, it is hardly a tenable explanation since it leaves many uncomfortable facts unexplained – most prominently, the whole of the constitutional order of the early Republic.

---

* This article is part of Fondecyt Project 1180022.
[1] See, for instance, Schiavone 2012, 88–90.
[2] See Pohlenz 1924. For a critical approach, see Balsdon 1971.
[3] Kaser 1938, 1960, and 1971, 30; Crawford 1996, 2:561; Arangio-Ruiz 2006, 22; Stanzione 2010.
[4] This last interpretation ultimately comes from Pomponius' statement that in its origin, the city lacked any sort of *lege certa* (D. 1.2.2.1), and everything was in the hands of the kings; see Elmore 1922; Pugliese 1973. In any case, D. 1.2.2.1 seems to be an introductory statement, explicitly made to enhance the importance of the laws of the kings, which are presented immediately afterwards, in D. 1.2.2.2-3. In other words, what Pomponius seems to mean is that in a very Archaic Period there was no law, but later the kings started to legislate, not that the kings never made any kind of statute; see Mantovani 2016, 1.910.

As far as we know, unless we are severely misled by the extant evidence, the Twelve Tables seem to focus on what we would refer to as private law.[5] Although there are some rules related to what later would be called public law,[6] such as the one referring to the *comitatus maximus* (XIIT 9.1-2), the lack of regulation of the foremost magistracies of the city is striking, especially since tradition states that the main purpose of decemviral legislation was to control the power of the consuls (Liv. 3.9). Whatever the cause for this omission, the fact remains that the most important public institutions of the early Republic do not seem to be regulated by the Twelve Tables, and tradition usually points to the earlier kings of Rome to explain their creation. The standard answer to this obvious contradiction is that this may be a later rationalisation of the role of custom in early Roman law. Most public institutions were created by custom, and later republican scholars simply ascribed them to the early Roman kings in order to explain their existence. Therefore, when they felt an institution needed an origin, they would point to Romulus as its creator, for his position as the founder of the city would allow it.

Although this theory has its merits, and it is probably true in some cases, it overlooks some decisive facts. Firstly, Romulus is not the only royal character supposed to have legislated before the Republic. In fact, according to tradition most Roman kings created statutes, including characters rooted in much more solid historical fact than the founder of the city, such as Tarquin the Elder and Servius Tullius. Secondly, we happen to have some material evidence that seems to support the idea that early kings of Rome could in fact legislate. As it is well known, in 1899 the Italian archaeologist Giacomo Boni found in the area of the Vulcanal a cippus made of a black marble slab inscribed with archaic characters, now known as the *Lapis Niger*.[7] Although the text is written in Latin, its meaning is almost impossible to grasp. Its reading is very uncertain (*ILS* 4913), the king (*recei*) is certainly mentioned, as well as *sakros* (as in *sacer*, the typical sanction in many dispositions of the Twelve Tables), a *calator* (as in the *comitia calata*), and the word *iovestod* (possibly an ancient form of *ius*). The cippus seems to have been made to display the text publicly, possibly in the early sixth century BCE. Although there is debate, consensus has been reached around the fact that the slab seems to contain a statute to be displayed in a way similar to the later Twelve Tables, following the traditional model common to the entire Mediterranean area. There also seems to be some indirect evidence for other, similar monuments that no longer survive. For instance, Dionysius tells us about a certain law of Tullus Hostilius composed in Greek characters, cast in bronze tablets, and fixed into the Temple of Diana and still extant in his time (Dion. Hal. *Ant. Rom.* 4.26.5). Although we can only speculate about the specific content of the disposition, it specifically points to material evidence of legislation made by the early kings.

---

[5] Pugliese 1973, 24; Guarino 1975, 208; Watson 1995, 471; Capogrossi Colognesi 2007, 93; Schiavone 2012, 97.

[6] Crawford 1996, 2:561.

[7] See Holloway 1996, 81; Lepore 2010, 55–62.

And finally, there is one other aspect that is not sufficiently considered by legal scholars: reform. Whatever virtues one might ascribe to custom, it lacks the specific ability to self-reform. As a source of law, custom always preserves the laws of the past, and even when it creates new institutions, it usually connects them with older material to create a smooth transition from older laws to new ones. Custom is the result of blind historical developments, and therefore it lacks a rational texture. Where custom has no planning and no conscious aim, legislation is the result of deliberation, contains objectives, and implies design. Custom does not usually reform custom for the simple reason that to amend means to plan, and that can only be done through legislation.

Early Roman public institutions present different layers, where some are deeply rationalistic and do not appear to be the result of simple historical developments. In other words, many of the institutions of early Rome seem to be the result of planning and design, even when they might have a customary origin. Take, for instance, the *curiae*. They seem to have an origin compatible with custom.[8] In fact, the names of the *curiae* that we know about do not hold a definite pattern.[9] Where some seem to be locative (*Veliense, Foriense*), others may be patronymic and linked with *gentes* (*Titia, Faucia, Acculeia*), while still others are unclear (*Rapta, Velitia, Tifata?*).[10] Seven of these were older (*veteres*) than the others (*novae*) (Fest. 174L; Varr. L.L. 5.155; Tac. Ann. 12.24), and they even seem to have different buildings:[11] one is in the oldest area under occupation on the Palatine hill, while the others seem to be located in a different zone, perhaps between the Palatine and the Caelian, an area which came under occupation only during the late seventh century BCE.[12] Each seems to have a chieftain of sorts (the *curio*), while there was also a *curio maximus* who was a patrician and held some kind of leadership position[13] (Dion. Hal. Ant. Rom. 2.14.3; Fest 113; Liv. 27.8.1–3). Put simply, their unpredictable nature reveals traces of a customary institution. They show development from seven original groupings to a larger number in a subsequent period. Their names do not follow a fixed pattern, as one would expect from different groupings that emerged in different moments in time. They have independent chieftains, which does not seem to fit in with the general public organisation of the later monarchy, let alone the early Republic, as one would expect from a political institution that no longer fulfils a clear political role, but held one at an earlier stage.

Regardless, on top of this random customary institution lies a rational structure, which tradition commonly ascribes to the fictional character Romulus.[14]

---

[8] Their name seems to point to a group of men (*co-viria*), and can mean the group or the building where they are gathered. See Terrenato 2010, 510; Carandini 2011, 24–5.
[9] Cornell 1995, 117; Momigliano 1989, 104; Smith 2006, 188.
[10] Cornell 1995, 117.
[11] The discovery of the building of the *curiae veteres* was claimed, apparently in the area of the Palatine hill. See Carandini 2006, 60–1; Smith 2006, 188.
[12] See Richardson, Jr 1992, 104.
[13] Drummond 1989, 178; Richard 1993, 29; Mitchell 2005, 130; Richard 2005, 109; Smith 2006, 216.
[14] Some scholarship is increasingly serious about the real character of the latter. For instance, see Carandini 2007 (translated as Carandini 2011). Carandini's rather polemical theories have been subject to criticism: see Wiseman 2001 and 2011–12.

According to this tradition, the first king of Rome divided the Roman population into three tribes and thirty *curiae* in the aftermath of the legendary Rape of the Sabines (Liv 1.13.6; Cic *Rep.* 2.14; Plut. *Rom.* 14.6). Their names would honour some of the women who were taken and it would give Rome a popular organisation, for they could be summoned in the *comitia* and manifest their intentions. In fact, these *curiae* would hold one of the most important political functions in the monarchy: to ratify the nomination of a king through the *lex de imperio*,[15] a faculty they preserved through the Republican Period and even into the Empire, although then in a purely ritualistic fashion. They could be summoned by the king through the *comitia calata*, apparently held thrice a year, maybe in the days marked in the calendar as QRCF.[16] The curial structure seems to mimic that of international relations, with the number thirty standing in contraposition to the thirty Latin communities of the Alban Hills, which were fossilised in the Latin Fairs (Tac. *Ann.* 6.11; Liv. 32.1.9.1).[17]

The organisation attributed to Romulus seems to be deeply rational and even anachronistic.[18] However, it does reflect a stage of Roman public organisation, which might not fit the eighth century BCE, but certainly does seem to be consistent with the early sixth century. In fact, during the late seventh and early sixth centuries BCE there are traces of a strong central authority, which was able to realise impressive public construction projects,[19] including the drainage of the forum,[20] the construction of the Senate house (*Curia*),[21] and even the *Comitium*, the very place where all the *curiae* could be summoned. Additionally, according to tradition, Tarquin the Elder reformed the Senate and populated it with three hundred members, coordinating its size with the actual number of *curiae*. In fact, we know that until the late fourth century BCE, when the *Lex Ovinia* reformed the institution, its members were elected from among the *curiae* (Fest. 246).[22]

In any case, this rational reform did not last long, for a different organisation of the city came along shortly after by the hand of Servius Tullius. According to tradition, he created a new organisation of the city, dividing it into a number of territorial tribes, grouping the population into classes according to their wealth, and creating a competing assembly of the population divided by *centuriae*. This is the basic organisation of the early Republic, which was superimposed on the declining curial configuration of the city, and seems to have its first developments in the late monarchy.

---

[15] With most of the older relevant scholarship, see Develin 1977; and for recent discussions, see Magdelain 1990a, 307–11; Forsythe 2006, 143; Serrao 2006, 74; Beck 2011.
[16] Forsythe 2006, 135.
[17] See Cornell 1989.
[18] Forsythe 2006, 117; Smith 2006, 168.
[19] Momigliano 1989, 95–6; Torelli 1989, 37; Smith 1996, 150; Edlund-Berry 2013.
[20] Cornell 1995, 102.
[21] See Bartoli 1963.
[22] Develin 1977, 56; Magdelain 1990b, 396; Mitchell 2005, 130; Richard 2005, 109.

There seem to be at least three stages in the development of the organisation of the city of Rome in the Regal era. The oldest one featured the *curiae*, with an unknown and probably developing number of them, holding their own chiefdoms and maybe a common one. A second stage would match what tradition attributes to Romulus, which might be properly the organisation of the late seventh and early sixth centuries, and finally the Servian organisation in *centuriae*, which would have taken shape in the middle or late sixth century.

Although the first organisation might be understood as driven by custom, the later ones require a rational setting which would be more indicative of real legislation. The problem that lies ahead is that all this legislation is attached to mythical or semi-mythical characters, which indicate a strong link with divinity. Romulus is the son of a god and has an apotheosis that elevates him into the pantheon; Numa Pompilius is the lover of a goddess; and Servius Tullius also has a divine background, at least according to part of the tradition. In comparison, the decemvirs appear as quite mundane characters, while their leader Appius Claudius is vile and his own evilness makes the second decemvirate seem unlikely. A magistracy created to design the new laws of the city, while its unofficial leader is deeply evil, seems more appropriate for a soap opera than cold historical facts. In fact, his attempt to rape Verginia seems to mirror the crimes of Tarquin the Proud's relatives.[23]

The change in the status of the lawgivers is quite evident, when the earliest legislation is accounted for as the work of a god while the later is the result of a criminal mind. The main focus of this paper will be to explain this difference and to offer a hypothesis on the relation between statutes and their legislators. The central question is: why did early Romans need to make their lawgivers divine figures, while during the early Republic they were not only men but also felons?

2. GREEK PATTERNS IN THE *LEGES REGIAE*?

Tradition is quite clear in attributing a Greek influence to the Twelve Tables. In fact, two different stories attempt to explain the matter: one by a presumed embassy to Athens in order to gather information about Solon's laws (Liv. 3.31; Dion. Hal. *Ant. Rom.* 10.51), while another tradition (Pomponius' *enchiridii* in D.1.2.2.3–4; Plin. *HN* 34.21; Strabo 14.1.25, p. 642c) seems to hold that the Greek philosopher Hermodorus was responsible for some of their Hellenising ideas. Although the idea of having an embassy to Athens is usually dismissed by scholarship[24] and Hermodorus was probably long since dead by the time the decemvirs started legislating,[25] most scholars now agree that the Twelve Tables

---

[23] See Girard 1977, 25; Drummond 1989, 230; Cornell 1995, 273.

[24] Although in the eighteenth century the credibility of the story was rather high, Gianbattista Vico was the first to doubt the traditional account. During the nineteenth and first half of the twentieth centuries, the majority of Roman law scholars denied the influence of Greek ideas in the Twelve Tables. See Niebuhr 1812, 102 ff.; Ciulei 1944; Gioffredi 1947–8; De Francisci 1948; Wenger 1953, 364 ff.

[25] He was a friend of Heraclitus, who died in 484 BCE, that is to say, some thirty years before the decemvirs started legislating.

have at their core some elements of Greek influence.[26] These arguments are quite sound, including the fact that the Greek word *poena* is commonly used in the Twelve Tables (XIIT 3.5; 6.2; 8.3–4 *inter alia*), and that the tenth table limits burial paraphernalia. The latter practice seems to have been out of practice for more than a hundred years in early Rome[27] and mirrors similar regulations in Hellenic legislation, as Cicero himself noted (Cic. *Leg.* 2.59).

The very idea of legislating – that is to say, giving to the political powers the capacity to create normative rules of law – seems to come into Italy through the Greek world.[28] Broadly speaking, between the seventh and fifth centuries the Mediterranean witnessed an age of legislators. During that period many important Greek *poleis* were under social stress due to the emergence of middling sectors of society, which exercised their influence in order to claim political rights. Hoplitism seems to be at the heart of these social confrontations, for this new military strategy made the foot soldier the axis of the army and, consequently, gave farmers with small plots of land – who possessed the minimum resources necessary to maintain this expensive outfit – a new role in the city's life.[29] These individuals seem to have claimed more political participation, and lawgivers provided the answer by engaging them institutionally in the life of the city. The activities of these lawgivers are evident not only in mainland Greece, where Draco and Lycurgus are early examples of the kind, but also in Magna Graecia, where Charondas, Andromadas, and Zaleucus appear active during the late seventh and early sixth centuries. As Eder puts it, there is usually social unrest (*anomia*) first, followed by a legislator, who is brought forward as an arbitrator to put in place reasonable social order (*eunomia*).[30]

As far as we know, legislative activity seems to have emerged in the Greek world during the seventh century BCE as a result of growing social pressure. Laws were engraved in stone to give them permanency. The oldest extant statute belongs to the Cretan city of Dreros.[31] Another early example of these legislative activities is the Gortyn Code, which is also divided into twelve groups of laws and seems mainly to regulate trials, property, and inheritance. In the Tyrrhenian area, the *Lapis Niger* seems to have been engraved in the same period when we can detect material evidence of similar activity in the Hellenic region. The possibility of Greek influence should, therefore, be considered not only for the Twelve Tables, but for the *leges regiae* as well. As far as we can judge, Greek influence in early Rome was very strong. From the founding of a colony at the Bay of Naples in Ischia, Greeks seem to have shaped the Tyrrhenian area in a considerable way.

---

[26] Wieacker 1956, 1971; Steinberg 1982; Ferenczy 1984; Cornell 1995, 274; Bauman 1996; Toher 2005, 268–92; Forsythe 2006, 210.
[27] Cornell 1995, 105; Toher 2005, 279.
[28] See also Clackson's chapter in this volume.
[29] Gschnitzer 1981, 75; Pallottino 1984 [2014], 86; Ferenczy 1984, 2001–12; Toher 2005, 276.
[30] Eder 2005, 241.
[31] BCH 70 (1946) 600, n. 4; Fornara 1983.

Unrest in the island of Euboea caused a major colonisation movement by the Chalcedonean Hellenes both to the east, where they established a colony at Al-Mina, and to the west, where they founded a colony at Ischia, in the Bay of Naples.[32] The Euboean example was shortly followed by continental Greeks and, in a matter of decades, the south of Italy became so Hellenised that it came to be known as Magna Graecia. The presence of Euboean and Proto-Corinthian pottery became common. Luxury items circulated throughout Italian communities, where they may have served as princely gifts. The attraction of Etruria's mineral ores for Greek merchants is apparent,[33] and it triggered the rapid Hellenisation of its indigenous culture. The process of urbanisation in the Villanovan area seems to develop under Greek influence.[34]

Greek exchange led to the rise of Etruscan commerce. Soon after the foundation of Pithekoussai in Ischia, Tyrrhenian amphorae (Zit-A or *Zentral Italische Amphoram*) – possibly used to transport wine or oil – are found in different contexts around the Mediterranean, such as Carthage, Spain, and Sicily,[35] and a bit later even in continental Greece.[36] During Latial Period II (1000–770 BCE), the presence of Villanovan goods in Latium is rather scant, except for metal items,[37] while Greek influence and trade goods are simply non-existent. If Latial culture should be related to any other culture during this period, pottery seems to put it in relation with the *fossa* grave culture of Campania,[38] but not with its Etruscan neighbour. This changes dramatically during Latial Period III. In coastal settlements, such as Lavinium-Prattica di Mare, Adrea, Anzio, and Satricum, the presence of bronze items of Villanovan origin is abundant and visible from Period IIB,[39] which implies an important escalation in exchange. Apparently, a network of commerce was established by sea, connecting with the inner region of Latium through a terrestrial axis in the Alban Hills and its settlement network. At the beginning of Latial Period III, there seems to be a geopolitical change in southern Etruria, where Veii takes a leading role in commerce with Latium, superseding neighbouring Caere.[40] This fuelled the use of a fluvial trade route through the Tiber and Aniene rivers, making the future site of Rome of seminal importance. The distribution system of metal items (and later other goods as well) changed with the rise of Veii, and the importance of the Alban Hills as an axis of distribution and exchange diminished drastically in favour of the future Rome. In fact, with the beginning of Latial Period III, the stagnation of the Alban Hills' settlements became apparent, while the protohistory of Rome begins. Still,

---

[32] Turfa 1986, 69.
[33] Pallottino 1984, 66; Morel 2007, 490.
[34] Cornell 1995, 86–7.
[35] Morel 2007, 491.
[36] Bietti Sestieri 1992, 45. <Add Ibid. as appropriate up to note 40>
[37] Bietti Sestieri 1992, 27.
[38] Bietti Sestieri 1992, 27.
[39] Bietti Sestieri 1992, 71.
[40] Bietti Sestieri 1992, 243.

during the entire Archaic Period, the Latin Fairs come to be part of Rome's ancestral memory[41] and, moreover, one of the key elements in defining the identity of the Latin peoples (Tac. Ann. 6.11; Liv. 32.1.9.1). They were continuously celebrated during the entire Republican Period and even during the Empire, at least until the age of Hadrian (SHA Ant.Phil. 4.6.2), although their economic importance had long since passed. From this period onward, Greeks and Phoenicians would sail the Tiber, bringing new cultural horizons to the Latin communities along with their cargo.[42]

As a consequence, Latial Period III begins with a technological revolution. Pottery experiences a massive change with the introduction of the potter's wheel, probably imported from Greece,[43] the diaphragm kiln (which allows a better control of temperature), and painted pottery. With these technological improvements, high-quality pottery emerges with very different features from the home-made wares of the preceding phase, and the professional potter appears.[44] In fact, stylistic variations cease to be distinctive between grave groups and become common to wider communities.

During this same period arboriculture seems to have been introduced in the Tyrrhenian area in the form of vines and olives (possibly by Phoenicians or Greeks[45]) to produce wine and oil. This implies a substantial change in agricultural exploitation techniques and the possible emergence of the so-called *coltora promiscua* and the Mediterranean triad. In the Villanovan and Latial areas, arboriculture is well established during the seventh century BCE,[46] although its presence in the Etruscan area could be from quite some time earlier, especially considering that there is evidence for vine exploitation during the ninth century BCE in Gran Carro[47] that enables us to speculate its first introduction in Latium around the beginning of Period III.[48] Another important technical advance is the introduction of literacy in central Italy (Osteria dell'Osa), where, surprisingly, the oldest inscription of Western Europe in alphabetical characters has been found (c. 770 BCE),[49] which is even earlier than the first Greek colony in Ischia.[50]

This technological revolution means that a whole new set of techniques could be applied to the productive processes, which allowed for population growth and the expansion of the settlements to previously unseen limits in central Italy. The settlement patterns widen with the occupation of new lands, especially volcanic

---

[41] See Cornell 1989.
[42] Holloway 1994, 165.
[43] Torelli 1986, 51.
[44] Torelli 1986, 51; Bietti Sestieri 1992, 94; Cornell 1995, 81; Forsythe 2006, 56.
[45] Turfa 1986, 67.
[46] Torelli 1986, 52; Forsythe 2006, 56.
[47] Barker and Rasmussen 1998, 73.
[48] Cornell 1995, 81.
[49] It is a globular jar found in the 482 tomb for a male, where five Greek letters can be read. See Bietti Sestieri, De Santis and La Regina, 1989–90 and Bietti Sestieri 1992, 184.
[50] Holloway 1994, 167.

soils, which present a comparative advantage for arboriculture. Higher-altitude lands also enter into the productive processes, with a sharp expansion.[51]

As a consequence, during Latial Period III an important process of nuclearisation takes place. Settlements enlarge and extend their influence into new areas.[52] Smaller settlements are absorbed by larger ones, configuring each settlement's area of influence.[53] The villages on the volcanic plateaus of southern Etruria and the Latial area begin a process of fusion that gives rise to larger settlements that are usually described as proto-urban.[54] It is likely that this process, which is essentially an internal process in the Latial area, was triggered by foreign cultural influence, principally Etruscan and Greek. During the sixth century BCE, Greek influence intensified still further. There is evidence of individuals bearing a Greek name living in the Tyrrhenian area,[55] such as a certain Rutile Hipukrates in Tarquinii (*TLE* 155). There are also Greek inscriptions in Rome itself, providing evidence of the strength of these contacts.[56] Additionally, there seems to be an increase in commerce between the Greek mainland and Rome. In fact, a plethora of archaeological evidence, including the discovery of proto-Corinthian and Attic luxury pottery, supports this assertion.[57] Apparently, the area occupied by Rome during the late seventh and sixth centuries did not only experience a large urban transformation, but also a sharp increase in commerce which integrated the Latial area into the exchange networks of early antiquity. In summary: the Greek presence in Latium is quite early and shaped the emerging city-states of the Tyrrhenian area from the very beginning of their existence, reaching its zenith during the sixth century BCE.

The importance of exchange between the peoples of the Tyrrhenian area and Greeks allows us to postulate that the idea of introducing dispositions through acts of political power – that is, legislation – might have been introduced precisely by Greek standards, especially when southern Italy was going through this process at exactly the same time. At the same time as Rome was being organised into a properly urban settlement, including the construction of the large and labour-intensive public works that would shape its public life, the age of lawgivers was taking place in southern Italy at the hand of Charondas, Andromadas, and Zaleucus.

The material reorganisation of the city itself can be interpreted as a manifestation of its ideological reconfiguration. Massive building projects imply a strong, centralised authority capable of organising complex activities. Many of the structures erected were, in fact, to house the political institutions that tradition attributes to the kings, including the *Curia Hostilia*, the *Comitium*, and the

---

[51] For a detailed soil study, see Fulminante 2007, 152–83.
[52] Morel 2007, 493.
[53] Ampolo 1976–7; Torelli 1989, 35; Cornell 1995, 90.
[54] Bietti Sestieri 1992, 45.
[55] See Torelli 1986, 54.
[56] Edlund-Berry 2013, 419.
[57] Turfa 1986, 79; Drummond 1989, 128; Holloway 1994, 22.

Regia. Just as the proto-urban settlement of the Palatine was superseded by an urban site that was focused in the newly developed area of the Forum valley, so the customary political order would be superseded by a new rationalistic system constructed through statutes.

While the annalistic tradition attributes to the kings much of the construction activity that took place during the late seventh and early sixth centuries, the most prominent rationalistic features of the Roman legislative constitution are retrospectively projected onto legendary and divine actors, especially Romulus and Numa Pompilius. The later monarchy seems schematic, with a founder, a legislator, and a tyrant.[58] While the founder, Tarquin the Elder, appears to be responsible for many of the physical traits of early Rome, he does not appear as a lawmaker in the tradition, besides elevating the number of senators and coordinating it with the *curiae* (Liv. 1.8.7; Dion. Hal. *Ant. Rom.* 2.12.1–2; Plut. *Rom.* 13.2; Vell. Pat. 1.8.5–6; Fest. 454; Zonar. 7.3). He even seems to be in open conflict with the religious authorities of the monarchy. Tradition puts him at odds with a certain augur named Attus Navius (Dion. Hal. *Ant. Rom.* 3.70; Liv. 1.36; Cic. *Rep.* 2.36; Fest. 169.25; Flor. *Epit.* 1.1.150). The incident is interesting for our argument. Tarquin the Elder wanted to increase the number of equestrian units, while Navius opposed his attempt to alter the institutions of the city. Consequently, Navius demonstrated his divine powers by cutting a whetstone with his razor. This made Tarquin back down from his reform.

His successor, Servius Tullius, on the other hand, does have the legendary origins needed, not only to grant him the crown, but also to make him a legislator. In fact, the figure (or figures) behind the traditional character seems to be responsible for the most dramatic reorganisation of the city during the sixth century BCE. The whole *curia* system was superseded by a new configuration of territorial tribes, while an assembly of plutocratic *centuriae* was created. Because this system overlaps with the three genetic tribes and the thirty *curiae*, it seems to be a reform of the previous organisation, which is preserved as an institutional fossil during the later Republic. Characteristically, Tarquin the Proud lacks not only a divine pedigree but also undertakes no permanent legislation. Tradition attributes to him only some misguided political measures, including his failure to consult the Senate (Liv. 1.49.4–7), his attempt to abolish the census (Dion. Hal. *Ant. Rom.* 4.43.2), and his infamous *poena cuello* for *parricidium* (Cic. *pro Rab. Perd.* 4.13; Val. Max. 1.1.13; Zonar. 7.11), which would in itself grant him a place among the most hideous characters in Roman historiography.

Apparently, during the monarchy – at least according to tradition – lawmaking ought to consist of some kind of divine powers. This is quite interesting, for the later Twelve Tables are not only relatively secular, but seem to emanate from characters who are openly vile and unreligious. There is a sharp contrast between the regal demigods and the mundane decemvirs.

---

[58] Eder 1993, 109–10.

3. A QUESTION OF VALIDITY?

The problem of validity seems obvious for modern legal theory. A statute is valid if it has been approved through the legal mechanisms prescribed for it. However, in classical antiquity there was nothing similar to a legal theory of ensuring enforcement to the rules of law created by the political power. This seems evident from the Mesopotamian legal codes, which seem to derive their authority from the very will of the king, who was, in fact, a physical person. After his death, enforcement depended on his successors, who could as readily maintain his will or alter it. In the epilogue to Hammurabi's code we find a whole set of recommendations and damnations to future rulers who might be tempted to alter his judgements.[59] This is particularly clear with international treaties, which seem to commit 'only the person who swore the oath. When a king died, they had to be renewed with his successor.'[60]

The situation seems to evolve in the peripheral coastal areas of the Middle Eastern empires in a rather late period, during the eighth and seventh centuries BCE.[61] In Deuteronomy and Leviticus, for instance, statutes were not acts of a political power, but were directly attributed to a permanent legislator. As Westbrook puts it, '[s]omewhere within this transition also lies the whole conceit of the Bible's historical narrative, assimilating the paragraphs of several codes to a single act of legislation, but projecting that act of legislation into the distant past'.[62]

The first Greek legislators seem to be encompassed in the same intellectual traditions. In fact, Minos, Lycurgus, and Draco were semi-mythical figures whose legal merits are shored up by the gods themselves. Even Solon, famously, made the Athenians swear to respect his laws until he returned to the city, something he never did, in order to ensure the biding force of his laws. In the Greek tradition, some of the lawgivers had a mythical status and this helped to lend permanency to their statutes.[63]

This tradition seems to be revisited by the Romans in the laws attributed to their earliest kings. In fact, those who had the most noticeable authority as lawgivers have the most shadowy and sacred origins. Romulus became Quirinus, who shared a place with Jupiter and Mars as the central deities of the city. Numa Pompilius was the lover of a goddess, who whispered to him the framework for his laws. Even Servius Tullius has a divine conception, which would enable him to bring up a new constitution to Rome. In this context, later laws made by historical kings might have been attributed to earlier mythical characters in order to grant them legitimacy.

---

[59] On the problem of validity, see Renger 1994; Westbrook 2015.
[60] Charpin 2010, l.1632.
[61] As Westbrook (2003, 20) puts it, 'References are found in the Hebrew prophets to obeying the law (torah) of God as an independent body of rules rather than simply the will of God . . .'.
[62] Westbrook 2003, 21.
[63] Harries 2007, 86.

There is an interesting scene in the literary tradition that might very well point in this direction. According to tradition, when Tarquin the Elder wanted to modify Rome's laws and expand the traditional numbers of knights from the Ramnes, Tities, and Luceres, the augur Attus Navius opposed him (Dion. Hal. *Ant. Rom.* 3.70; Liv.1.36; Cic. *Rep.* 2.36; Fest. 169.25; Flor. Epit. 1.1.150). Famously, to prove he was a charlatan, Tarquin ordered Navius to cut a whetstone with his razor, which he accomplished, leaving Tarquin perplexed. This intriguing scene seems to point to a kind of incapacity of the kings to alter the basic framework of the *res publica* without religious approval.

It is important to mention that the period which tradition ascribes to Tarquin the Elder was characterised by an enormous expansion of the city's material infrastructure,[64] which included the forum,[65] the Senate,[66] and the Comitia. The entire infrastructure of the Roman legal and political superstructure was built during this time period. This is evidently indicative not only of a strong central authority,[67] but also of a possible reconfiguration of the constitutional framework that allowed this power to be exercised.

Another piece of the tradition might be helpful in order to understand the phenomenon. Pomponius, in his famous *Enchiridii*, quotes a legal text that would have been written during the time of the kings by a certain Sextus Papirius (D.1.2.2). The text is unclear on whether the character would have lived during the reign of Priscus or Superbus, for it refers to *superbus*, the nickname of the last king of Rome, and yet calls him *Demarati Corinthii filius* (son of Demaratus of Corinth), who would be *Priscus*, the first king of the dynasty.[68] According to Dionysius, his *praenomen* was Gaius and he would have written the text shortly after the expulsion of the kings (Dion. Hal. *Ant. Rom.* 3.36.4). According to Paulus, the jurist Granius Flaccus, quite possibly during Caesar's time, wrote a book on Papirius' work (D.50.16.144). Although such a document – supposedly written during the late seventh or sixth centuries BCE – might have been almost impossible to read for a scholar of the first century BCE, we should not simply dismiss the tradition as a fabrication,[69] as the hypercritical school did during the early twentieth century.[70] During the century that separates us from these studies, we have learned that the Romans' most distant past was closer to what the tradition states than what earlier historiographical scholarship thought. There are a number of public works that seem to fit into the time frame that the tradition sets,[71]

---

[64] Torelli 1989, 37; Momigliano 1989, 95–6; Smith 1996, 150; Edlund-Berry 2013.
[65] Cornell 1995, 102.
[66] See Bartoli 1963.
[67] See Coarelli 1983, 119–60; Ammerman 1990; and Smith's chapter in this volume.
[68] On the uncertainties regarding Sextus Papirius, see Watson 1972, 100–5 and Momigliano 1989, 107–8.
[69] This is the most important conclusion of Watson 1972.
[70] See von Hirschfeld 1903.
[71] Cornell 2005, 55.

including the draining of the Forum area, and the construction of several temples, the Senate House, and the Regia. We know there were kings in Rome, and we can even guess the meaning of one of their laws. Some of the characters that the tradition presents have even emerged out of legend and into history, such as Valerius Poplicola, who was confirmed with the discovery of the *lapis satricanus*.[72]

As improbable as it may seem, some information about the archaic community survived from the earliest time of Rome into the third century BCE, when the first historical narratives were written.[73] The narrative concerning Romulus' laws seems quite compact and coherent (Dion. Hal. *Ant. Rom.* 2.7–29). The text takes the appearance of a literary capsule self-contained and precise,[74] as if it was taken from a different document with several layers of re-elaboration. This would fit the commentaries made by the first-century BCE jurist Granius Flaccus, who apparently worked on some kind of earlier material attributed to a certain Papirius. Whatever its nature, it would be fitting that a document from the early Republic or the late monarchy contained some of the laws that the tradition attributes to the first kings of Rome, especially because although they do not figure in the Twelve Tables, they seem to be well known and even obsolete by the eve of the Republic. The rules on how to constitute the *curiae* and what to call them must have been quite clear, although their functions and powers were superimposed on and partially absorbed by the *centuriae* even at the earliest stages of development of the Republic.

Be that as it may, it is likely that the political configuration of the city should have been altered in a centralised and rationalistic fashion during a time frame that fits the Tarquinian dynasty, as the material remains suggest. The construction of the *curiae novae*, the House of the Senate (also known as *Curia*), the *comitium*, and the *Regia* points to it. The tradition seems to imply a certain supernatural incapacity of Tarquin the Elder to meet the challenge, so an appropriate way to face the problem would be to attribute the city's most basic institutions to the founding eponymous hero Romulus, who would hold enough divine authority to sustain a rational organisation of its basic institutions. The figure known to us as Servius Tullius would solve the problem in a different fashion, giving himself a divine status that would allow him to build a new organisation for the city. The fact remains that the most ancient laws of the city were retrospectively projected to give them a divine authority that seems coherent with Greek and Middle Eastern legislative models of the time period, as the laws attributed to Minos and to Moses imply. As we will see, a completely different approach is implied in the Twelve Tables.

---

[72] See Coarelli 1983, 79–83; Wiseman 1998, 76–89.
[73] Cornell 1995, 24.
[74] Balsdon 1971.

4. SECULAR LAWS

As has been often noted, the tradition is quite contradictory regarding the origins of the Twelve Tables. In particular, the whole story of the second decemvirate makes little sense.[75] Many aspects are open to debate, including the odd fact that the first time plebeians were admitted to a major magistracy, they legislated against their own intermarriage with patricians. Even so, one of the most intriguing sides of the tradition is the relationship between Appius Claudius and Verginia. The story is melodramatic and would perfectly fit in a modern soap opera. It was probably inspired by the story of Lucretia,[76] and would effectively encapsulate a powerful motto for Roman society: death is better than serfdom or humiliation (*mors servituti turpitudinique anteponenda* [*est*], Cic. *Off*. 1.81).

There is an interesting theory, first put forward by Noailles[77] and later by Ogilvie,[78] that considers the possibility that some of the dispositions of the Twelve Tables were accompanied by examples to make intelligible their meaning, added either during the early Republic or, perhaps, in later periods, as by Sextus Aelius Paetus (cos. 198 BCE). The case of Verginia would be one of these, exemplifying the *causa liberalis*. Tradition would interpret the cases as real events and, therefore, added them into the historical account. As tempting as it may sound, the theory still leaves the bigger question unanswered: why did the Romans make of their most important legislators a bunch of felons? Instead of surrounding them with divinity – as in the case of the fictional character of Romulus or the person known to us as Servius Tullius – they deliberately chose to make them tyrants. There seems to be a sharp contrast between the traditional Greek lawgivers and the Roman *decemvirate*, for the first were inspired by divinity, while the second were completely mundane.[79]

Another obscure aspect of the Twelve Tables is the procedure used to approve them. Tradition is contradictory on the matter. According to Livy and Dionysius (Liv. 10.34.6; Dion. Hal. *Ant. Rom.* 10.57.6), the first ten tables were publicly exposed and finally approved by the *comitia centuriata*, while the two last tables do not seem to have followed a similar constitutional procedure (Liv. 3.57.10; Dion. Hal. *Ant. Rom.* 10.60.5), but were simply included among the other ten as a sort of supplement. Diodorus (12.24–26) seems to believe that the Twelve Tables were not finished by the decemvirs, but by the consuls. The story mirrors the idea of a first virtuous decemvirate, followed by a tyrannical one, where the first would follow constitutional conventions, while the second would abuse its power. The same idea is present in the Romulan calendar, which was originally composed of

---

[75] De Martino 1972, 305; Drummond 1989a, 114 and Drummond 1989b, 230; Crawford 1996, 2:560; Capogrossi Colognesi 2007, 91; Forsythe 2006, 223. Only Cornell (1995, 273) seems inclined to give a little more credit to the story.
[76] See Girard and Senn 1977, 25; Drummond 1989, 230; Cornell 1995, 273.
[77] Noailles 1942.
[78] Ogilvie 1962.
[79] Humbert 2005, 6.

ten months, to which Numa Pompilius added two more (Plutarch, *Numa* 19). These contradictions led part of the twentieth-century scholarship to believe that the Twelve Tables were *leges datae* – that is to say, that they were simply imposed by the decemvirs, but never approved by the *comitia*, as the *leges rogatae* would be.[80]

It is interesting that there is no question in antiquity about the validity of the corpus as a whole. According to Pomponius, the decemvirs could create, interpret, and correct the laws as they wished (*datumque est eis ius eo anno in civitate summum, uti leges et corrigerent, si opus esset, et interpretarentur neque provocatio ab eis sicut a reliquis magistratibus fieret*, D.1.2.2.4). So by adding two more tables to the ten original ones, they would be simply exercising the power conferred to them. As Drummond puts it, '[w]hether or not the Tables were the subject of formal comitial approval, their acceptance rested on general public recognition of the law they enshrined'.[81]

The secular tone used in the laws as a whole is also of considerable interest. For even though there are some penalties that seem to imply a religious conception of the world, as the *sacer esto* sanction that some dispositions hold, neither in the surviving text nor in the tradition does there seem to be any kind of supernatural intervention to secure their enforcement. Simply put, the Twelve Tables are binding because they are laws, not on account of any divine backing they might have. This way, they depart not only from the older Greek tradition, but also from its Middle Eastern roots, which needed a permanent legislator to grant them permanency. The laws are separated from the legislator: they are not merely their will expressed in a written form, but furthermore a secular instrument with a validity of their own. Interpretation of the will of the lawgiver will never be a guessing act among the Romans, nor they will require a Ouija board to get in contact with the 'spirit' of the legislator. The law is simply a public promise (*communis rei publica sponsio*, D.1.3.1), as Papinian would put it, and its scope is provided by its rationality. In this sense, the Twelve Tables are the first secular and modern law recorded in Western history, separating their nature from the earlier laws of the kings. Centuries later, when the Donatist heresy would divide African public opinion in the wake of the legalisation of Christianity, the same arguments would influence the orthodoxy: even a felon can act validly, for his evildoing does not affect the nature of his acts.

Works Cited

Ammerman, A J, 1990. 'On the Origins of the Forum Romanum.' *AJA* 94.4:627–45.
Ampolo, C, 1976–7. 'Demarato.' *DialArch* 9–10 n. 1–2:333–45.
Arangio-Ruiz, V, 2006. *Storia del diritto romano*. Naples: Jovene.
Balsdon, J P V D, 1971. 'Dionysius on Romulus: A Political Pamphlet?' *JRS* 61:18–27.

---

[80] Binder 1909, 522; De Francisci 1943, 274; Guarino 1975, 210. *Contra*: de Martino 1972, 308.
[81] Drummond 1989, 231.

Barker, G and T Rasmussen, 1998. *The Etruscans*. Malden, MA: Blackwell.
Bartoli, A, 1963. *Curia Senatus. Lo scavo e il restauro*, vol. 1. Rome: Istituto di Studi Romani.
Bauman, R A, 1996. 'The Interface of Greek and Roman Law.' *RIDA* 43:39–62.
Beck, H, 2011. 'Consular Power and the Roman Constitution: The Case of imperium Reconsidered.' In *Consuls and* Res Publica: *Holding High Office in the Roman Republic*, edited by H. Beck et al., 77–96. Cambridge: Cambridge University Press.
Bietti Sestieri, A, 1992. *The Iron Age Community of Osteria dell'Osa. A Study of Socio-political Development in Central Tyrrhenian Italy*. Cambridge: Cambridge University Press.
Bietti Sestieri, A M, A De Santis, and A La Regina, 1989–90. 'Elementi di tipo cultuale e doni personali nella necropoli laziale di Osteria dell'Osa.' *ScAnt* 3-4: 65–88.
Binder, J, 1909. *Die Plebs: Studien zur Römischen rechtsgeschichte*. Leipzig: Deirecht.
Capogrossi Colognesi, L, 2007. *Diritto e potere nella storia di Roma*. Naples: Jovene.
Carandini, A, 2006. *Remo e Romolo: Dai rioni dei Quiriti alla città dei Romani (775/750–700/675 a.C. circa)*. Turin: Einaudi.
——, 2007. *Roma: Il primo giorno*. Rome: Bari.
——, 2011. *Rome. Day One*. Princeton and Oxford: Princeton University Press.
Charpin, D, 2010. *Writing, Law, and Kingship in Old Babylonian Mesopotamia*. Kindle edition. Chicago: University of Chicago Press.
Ciulei, G, 1944. 'Die XII Tafeln und die römische Gesandtschaft nach Griechenland.' *ZSav* 64: 350–4.
Coarelli, F, 1983. *Il foro romano: periodo arcaico*. Rome: Quasar.
Cornell, T J, 1989. 'Rome and Latium to 390 BC.' In *CAH*, vol. 7.2, edited by F W Walbank, E A Astin, M W Frederiksen, R M Ogilvie assisted by A Drummond, 243–308. Cambridge: Cambridge University Press.
——, 1995. *The Beginnings of Rome. Italy and Rome from the Bronze Age to the Punic Wars (c. 1000–264 BC)*. London: Routledge.
——, 2005. 'The Value of the Literary Tradition Concerning Archaic Rome.' In *Social Struggles in Archaic Rome. New Perspectives on the Conflict of the Orders*, edited by K A Raaflaub, 47–74. Oxford: Blackwell.
Crawford, M H, 1996. *Roman Statutes*, vol. 2. London: Institute of Classical Studies.
De Francisci, P, 1943. *Storia del diritto romano*, vol. 1. Milan: Giuffrè.
——, 1948. *Arcana imperii*, vol. 3.1. Milan: Giuffrè.
De Martino, F, 1972. *Storia della costituzione romana*, vol. 1. Naples: Jovene.
Develin, R, 1977. '*Lex curiata* and the Competence of Magistrates.' *Mnemosyne* 30.1:49–65.
Drummond, A, 1989a. 'Rome in the Fifth Century I: The Social and Economic Framework.' In *CAH*, vol. 7.2, edited by F W Walbank, E A Astin, M W

Frederiksen, R M Ogilvie assisted by A Drummond, 113–71. Cambridge: Cambridge University Press.

——, 1989b. 'Rome in the Fifth Century II: The Citizen Community.' In *CAH*, vol. 7.2, edited by F W Walbank, E A Astin, M W Frederiksen, R M Ogilvie assisted by A Drummond, 172–242. Cambridge: Cambridge University Press.

Eder, W, 1993. 'Zwischen Monarchie und Republik: das Volkstribunat in der frühen römischen Republik.' In *Atti dei convegni Lincei 100: Convegno sul tema: Bilancio critico su Roma arcaica fra monarchia e repubblica in memoria di Ferdinando Castagnoli (Roma, 3–4 giugno 1991)*, edited by Accademia Nazionale dei Lincei, 97–127. Rome: Accademia Nazionale dei Lincei.

——, 2005. 'The Political Significance of the Codification of Law in Archaic Societies: An Unconventional Hypothesis.' In *Social Struggles in Archaic Rome. New Perspectives on the Conflict of the Orders*, edited by K A Raaflaub, 239–67. Oxford: Blackwell.

Edlund-Berry, I, 2013. 'Early Rome and the Making of "Roman" Identity through Architecture and City Planning.' In *A Companion to the Archeology of the Roman Republic*, edited by J DeRose Evans, 406–25. Malden, MA: Blackwell.

Elmore, J, 1922. 'The Purpose of the Decemviral Legislation.' *CP* 17.2:128–40.

Ferenczy, E, 1984. 'La legge delle XII Tavole e le codificazioni greche.' In *Sodalitas. Scritti in onore di Antonio Guarino*, edited by V Giuffrè, vol. 4: 2001–12. Naples: Jovene.

Fornara, C W, 1983. *Translated Documents of Greece and Rome*, vol. I. Cambridge: Cambridge University Press.

Forsythe, G, 2006. *A Critical History of Early Rome*. Berkeley: University of California Press.

Fulminante, F, 2007. 'Environment and Settlement Analysis: Investigating the Bronze and Iron Age *Latium Vetus* Physical and Political Landscape.' In *Broadening Horizons, Multidisciplinary Approaches to Landscape Study*, edited by B Ooghe and G Verhoeven, 152–83. Newcastle: Cambridge Scholars Publishing.

Gioffredi, C, 1947–8. 'Ius, lex, praetor.' *Studia et documenta historiae et juris* 13–14:7–140.

Girard, P F and F Senn, 1977. *Les lois des Romains*. Naples: Jovene.

Gschnitzer, F, 1981. *Sozialgeschichte von der mykenischen bis zum Ausgang der klassischen Zeit*. Wiesbaden: Steiner.

Guarino, A, 1975. *La rivoluzione della plebe*. Naples: Liguori Editore.

Harries, J, 2007. 'Roman Law Codes and the Roman Legal Tradition.' In *Beyond Dogmatics. Law and Society in the Roman World*, edited by J W Cairns and P. du Plessis, 85–104. Edinburgh Studies in Law 10. Edinburgh: University of Edinburgh Press.

von Hirschfeld, O, 1903. *Die Monumenta des Manilius und das Ius Papirianum*. Berlin: Deutsche Akademie der Wissenschaften zu Berlin.

Holloway, R R, 1994. *The Archaeology of Early Rome and Latium*. London: Routledge.
Humbert, M, 2005. 'La codificazione decemvirale: tentativo d'interpretazione.' In *Le Dodici Tavole. Dai Decemviri agli Umanisti*, edited by M Humbert, 1–50. Pavia: Iuss Press.
Kaser, M, 1938. 'Der Inhalt der Patria Potestas.' *ZSav* 58: 62–87.
———, 1960. 'La famiglia romana arcaica.' In *Conferenze Romanistiche*, edited by Istituto di Diritto Romano e Storia del Diritto, 37–62. Milan: A Giuffrè.
———, 1971. *Das römische Privatrecht*, vol. 1. Munich: Beck'sche.
Lepore, P, 2010. *Introduzione allo studio dell'epigrafia giuridica latina*. Milan: Giuffrè.
Mantovani, D, 2016. 'Roman Ways of Organising and Giving Access to Legal Information.' In *The Oxford Handbook of Roman Law and Society*, edited by P du Plessis, C Ando, and K Tuori, 23–42. Oxford: Oxford University Press.
Magdelain, A, 1990a. 'Note sur la loi curiate et les auspices des magistrats.' In *Jus imperium auctoritas. Études de droit romain*, edited by A Magdelain, 307–11. Collection de l'École française de Rome 133. Rome: École française de Rome.
———, 1990b. 'De L'auctoritas patrum à l'auctoritas senatus.' In *Jus imperium auctoritas. Études de droit romain*, edited by A Magdelain, 385–403. Collection de l'École française de Rome 133. Rome: École française de Rome.
Mitchell, R E, 2005. 'The Definition of *patres* and *plebs*: An End to the Struggle of the Orders.' In *Social Struggles in Archaic Rome. New Perspectives on the Conflict of the Orders*, edited by K Raaflaub, 128–67. Expanded and updated edition. Malden, MA: Blackwell.
Momigliano, A, 1989. 'The Origins of Rome.' In *CAH*, edited by F W Walbank, E A Astin, M W Frederiksen, R M Ogilvie assisted by A Drummond, vol. 7.2: 52–112. Cambridge: Cambridge University Press.
Morel, J-P, 2007. 'Early Rome and Italy.' In *The Cambridge Economic History of the Greco-Roman World*, edited by I Morris, W Scheidel, and R P Saller, 487–510. Cambridge: Cambridge University Press.
Niebuhr, B G, 1812. *Römische Geschichte*. v.2. Berlin: Realschulbuchhandlung.
Noailles, P, 1942. 'Le procès de Virginie.' *REL* 20: 106–38.
Ogilvie, R M, 1962. 'The Maid of Ardea.' *Latomus* 21–23:477–83.
Pallottino, M, 1984 [2014]. *A History of Earliest Italy*. London: Routledge.
Pohlenz, M, 1924. 'Eine politiche Tendenzschrift aus Caesars Zeit.' *Hermes* 59:157–89.
Pugliese, G, 1973. 'Customary and Statutory Law in Rome.' *Israel Law Review* 8.1:23–31.
Renger, J, 1994. 'Noch einmal: Was war der "Kodex" Hammurapi – ein erlassenes Gesetz oder ein Rechtsbuch?' In *Rechtskodifizierung und soziale Normen in inetrkulturellen Vergleich*, edited by H-J Gehrke, 27–58. Tübingen: Narr.
Richard, J-C, 1993. 'Réflexions sur les "origines" de la plebe.' In *Atti dei convegni Lincei 100: Convegno sul tema: Bilancio critico su Roma arcaica fra monarchia e repubblica in memoria di Ferdinando Castagnoli (Roma, 3–4 giugno 1991)*, edited

by Accademia nazionale dei Lincei, 27–41. Rome: Accademia Nazionale dei Lincei.
——, 2005. 'Patricians and Plebeians: The Origin of a Social Dichotomy.' In *Social Struggles in Archaic Rome. New Perspectives on the Conflict of the Orders*, edited by K Raaflaub, 107–27. Expanded and updated edition. Malden, MA: Blackwell.
Richardson Jr, L, 1992. *A New Topographical Dictionary of Ancient Rome*. Baltimore: Johns Hopkins University Press.
Schiavone, A, 2012. *The Invention of Law in the West*. Cambridge, MA: Harvard University Press.
Serrao, F, 2006. *Diritto privato economia e società nella storia di Roma*. Naples: Jovene.
Smith, C J, 1996. *Early Rome and Latium. Economy and Society c. 1000–500 BC*. Oxford: Clarendon.
——, 2006. *The Roman Clan. The Gens from Ancient Ideology to Modern Anthropology*. Cambridge: Cambridge University Press.
Stanzione, N J, 2010. 'Reconstructing the Twelve Tables: Some Problems and Challenges.' *The Digest. National Italian American Bar Association Law Journal* 21:21–36.
Steinberg, M, 1982. 'The Twelve Tables and Their Origins: An Eighteenth-Century Debate.' *Journal of the History of Ideas* 43.3:379–96.
Terrenato, N, 2010. 'Early Rome.' In *The Oxford Handbook of Roman Studies*, edited by A Barchiesi and W Scheidel, 507–18. Oxford: Oxford University Press.
Toher, M, 2005. 'The Tenth Table and the Conflict of the Orders.' In *Social Struggles in Archaic Rome. New Perspectives on the Conflict of the Orders*, edited by K Raaflaub, 268–92. Oxford: Blackwell.
Torelli, M, 1986. 'History: Land and People.' In *Etruscan Life and Afterlife*, edited by L Bonfante, 47–65. Detroit: Wayne State University Press.
——, 1989. 'Archaic Rome Between Latium and Etruria.' In *CAH*, edited by F W Walbank, E A Astin, M W Frederiksen, R M Ogilvie assisted by A Drummond, vol. 7.2: 30–51. Cambridge: Cambridge University Press.
Turfa, J M, 1986. 'International Contacts: Commerce, Trade, and Foreign Affairs.' In *Etruscan Life and Afterlife*, edited by L Bonfante, 66–91. Detroit: Wayne State University Press.
Watson, A, 1972. 'Roman Private Law and the *Leges Regiae*.' *JRS* 62:100–5.
——, 1995. 'From Legal Transplants to Legal Formants.' *The American Journal of Comparative Law* 43.3:469–76.
Wenger, L, 1953. *Die Quellen des romischen Rechts*. Vienna: Holzhausen.
Westbrook, R, 2003. 'The Character of Ancient Near Eastern Law.' In *A History of Ancient Near Eastern Law*, edited by R Westbrook, 1–92. Leiden: Brill.
——, 'Codification and Canonization.' In *Ex oriente lex. Near Eastern Influences on Ancient Greek and Roman Law*, edited by D Lyons and K Raaflaub, 181–93. Baltimore: Johns Hopkins University Press.

Wieacker, F, 1956. 'Zwolftafelprobleme.' *RIDA* 3:456–91.
——, 1971. 'Solon und die XII Tafeln.' In *Studi in onore di Edoardo Volterra*, edited by P De Francisci, vol. 3: 757–84. Milan: Giuffrè.
Wiseman, T P, 1998. *Roman Drama and Roman History*. Exeter: University of Exeter Press.
——, 2001. 'Reading Carandini.' *JRS* 91:181–93.
——, 2011–12. 'Review of Rome: Day One.' *CJ* 107.2:248–50.

Chapter 5

The *leges regiae* in Livy: Narratological and Stylistic Strategies

Marco Rocco

1. INTRODUCTION

Although the *leges regiae* are mainly transmitted by Greek sources, Livy in the first book of *Ab Urbe Condita* records many legislative measures that were issued by kings. These 'laws' can be framed in various ways within the context of the kings' legislative activity. All the passages related to this activity are ordered according to the type of measure considered and are examined from the narratological, lexical, and stylistic point of view, in order to verify what Livy is aiming at by choosing from time to time only certain information offered by the sources and diversifying narrative and rhetorical techniques. It is possible to note that Livy adapts his story not only to the different types of measures considered, but also to the narrative function assigned to each of them. In general, at least two trends can be observed: Livy describes with particular care the sacred formulae of some laws, when he considers that their value is still foundational and exemplary for his time; at the same time, he makes sure to point out all aspects of the content of the law that may appear consistent with the overall portrait of the author of the measure, in order to increase the verisimilitude of the story.

Although much has been written about *leges regiae*, the topic is still very much debated. It has recently been observed that scholars of Roman law do not agree on whether the kings of Rome have ever legislated in the strict sense, namely according to what would later become the classic notion of *lex*. Furthermore, it has not so far been possible to draw up a collection of the legislative provisions mentioned by the sources of the regal period which is based on unanimously shared criteria of selection.[1] In a similar way, it has not yet been possible to establish unequivocally what measures, among those attributed to the Roman kings by the sources, should be understood as true *leges*, especially since it is almost never given to ascertain whether they were approved

---

[1] Carandini et al. 2011, 281–376; cf. Bujuklić 1998; Mantovani 2012, 287 n. 17.

by the *curiae* (*leges curiatae*), or simply imposed on them (*leges datae*).² In such a situation of uncertainty, Luigi Capogrossi Colognesi understands the *leges regiae* as 'solenni pronunce espresse unilateralmente dal *rex* di fronte all'assemblea cittadina'.³

According to a well-known tradition, the first written laws of Rome would have been collected in the last period of the monarchy by the *pontifex* Papirius.⁴ Reconsidering this tradition, Dario Mantovani has suggested approaching the question of the *leges regiae* by adopting a philological point of view, rather than a jurisprudential one.⁵ Such a perspective would make us realise that the term '*leges regiae*' is not a modern one. The expression, in fact, derives from a passage in Livy's book 6 which narrates how the new *tribuni militum consulari potestate* in 389 BCE ordered the recovery of the *foedera ac leges*, which had survived the Gallic occupation: among them, *quaedam regiae leges* are mentioned.⁶ Later, Livy uses the term in the singular form, when the tribune L Valerius Tappus, in the discussion about the abolition of the *lex Oppia* in 195 BCE, recalls the particular value of those laws that *perpetuae utilitatis causa in aeternum latae sunt*, among which were the *regia lex simul cum ipsa urbe nata*.⁷

Unfortunately, these passages in themselves do not throw much light on the issues mentioned above, not only because Livy's notion of *lex* is always somewhat indefinite and varied, as Thibaud Lanfranchi has noted,⁸ but also because in the first book of *Ab Urbe Condita* the aforementioned expressions are never employed: Livy only occasionally uses the terms *lex* and *ius* in reference to various kinds of measures adopted by kings and generically attributable to their legislative activity.⁹ Nonetheless, Livy remains an indispensable source on the subject. Although

---

² See in particular D'Ippolito 1998, 40–1. Franciosi (2003, xv) excludes the possibility that the *leges regiae* were *leges curiatae* and considers them *leges datae*. In contrast, Carandini et al. (2011, 293–301) believe that the *curiae* already participated in the process of formation of the rules of law, as demonstrated by the fact that their role was essential in conferring the *imperium* upon the kings. Bujuklić (1998, 106–13, 128–38) suggests that the *leges* issued by the kings were normative acts rather than laws in the strict sense, and he postulates that some of them were *leges curiatae*, others *leges centuriatae*, others *leges datae*, with a probable prevalence of the latter at the time of the military leadership of the so-called Etruscan kings.

³ Capogrossi Colognesi 2009, 35.

⁴ See especially Pomponius in D. 1.2.2.1–3; 1.2.2.7; 1.2.2.36, but also cf. Dion. Hal., *Ant. Rom.* 3.36.4; Macrob., *Sat.* 3.11.5–6; Serv., *ad Aen.* 12.836; D. 50.16.144; for more on the topic, see Santoro 1998. The *praenomen* of *Papirius* (*Sextus*, *Publius*, or *Caius*) is not certain, but all the sources agree in attributing the title of *pontifex* to him. The collection should date back to the age of Tarquinius Superbus, or to the years following the end of monarchy (Franciosi 2003, xvii). Many hints, including especially the inscription engraved on the so-called cippus of the *Lapis Niger*, let us suppose that some laws were put in writing well before the Decemvirate (Bujuklić 1998, 114–18; cf. Tondo 1971 and 1973, 17–34).

⁵ Mantovani 2012, 283–4.

⁶ Liv. 6.1.10.

⁷ Liv. 34.6.7.

⁸ Lanfranchi 2012, 339.

⁹ Liv. 1.8.1; 1.17.9; 1.19.1; 1.26.6–7.

the *leges regiae* are mainly transmitted by Greek authors, primarily by Dionysius of Halicarnassus and Plutarch (the latter exclusively focuses on Romulus and Numa), the Roman historian sometimes is the only author to inform us about some of these measures.[10]

Almost all the passages concerning legislative actions issued by Roman kings in the first book of *Ab Urbe Condita* have already been studied exhaustively from a legal point of view. However, an analysis of their narrative, lexical, and rhetorical characteristics, as well as their purposes, has not yet been attempted. This analysis seems, however, indispensable if we consider that, as Torrey James Luce noted, 'ancient historiography was concerned primarily with narrative'.[11] This paper, therefore, considers the tradition of the *leges regiae* in Livy within an historical and literary framework. The main aim is not to interpret the *leges* in a formalistic way, but to contextualise them in the political and cultural climate in which the literary works which transmit them were written.[12]

By means of selected examples, I will explore how Livy interpreted the content of some of the *leges regiae* and which specific narrative and rhetorical techniques, and vocabulary he used to present them. I suggest that Livy included and revised the *leges regiae* in his work according to a twofold aim: 1) to give particular emphasis on founding traditions, in order to show their particular value as a lesson for the present; 2) to help outline coherent portraits of the different kings, though often including both positive and negative elements (with the prevalence of the former except in one case, as we shall see).

The laws examined here are grouped according to the categories used by Lanfranchi to group the comitial laws in Livy's first decade. Some of the laws I have considered in this contribution do not appear in modern collections of the *leges regiae*, as they have never been considered in light of Lanfranchi's approach. I made this choice not because I assume an identification between the *leges regiae* and comitial laws, but rather because the typologies proposed by Lanfranchi fit well into the extremely varied nature of the regulations recalled by Livy in the first book. Following Lanfranchi's typologies, I grouped the *leges regiae* into six categories. The first one I will focus on in the following section concerns the regulations of religious life. I have excluded from this section the *sacra* attributed to Numa because, as Dario Mantovani argued, they are conceived as precepts and technical standards related to priestly practices, rather than as statutes of private and/or constitutional law.[13] The other categories concern the *civitas*' fundamental institutions; political life; war and army; agrarian laws; and granting of citizenship.

---

[10] Franciosi 2003.
[11] Luce 1977, 158.
[12] Cf. Mantovani 2012, 284. A similar operation was carried out by Emilio Gabba regarding Dionysius of Halicarnassus (Gabba 1996, 137–46; 2000, 69–150). For the study of the *leges regiae* in Dionysius, regarding the Latin-Sabine monarchy only, see most recently Di Trolio 2017 (*non vidi*).
[13] See most recently Mantovani 2012; cf. Tondo 1973, 33–4.

2. RELIGIOUS LIFE

Excluding the passages related to Numa's *sacra*, in the first decade Livy records two *leges* that are connected with religious life. These represent sacred procedures to conform Rome's relations with foreign peoples to the will of the gods. In the first case, Livy describes the *foedus* with Alba before the duel between *Horatii* and *Curiatii*, at the time of Tullus Hostilius;[14] while, in the second case, we find the mention of the rite of declaration of war by Ancus Marcius.[15]

In both episodes the priests, the *Fetiales*, are involved. Livy does not reveal anything about the origins of this priesthood; however, Dionysius informs us that it was instituted by Numa.[16] While the two passages contain a rather technical formulation, they do not record, differently from Numa's *sacra*, norms and precepts pertaining to religious practices in the strict sense. Rather, they contain references to fundamental institutions of 'international law', which were vital to the politics of Rome. In this regard, it seems that Giovanni Torelli is correct when he writes that 'l'elevato tecnicismo delle procedure [...] fa risaltare la funzione giuridico-religiosa dei feziali. [...] l'attività diplomatica, se intesa quale apparato organizzato di persuasione e convincimento della controparte, [...] non rientra nel panorama delle incombenze sacerdotali.'[17]

It is not to be excluded a priori that the presence of specific, archaising formulae, so evident in both of the texts from Livy, is the result of the perpetuation of their use in diplomatic contexts rather than of their religious significance.[18] Late Republican sources such as Varro and Cicero sometimes refer to some of the jurisdictions of the *Fetiales*, especially those related to the signing of the *foedera*, as these were still in use in their own time.[19] Similarly Livy, in narrating the detailed dialogue between Tullus Hostilius and the Fetial Marcus Valerius on the occasion of the *foedus* between Rome and Alba, states that the ceremonial of the *foedera* has never changed and that it still remains unchanged in his own time. The verb *fiunt* in the present tense seems to further strengthen his point.[20] On the other hand, in the same passage, Livy points out that *foedera*'s specific clauses may vary depending on the agreements. In order to highlight the importance of the passage Livy uses a concise, chiastic expression accompanied by polyptoton, *foedera alia*

---

[14] Liv. 1.24.3–9.
[15] Liv. 1.32.5–14.
[16] Dion. Hal., *Ant. Rom.* 2.72; cf. Plut., *Num.* 12. Cic., *Rep.* 2.31 traces them back to Tullus Hostilius. Cf. Ogilvie 1965, 110–12, 130–6. Some scholars see a link between the *Fetiales* and Jupiter Feretrius, suggesting therefore that the priesthood can even go back to Romulus (Carandini et al. 2011, 275–6; cf. Mora 1995, 253–5).
[17] Turelli 2011, 122–3.
[18] Cf. Hickson 1993, 134.
[19] Varro, *Ling.* 5.86; Cic., *Leg.* 2.21. For the interpretation of these passages, see in particular Santangelo 2014, 88–9, 94–5. The *vetus praefatio fetialium* continued to be used for the *foedera* until the imperial age: Suet., *Claud.* 25.14. For the continued existence of the *Fetiales* and their rituals until the beginning of the third century CE, cf. Latte 1960, 123–4, 297; Carandini et al. 2011, 275.
[20] Liv. 1.24.3.

aliis legibus (*fiunt*), which tends to contrast the extreme variety of the contents of the individual treaties with the immutability of their form.[21] For a similar reason and not just for narrative convenience, perhaps, Livy, while recording the words of the *pater patratus* Spurius Fusius before the sacrifice which sealed the treaty with Alba, says that *non operae est referre* the *longum effatum carmen* (the latter being the one used in the final oath).[22] Again, the verbs in the present tense (*fit, peragit*), in a narrative context in which the other predicates are all conjugated in the perfect tense, seems to suggest that the formula was still in use in Livy's own time and that it was also well-known to Livy's readers.

Similarly, in the passage relating to the introduction of the fetial declaration of war by Ancus Marcius, Livy initially states that it still makes use of the *Fetiales*.[23] Throughout the first part of the description of the ritual, Livy regularly uses the verbs in the present tense, while in the second part, specifically in the narration of the episode of war declared by Ancus to *Prisci Latini*, he employs the imperfect and perfect tenses, before reaffirming that *hoc tum modo ab Latinis repetitae res ac bellum indictum, moremque eum posteri acceperunt*.[24] Livy possibly was influenced in this by Augustus' attempt to revitalise the fetial ceremonial, which the latter himself used as a *pater patratus* to declare war on Cleopatra.[25] But it is difficult to accept the hypothesis, according to which the Augustan historians falsely attested the very existence of the fetial priesthood, and its relative functions, before the *princeps*' religious reforms.[26]

In fact, Livy's statements do not seem to be an anachronistic fabrication, if we consider that, as Federico Santangelo pointed out, even if the earliest sources on the *Fetiales* cannot be considered as an accurate historical evidence of the origin of that priesthood,[27] at least starting from the middle-Republican Age the *Fetiales* acted as advisors in the management of the preliminaries of a declaration of war and, above all, they were actively involved in the conclusion of the treaties.[28]

On the other hand, the fact that Livy dates the involvement of the *Fetiales* in these two fundamental functions to the time of the early kings should not be considered only for its possible historicity, which remains uncertain. In order to understand the author's purposes, it is much more meaningful to ask why he emphasises the immutability of ritual formulae and their symbolism. Livy is not interested here in the accuracy of the historical data, but, rather, in their deepest value: that is, the idea that the sacredness of an ancient tradition requires the

---

[21] Cf. de Martino 1972, 39.
[22] Liv. 1.24.6.
[23] Liv. 1.32.5: *nunc fetiales habent*. Cf. Ov., *Fast.* 6.207–8.
[24] Liv. 1.32.14. Cf. Rich 2011, 199–209.
[25] Cass. Dio 50.4.4; cf. *Mon. Anc.* 7.3: '*fetialis fui*.' See also Turelli 2014, 469 n. 62.
[26] See Bianchi 2016, 48; cf. Champion 2017, 83–4.
[27] Santangelo 2014, 99–100; cf. Rich 2011, 202–4. However, with regard to Livy it should be noted that 'the antiquity of the procedure in general [. . .] seems to be confirmed by its similarity to the procedures of early Roman civil law' (Beard et al. 1998, 7; cf. Martin 1982, 156).
[28] Santangelo 2014, 91.

relations between Rome and foreign *civitates*, both in peace and war, to be connected with the observance of an impeccable religious ritual, in order to avoid the risk that the impiety of a political decision could become an injustice in international relations. This close ideal correlation is made evident by the repeated juxtaposition, strengthened by the enclitic particle *-que*, between the adjectives/adverbs *iustus/iuste-iniuste/purus* and *pius/pie-impie*.[29] And it is precisely in this sense that Livy's blatant fabrication of the consultation of the Senate by Ancus, after the expiry of the ultimatum imposed on the *Prisci Latini*, should be interpreted:[30] the recurrence of the sacral and legal vocabulary and the almost obsessive repetition of the formulae seem to emphasise the need to conform to a ritual that also shows the favour of Jupiter, who is called several times in the passage as a witness of the war ritual.[31]

3. THE *CIVITAS*' FUNDAMENTAL INSTITUTIONS

Livy traces these *leges* back to specific kings, in particular to Romulus, the *conditor*, whom he presents in three passages as the creator of the basic institutions of the civic body.[32] In the first episode it is stated very generically that the king, who in the previous chapter is described in the act of fortifying the Palatine and performing the sacred ceremonies, *iura dedit* to the people for the first time gathered in assembly. Then Livy focuses on the establishment of the twelve lictors as *insigna imperii*, and reports two different traditions on the origin of their number, expressing himself in favour of the one that has them borrowed from the Etruscan world.

In the second passage, at the end of the same chapter, Romulus decides to support the already flourishing *vires* of the *civitas* by instituting a *consilium* of one hundred senators. Similarly to the previous case Livy provides, albeit very briefly, two different possible aetiologies for the number of members of the longest-established Romulean institution. This time, however, he does not express preferences for any of the traditions he mentions; rather, he seems to consider them both valid, as the anaphoric use of the *sive quia* would suggest.

In the last episode regarding Romulus, Livy describes the king as the one who, after having made peace with the Sabines, established the 30 *curiae*, naming them after some of the abducted women. The passage is quite interesting, for two reasons. Firstly, here Livy introduces an issue which is halfway between aetiology and historiography: once again, the author tends to consider antiquarian issues, which are missing in the text from Dionysius.[33] Secondly, Livy relies on a tradition,

---

[29] Liv. 1.32.6–7, 12.
[30] Liv. 1.32.11–12; on this fabrication see also Rich 2011, 203–4, who offers a different interpretation of Livy's intentions.
[31] Liv. 1.32.7; 9. Cf. Dangel 1982, 59; Hickson 1993, 114, 115–16. On the 'funzione cogente del rito, che da una parte impegna gli dei, dall'altra condiziona gli uomini', see Turelli 2014, 469.
[32] Liv. 1.8.1–3; 8.7; 13.6–7.
[33] Cf. Dion. Hal., *Ant. Rom.* 2.7.2–3; 12; 29.1.

already present in Cicero, which links the legal measure with the reconciliation and the alliance between the Romans and the Sabines;[34] Dionysius, on the other hand, mentions the same *lex* immediately after the founding of the city.[35]

It is very likely that Livy dwelled on these particular traditions according to a specific agenda. The aim was to portray Romulus as a wise king, conscious of the usefulness of peace and concord. These traits of the *conditor* are somehow highlighted by Livy's recurrent use of aetiology which, as Matthew Fox has noted, not only has the function of creating a narrative pause at the end of an episode, but also of emphasising, especially in the first book, 'a sense of connection between the Rome of now and the Rome of the distant past'.[36]

Livy's intent to portray kings in a coherent way appears even more evident from the comparison between two other passages, specifically those concerning Tarquinius Priscus and Tarquinius Superbus. In the first, the doubling of the number of senators is recorded.[37] Here too, the normative action clearly reveals the king's political behaviour: Tarquinius, in fact, by enlarging the senatorial assembly with the introduction of a *factio haud dubia regis*, aims not only to increase the power of the *res publica*, but also to strengthen his own. This explicit judgement about the king is coherent with other passages in Livy, and it further contributes to the overall portrait of Tarquinius. The latter is portrayed as an excellent man in all other respects. However, he also appears to be aiming in all of his political actions less to the good of the state and more to the *ambitio*; that is, the tendency to intrigue for political support.[38] This is a behaviour that Livy does not attribute in any way to Tarquinius' predecessors, unlike the contemporary Greek sources.[39]

Connected to this passage is the one related to Tarquinius Superbus, who, after having assassinated the senators who he believed to have sided with Servius Tullius, decided not to replace them, in order to discredit the whole assembly.[40] Livy here draws on a tradition already established, as emerges from the comparison with Dionysius.[41] However, he intervenes in making the picture given by his sources homogeneous in every aspect. There is no doubt that this operation should be read in light of Livy's continuous search for exemplarity in his work.[42] But it can also be interpreted as an attempt to adhere to tradition, on the one hand, and to confer verisimilitude on the narration, pursued by means of its adherence to the

---

[34] Cic., *Rep.* 2.14. *Contra* Plut., *Rom.* 20.3 (cf. 14.1–2; 14.8).
[35] Dion. Hal., *Ant. Rom.* 2.7.2–3.
[36] Fox 2015, 291.
[37] Liv. 1.35.6.
[38] Cf. Liv. 1.35.2. For the meaning of *ambitio* referred to Livy's Tarquinius Priscus, see Penella 2004.
[39] Penella 2004, 631–2; Vasaly 2015, 43–5.
[40] Liv. 1.49.6.
[41] Dionysius, relying on previous historians, only briefly recalls that Romulus became a tyrant in the last years of his reign (Dion. Hal., *Ant. Rom.* 2.56.3). On the contrary, Plutarch describes Romulus as a tyrant: Plut., *Rom.* 26.1–3; 31.
[42] Stem 2007; cf. Vasaly 2015, 37–40.

natura of the characters, on the other. It seems that the verisimilitude of the story is functional for Livy in the search for historical truth, according to Cicero's ideal that the narration to be *probabilis* must conform to the truth of facts and characters, thus pursuing the first *historiae lex*: the search for truth.[43]

Two other *leges* are attributed to Servius Tullius.[44] In the first passage Livy illustrates the census reform, probably the best known among the *leges regiae*. The second one is a brief and enigmatic mention of norms for the election of the consuls, which draws from some *commentarii* of the king used in the centuriate assembly at the time of the expulsion of the *Tarquinii* from Rome.

Immediately before the description of the reform of the census, Servius Tullius is presented by Livy as a man who tried to legitimise and strengthen his power 'nec iam publicis magis consiliis [. . .] quam privatis'.[45] This positive portrait emerges also in the account of the reform itself: firstly in an explicit form, with the praise given to it as *pacis longe maximum opus*,[46] and then more indirectly, when Livy stresses how the new system combined the preservation of the right to vote for all citizens with the actual transfer of all the decision-making capacity ('*vis omnis*') in the hands of the magnates, a measure which was due to the overwhelming number of centuries in which the latter were distributed.[47]

The quick mention by Livy of certain *commentarii Ser. Tulli*, which appears at the end of the book, could be similarly read. According to these *commentarii* the liberators of the city would have obtained the rules for the election of the two consuls through the convocation of the centuriate assembly presided by the *praefectus Urbis*. The information is mostly considered a late fabrication, perhaps from the age of Sulla,[48] but what is interesting here is that Livy uses it in a strategic way, to symbolically associate Servius Tullius with the birth of the Republic: the very king who had already been presented in an earlier chapter as being eager to lay down power and to donate *libertas* to Rome.[49]

More than any other work, Livy's AUC depicts clearly and insistently Servius Tullius as a champion of the people, even though not as a 'revolutionary king', as we shall see.[50] Dionysius also reports the widespread conviction that Servius

---

[43] Livy probably knew about Cicero's passages on this subject (Cic., *De or.* 2.62–3; *Inv. rhet.* 1.29; *Top.* 97) See McDonald 1957, 160; cf. Luce 1977, 182.
[44] Liv. 1.42.4–43.13; 60.4.
[45] Liv. 1.42.1.
[46] Liv. 1.42.4: *Adgrediturque inde ad pacis longe maximum opus, ut quemadmodum Numa divini auctor iuris fuisset, ita Servium conditorem omnis in civitate discriminis ordinumque quibus inter gradus dignitatis fortunaeque aliquid interlucet posteri fama ferrent. Censum enim instituit, rem saluberrimam tanto futuro imperio [. . .]*.
[47] Liv. 1.43.10.
[48] For example, see Thomsen 1980, 22, 247–8; Marastoni 2009, 78–85, 260–1; Ridley 2014, 98–9.
[49] Liv. 1.48.9.
[50] We must observe that Servius '*primus iniussu populi, voluntate patrum regnavit*' (Liv. 1.41.7). Other authoritative sources remember this detail (Cic., *Rep.* 2.37; Dion. Hal., *Ant. Rom.* 4.40.1; cf. Flor. 1.6.1–2). However, Poletti (2013) underlines how Livy, unlike other authors, shows how Servius Tullius acted irregularly, but not illegitimately.

intended to turn the monarchy into a democracy, but the Greek historian completely omits the information about the *commentarii*.[51] Cicero does the same in the *De republica*.[52] It is commonly believed that, in his idealisation of Servius, Livy was influenced by the late Annalists and that he chose to depict him in this way in order to praise indirectly Sulla or, possibly, Augustus.[53] Although this theory is plausible and intriguing, it remains unfortunately hard to demonstrate; in addition, it risks leading to the unsolvable question of whether Livy was an Augustus supporter or not.

Rather, what seems to emerge clearly from the analysis of Livy's text is that the author intends to emphasise as much as possible the contrast between the 'good' Servius, who would have transformed the Roman monarchy into a Republic had he not been assassinated, and the 'bad' Tarquinius, who represents a sort of tragic, though necessary, anomaly in this natural evolutionary process.[54] This is demonstrated by the fact that Livy not only reports the rumour according to which Servius intended to give freedom to the Roman people, but also explicitly points to the king almost as the ideal sovereign.[55]

The famous passage in which Livy describes the institution by Tullus Hostilius of the *duumviri / duoviri perduellionis* and of the *provocatio* deserves particular consideration.[56] It is not necessary here to consider the juridical implications of the passage, which is for the most part considered to be the result of mere legend.[57] Rather, it seems interesting to note that here Livy includes in the narrative numerous direct discourses, as well as formulae that this time, however, do not seem connected to a sacral rituality in the strict sense, as previously noted, but to the use of more frankly legal expressions, even though typical of a later age.[58] This is demonstrated by the syntactic scheme, consisting of very brief main, independent, and hypothetical phrases, and by the juxtaposition of subjunctive (*iudicent*), indicative (*provocarit, vincent*), and imperative (*certato, obnubito, suspendito, verberato*) tenses.[59] It is no coincidence that, in this single passage, the term *lex* is used by Livy five times, but nowhere else in the first book. The *pietas* and the religious inspiration return only in the final part of the passage, which, however, no longer concerns the *lex* established by Tullus Hostilius, but the introduction of a *mos*: the regular fulfilment of *piacularia sacrificia* to expiate the murder of Horatia, a practice related still in the days of the author to the conservation of the

---

[51] Dion. Hal., *Ant. Rom.* 4.40.3.
[52] Cic, *Rep.* 2.37-43; cf. Accius ap. Cic., *Sest.* 123 = TRF praet. 40: '*libertatem civibus stabiliverat*.' Also Plut., *De fort. Rom.* 10 remembers that Servius intended to abdicate, adding that Tanaquil, on the verge of death, dissuaded him.
[53] Ogilvie 1965, 185, 194; Ridley 2014, 98-9; Marastoni 2009, 51-85, 180-8.
[54] See also Bernard 2000, 197-99; Fromentin 2003.
[55] Liv. 1.48.8.
[56] Liv. 1.26.2-14.
[57] See among others Liou-Gille 1994, 6.
[58] For an overview on the authenticity of these formulae, see Turelli 2014, 475 n. 91.
[59] Ogilvie 1965, 115; Powell 2011, 471-2.

so-called *sororium tigillum*. The episode receives further emphasis with the adoption of a particular mixture of narration, dialogue, rhythmically constructed formulae, and topographical and juridical aetiologies:[60] everything revolves around the ideal contrast between the ruthlessness of the '*lex horrendi carminis*', on the one hand, and the wise *clementia* of its interpreters, the *rex* and the *populus*, on the other.[61] Also in this case, Livy wants to present both these conceptions as archetypal and innate in the institution itself, to affirm implicitly the rightness and paradigmatic value of the latter.

4. POLITICAL LIFE

All five texts in this section, with only one exception,[62] concern individual *foedera* of alliance between Rome and other *civitates*.[63] They differ from the *foedus* between Rome and Alba as they do not contain any formulae. This is probably due to the fact that Livy has already mentioned the formulae when narrating the details of that *foedus*, whose rite, according to the author, is the oldest among those known.[64]

Livy is to adopt a formulaic and archaic language again only in the short story of the surrender of Collatia to Tarquinius Priscus.[65] This *deditio* was not a true treaty of alliance, but a peculiar kind of international agreement, and this might explain Livy's language. Here Livy again returns to focus on the formulae of the treaty, overlooking the characterisation of the king. Again, as in the case of the Fetial formulae, the tripartite structure reappears, here in the form of questions posed by Tarquinius to the Collatia's delegates and their answers, consisting of a single verb. However, unlike previous cases, Livy here does not employ a lexicon related to the concepts of *iustus* and *pius*, nor does he highlight the contrast between the variability of individual conditions and the immutability of formulae through a diversified use of verbal tenses. The story is on the whole much more concise, although here Livy, in contrast to the norm, dwells on the subject more than Dionysius, who does not report the formulae handed down by the Annalists.[66] This could depend on the fact that the *deditio*, unlike a *foedus*, did not provide (at least until the end of the Republic) contractual guarantees. Rome offered only its own *fides*, which the *dediti* could choose to accept or reject.[67]

---

[60] Cf. Solodow 1979, 261–4; Fox 2015, 292–3. For the use of references to specific places, especially those that bear vestiges of the past, in order to *movere* the reader, see Vasaly 1993, 26–39.
[61] On this ambivalence see Solodow 1979, 255–6, 257.
[62] Liv. 1.44.1.
[63] Liv. 1.13.4–5; 38.1–2; 52.1–5; 55.1. The treaty signed by Tullus Hostilius with the Latins was excluded from the list, because Livy recalls it only retrospectively, and incidentally, at the beginning of the reign of Ancus Marcius: Liv. 1.32.3.
[64] Liv. 1.24.4.
[65] Liv. 1.38.1–2.
[66] Dion. Hal., *Ant. Rom.* 3.50.2–3.
[67] Auliard 2006, 40, 42–3.

The best-known *foedus* is perhaps the one signed by Romulus and Titus Tatius, at the end of the war triggered by the Rape of the Sabine Women: the kings thereafter made peace and united with the Latins and Sabines into one people.[68] Here too, as in the case of the other *leges regiae* that Livy attributes to the founder, the facts are told very briefly, as they are considered to be a simple completion of the common desire for pacification and integration. Livy, on the other hand, prefers to add at the end of the story two antiquarian notes on the Sabine origin of the term *Quirites* and on the toponym *lacus Curtius*.[69] In this, he differs from Dionysius, who devotes almost a whole chapter to narrating the details of the *foedus*, recalling only in the end the aetiology of *Quirites*. Livy will then be followed by Plutarch, who uses a more dramatic narrative technique, accentuated both by the broken syntax and by the description of the sudden silence between the two armies immediately before the agreement.[70]

Of particular interest are the passages concerning the *foedera* which Tarquinius Superbus agreed upon with several neighbouring peoples: while one of them consists only of a quick mention of peace treaties which had been renewed, or stipulated, with Aequi and Etruscans,[71] the other one is part of a longer account (extending for three chapters) aimed at demonstrating the king's political ability to employ tricks and scams to achieve his goals.[72] Tarquinius, by means of an elaborate and clever plan, takes revenge on Turnus Herdonius, an Arician nobleman, who strongly criticised the king during the meeting of the Latin leaders summoned at *lucus Ferentinae*, and thus manages to gain the Latin League's trust. This resulted in the renewal of the ancient *foedus* by the king, who left the counterparts without a doubt that this time *superior Romana res erat*. This *foedus* was therefore concluded on unequal terms and obtained through deceit and threats: it is no coincidence that Livy, as soon as the episode is over, defines Tarquinius *iniustus in pace rex* in the next chapter. This trait assigned by Livy to the king is consistent with the other elements of Tarquinius' negative characterisation, and the acknowledgement of the king's great talent as a commander does little to improve it.[73]

Livy dedicates only a very thin note to the last measure belonging to this section, namely the *lex de incensis* promulgated by Servius Tullius in conjunction with the institution of the census, presenting it as a mere appendix to the centuriate reform.[74] The extremely severe penalties provided for by this law are presented as a merely functional instrument to accelerate the operations of the census.

---

[68] Liv. 1.13.4–5.
[69] For a different aetiology of the toponym *lacus Curtius* cf. Liv. 7.6.6.
[70] Dion. Hal., *Ant. Rom.* 2.46; Plut., *Rom.* 19.9–10; 18.6.
[71] Liv. 1.55.1.
[72] Liv. 1.52.1–5. On the inconsistencies of Livy's story and a proposal for their resolution, see Barzanò 1991.
[73] Liv. 1.53.1.
[74] Liv. 1.44.1.

It would seem that Livy emphasises this use, aimed at beneficial and necessary purposes, choosing from his sources a more severe version of the law than that handed down by Cicero and Dionysius, and by third-century CE jurists. In fact, according to Livy, *incensi* can be punished with imprisonment and even death, while the other authors recall only confiscation of property, flogging, and slavery among the penalties.[75] In other words, it seems that Livy presents this law in such a way to portray Servius Tullius as a just and libertarian king, who also knows how to apply strict laws for the good of the *res publica*.

5. WAR AND ARMY

This section focuses on four *leges* dealing with the increase of army strength.[76] Almost all of them are reported by Livy in an extremely synthetic, and sometimes inaccurate, form. Livy, in the first passage, highlights how Romulus and Titus Tatius created the oldest cavalry centuries, named *Ramnenses, Titienses, Luceres*.[77] As in other cases, this episode allows the author to insert an antiquarian note in the story and to trace back the origins of the name *Ramnenses* to Romulus and that of the *Titienses* to Titus Tatius, while leaving unexplained the third etymology with the justification of the uncertainty of the sources. Interestingly, as it is well known, other authors do not associate the names mentioned by Livy with the cavalry centuries, but rather link them to the original tribes and attribute to them an Etruscan origin.[78] Livy, on the contrary, seems to condense the information at his disposal, merging the cavalry centuries, which were created with people from the tribes, with the tribes themselves (although the latter are mentioned as such only much later in the decade).[79] In addition, he probably uses two false etymologies to reinforce, once again, the bond between ancient institutions and the founding king, as it was also the case with *curiae*.[80]

Later, Tullus Hostilius would take care of the army. After destroying Alba and granting Roman citizenship to the population, he increases the cavalry and infantry numbers, introducing rules that Livy describes in an unclear way.[81] For on the one hand, the king adds ten cavalry *turmae* recruited among the Albans, which, if we count thirty knights *per turma*,[82] would seem to imply an overall doubling of the cavalry (which until then was constituted only by the aforesaid three centuries created by Romulus and Titus Tatius). On the other hand, the king *legiones et*

---

[75] Dion. Hal., *Ant. Rom.* 4.15.6 (cf. 5.75.3); Cic., *Caecin.* 99–100; Ulp., fr. 11.11; Gai, *Inst.* 1.160.
[76] Liv. 1.13.8; 30.3; 36.2; 7–8; 52.6.
[77] Liv. 1.13.8.
[78] Varro, *Ling.*, 5.55; cf. Plut., *Rom.*, 20.2. Rix (2006, 167–75) denies the Etruscan origin of these names and believes that they are Latin. On the topic, see also Cornell 1995, 114–18.
[79] Liv. 10.6.7 (*Ramnes* instead of *Ramnenses*); cf. Festus, *Gloss. Lat.* 484. The implicit link between tribes and centuries in Livy is stressed by Oakley (2005, 94–5).
[80] Ogilvie 1965, 80; cf. Mora 1995, 214–15.
[81] Liv. 1.30.3. Dionysius only states that, after the capture of Alba, Tullus Hostilius could have a double amount of Roman soldiers and a number of allied troops (Dion. Hal., *Ant. Rom.* 3.33.3).
[82] Polyb. 6.20.9; 25.1; Festus, *Gloss. Lat.* 484; Isid., *Etym.* 9.3.51. See Dobson 2008, 50.

veteres eodem supplemento explevit et novas scripsit. The later information could mean that Tullus Hostilius enlisted a proportional number of Albans even among the infantry ranks; the existence of more than one legion in this age seems unlikely, however.[83] This could be an exaggeration by Livy or his source; however, it is more likely that the term *legio* here does not mean 'legion' but, in a broader sense, 'troops of infantry' or 'army', as it seems to be confirmed by the mention, in the same book, of a *legio Fidenatium* and *legiones Sabinas*.[84] In this light, the passage would no longer present difficulties of meaning, as it should be interpreted as an emphasis on the care of the army by Tullus Hostilius, who Livy wants to depict as an exemplary figure of a warrior and warlike king, even more so than Romulus.[85]

Livy deals again with the cavalry centuries when he illustrates the failed attempt by Tarquinius Priscus to create new ones. Tarquinius, who was successfully opposed in his plan by a negative prophecy by the augur Attus Navius, managed to overcome the problem by doubling the strength of the pre-existing centuries.[86] However, the figures transmitted by Livy fail to convince: in fact, by doubling the numbers of the Romulean centuries, an overall total of 600 horsemen rather than 1,800 would have been obtained. In addition, after Tullus Hostilius integrated the Albans into Roman citizenship, the number of horsemen inherited from Tarquinius amounted already to 600; therefore, their doubling would have led to a total of 1,200. The number of 1,800 *equites* coincides suspiciously with those of the eighteen cavalry centuries of the Servian reform, which suggests that Livy's detail here is probably anachronistic.[87]

The episode is connected to the Rome of Livy's own time by means of the aetiology of the so-called *sex suffragia*. Their origins are linked to the creation of the three centuries, although other authors attribute them to Servius Tullius.[88] It is not a coincidence that Livy associates the figure of Tarquinius with that of the author of the centuriate reform. Indeed, it is likely that the historian is aiming here to link Tarquinius to Romulus and to Servius Tullius (although in a subordinate position) within the wider framework of the establishment of the fundamental institutions of the city.

On the other hand, the confrontation with the priest Attus Navius, whose powers of divination are questioned by Tarquinius, contributes to accentuating the image of the king as a man who, although excellent in all other respects, will stop at nothing in order to realise his own personal *ambitio*, even if this leads to impiety.[89] Livy's use of the term *ambitio* to describe Tarquinius' behaviour in the

---

[83] Plut., *Rom.* 13.1 unconvincingly suggests that already in the time of Romulus there was more than a single legion of 3,000 infantry and 300 knights.
[84] Liv. 1.27.5; 37.3. See Luce 1977, 241.
[85] Cf. Bernard 2000, 198–9; Fox 2015, 293.
[86] Liv. 1.36.2; 7–8. At the end of the corresponding episode, Dionysius does not mention centuries doubling, but only states that Tarquinius gave up creating new ones: Dion. Hal., *Ant. Rom.* 3.71.5.
[87] Cf. Liv. 1.43.9. See Ogilvie 1965, 152.
[88] Festus, *Gloss. Lat.* 452; see Ogilvie 1965, 152.
[89] Cf. Penella 2004, 633.

text (concerning another *lex* by the same king) does not seem to be a coincidence.[90] Furthermore, in contrast to the Greek sources, Livy does not attribute this behaviour to Tarquinius' predecessors, but assigns it to the Etruscan king for the first time.

The same does not apply to Tarquinius Superbus, who doubles the army by creating new Roman-Latin mixed maniples after the imposition of the *foedus* to the Latins.[91] In imagining similar units, composed of Romans and allies, Livy is again anachronistic.[92] This is functional to represent the behaviour of Superbus as entirely consistent with the unfair actions he just undertook to the detriment of the Latins: by depriving the allies of their leaders and commands, and even of their *signa*, the king intends to make them docile tools of his ambitious expansionist aims, which are narrated by Livy in the next chapter.

6. AGRARIAN LAWS

In the entire first book, only one agrarian law is mentioned: an *adsignatio viritana* of newly conquered land, which was carried out by Servius Tullius to reconcile the people after Tarquinius had accused him of ruling *iniussu populi*.[93] The way that Livy remembers this *lex regia* aims once again to reinforce the image of a 'popular' king. In addition, the cursory mention of the *lex* seems intended to demonstrate the king's ability to defend himself against the threat posed by the young Tarquinius and to compare the fair and moderate behaviour of the former with the shady schemes of the latter.[94]

Of course, the aim here is not to depict Servius Tullius as a sort of forerunner of the reformers of the late Republic, although the episode – anachronistic as it is here – does present features that are affected by the political discourse of the Gracchan age.[95] This emerges also from a comparison with the corresponding passages from Dionysius. The historian from Halicarnassus states that, at the beginning of his reign, Servius redistributed land that had been illegally occupied by the rich to people with no property.[96] Dionysius places the assignment of conquered land at the end of Servius' kingdom, asserting that the beneficiaries were freedmen.[97] Livy, on the other hand, wants to highlight that the behaviour of the king does not appear revolutionary at all and that it can be considered within a 'constitutional'

---

[90] Liv. 1.35.6.
[91] Liv. 1.52.6.
[92] The anachronism is made even more evident by the use of the term *manipulus*: the manipular legion did not appear before the fourth century BCE (see for example Brizzi 2008, 33–7; cf. Ogilvie 1965, 204). In the corresponding passage Dionysius only mentions that Tarquinius collected a very large number of allied troops (Dion. Hal., *Ant. Rom.* 4.50.1).
[93] Liv. 1.46.1.
[94] See also Poletti 2013, 137–8; 141–3.
[95] Ogilvie 1965, 187; Gabba 1996, 156.
[96] Dion. Hal., *Ant. Rom.* 4.9.8–11.
[97] Dion. Hal., *Ant. Rom.* 4.27.1–6. See Marastoni 2009, 25–6.

framework. In order to make this point clear, Livy uses a lexicon typical of the *lex rogata*, when he relates in a statement that follows his description of the agrarian law,[98] that Servius submitted to the judgement of the people the legitimacy of his rule. The formula *vellent iuberentne* represents a clear example of this.[99]

7. GRANTING OF CITIZENSHIP

Livy tells us about three concessions of citizenship to enemies defeated in war, which had been carried out by Romulus, Tullus Hostilius, and Ancus Marcius.[100] In the first case, the king grants citizenship to the peoples of *Caenina* and *Antemnae* after only one clash and without further bloodshed: Hersilia, moved to compassion by the supplications of the girls kidnapped by these cities, convinces her husband Romulus to fulfil their requests. The episode ends with the exaltation of *concordia* as an instrument to consolidate the state, and is followed by a brief account of the defeat of *Crustumini* and the emigration of many of them in Rome.[101] The whole passage seems to anticipate the final outcome of the war, when Romulus and Titus Tatius, once again at the behest of women, seal the peace and decree the union of Latins and Sabines into a single civic body.[102] It cannot be excluded that by insisting on the use of *concordia* by Romulus, a trait mostly absent in the tradition of the character handed down by Cicero and Dionysius, Livy wants to establish a parallel with the politics of Augustus.[103] However, in these passages the figure of Hersilia and of the other women is undoubtedly much more central than that of Romulus,[104] who bends to their prayers but never spontaneously takes the peace-making initiative, in contrast to what Dionysius reports.[105] Livy is the first source to present Hersilia as the wife of Romulus and the promoter of a partial reconciliation before the end of the war; this is clearly aimed at giving women the role of protagonists in the conclusion of the peace and, consequently, in the very institution of the fundamental political category of *concordia*, which is readily accepted and translated into action by Romulus.[106]

In the second case, instead, citizenship was granted only after the total destruction of the city of Alba. The event presents the characteristics of a deportation, although with some advantages for the defeated enemy. Livy reports the measure using mostly a series of very brief main phrases. Livy inserts two antiquarian notes

---

[98] Liv. 1.46.1. Cf. Cic., *Rep.* 2.38; Dion. Hal., *Ant. Rom.* 4.12.2–3.
[99] Ogilvie 1965, 187.
[100] Liv. 1.11.2; 30.1–2; 33.1–2; 5–6.
[101] Liv. 1.11.3–4.
[102] Many authoritative sources consider Hersilia the key figure in this story as well: Dion. Hal., *Ant. Rom.* 2.45.2; 45.6; Ov., *Fast.* 3.203–12; Cnaeus Gellius, fr. 15 Peter ap. Gell., NA 13.23.13; Plut., *Rom.* 19.7; Cass. Dio 1.5.5. On the topic, see also Kowalewski 2002, 21–3.
[103] Cf. Cic., *Rep.* 2.13; Dion. Hal., *Ant. Rom.* 2.5.4. See Mineo 2015, 145. Cf. Stem 2007, 467–8.
[104] See for example Vandiver 1999, 212–17.
[105] Dion. Hal., *Ant. Rom.* 2.35.
[106] Brown 1995, 300–3; 306–10; 312–13.

in the story: the first concerns the enlargement of the city to include the Caelian hill to accommodate the new citizens; the second relates the entry into the Senate of some of the oldest Alban families in Rome by the will of the same Tullus Hostilius. Livy also appears in this passage above all to exalt the renewed harmony between ancient enemies, although the initial reference to the ruins of Alba differentiates this episode quite clearly from the previous one: here *concordia* does not prevail, but the right of the winner, despite the important advantages for the deportees that are also highlighted.

Ancus Marcius also arranges the transfer of defeated Latin populations in Rome.[107] In narrating the event, Livy clarifies almost immediately that Ancus followed *morem regum priorum, qui rem Romanam auxerant hostibus in civitatem accipiendis*, in order perhaps to justify the harsh action of the king. Seeking to strengthen this ideal of continuity, which is indispensable to the growth of Roman power, Livy also emphasises the further enlargements of the town due to the growth of the civic community. According to the same agenda, Livy too underlines the king's will to link old and new areas of the *Urbs*. In doing so, the historian at times forces the historical data, particularly when he claims that the *pons Sublicius* was built to connect the Janiculum hill to the city while, in fact, the latter was fortified to protect the western end of the pre-existing bridge.[108] This results in an overall quite positive portrait of Ancus Marcius. However, this is far less marked than that of other kings. Here, as elsewhere, the profile of the king is almost always quite blurred, especially when compared to the portraits of the kings Numa, Romulus, and Tullus Hostilius.[109]

8. CONCLUSION

To sum up and conclude: the *leges regiae* associated with religious life and international relations are characterised by formulaic language, direct discourses, archaic vocabulary halfway between the semantic field of religion and law, a high degree of detail, and an anticipation of institutions which were probably created later than the regal period. In this category, Livy tends to emphasise those founding traditions which could become an inspirational model for the decadent society of his own time. This is consistent with the programmatic invitation in Livy's *Praefatio* to take from history the *documenta* which should be imitated or avoided by both individuals and states.[110] In this sense Livy, who in the *Praefatio* also offers a profoundly pessimistic interpretation of contemporary Rome,[111] differs from Dionysius. For the latter, the glorious past of the *Urbs* finds its full realisation in the Augustan age.[112]

---

[107] Liv. 1.33.1–2, 5–6.
[108] Ogilvie 1965, 137.
[109] Bernard 2000, 198.
[110] Liv., *Praef.* 10.
[111] Liv., *Praef.* 9.
[112] As Emilio Gabba suggested: Gabba 1996, 80, 87–90.

In the episodes concerning the introduction of 'constitutional norms', not only does Livy write according to the same agenda, but he also aims at characterising the individual kings, calibrating the positive and negative traits of each of them. Positive traits generally prevail, the only exception being the portrait of Tarquinius Superbus.[113] Livy achieves this result in many ways: by choosing particular historiographical variants, sometimes not otherwise attested; by inserting several aetiologies; and by adopting an essential and concise style, characterised by a dense *brevitas*, which contributes to an accurate presentation of the features that are to be highlighted.[114] As a consequence, distinctive portraits of the kings are often significantly different from those found in other sources.[115]

In the remaining categories of *leges*, Livy's agenda is mostly the same. Not only does the historian use the techniques and procedures I have already mentioned above, in order to frame his own depiction of the Roman kings for his reader, but he also at times forces the historical data using false etymologies or anachronistic legal vocabulary. In light of all this, on the one hand, it seems that Livy insists on creating ideal and exemplary connections between the most remote past of Rome and the present. This would be consistent with the words the historian attributes, in book 34, to the tribune Valerius Tappus, who exalts the eternal *utilitas* of *regia lex simul cum ipsa urbe nata*.[116] On the other hand, Livy seems to emphasise the internal coherence of the portraits of each individual king, in particular by comparing an individual portrait with those of the other kings. This feature of Livy's narrative does not seem to be meant merely to embellish the story in order to make it more enjoyable and effective from the literary point of view. Rather, it seems to be a technique aimed at the pursuit of historical truth – a goal to be achieved by adapting the narrative to the characters.

This is certainly not a truth which derives from the objective documentation of Roman history of such an ancient age, which is quite difficult to reconstruct and therefore susceptible to adaptations and alterations.[117] Rather, this 'truth' represents *the image of that history which Livy wants to give*, according to his personal point of view.[118] As Joseph Solodow has stated, Livy's greatness as an historian

---

[113] Cf. Luce 1977, 239 n. 20: 'Most of the kings are represented as versatile and many-sided.' On the complexity of Livy's moral judgement regarding the characters of his work, see for example Solodow 1979.

[114] Cf. Fox 2015, 287.

[115] Cf. Luce 1977, 235–6.

[116] Liv. 34.6.7.

[117] As Livy acknowledges (6.1.2): *res cum vetustate nimia obscuras velut quae magno ex intervallo loci vix cernuntur, tum quid rarae per eadem tempora litterae fuere, una custodia fidelis memoriae rerum gestarum, et quod, etiam si quae in commentariis pontificum aliisque publicis privatisque erant monumentis, incensa urbe pleraeque interiere.* Cf. 5.21.9: *sed in rebus tam antiquis si quae similia veri sint pro veris accipiantur, satis habeam*; 7.6.6: [. . .] *fama rerum standum est, ubi certam derogat vetustas fidem*. Luce (1977, 224) remarks that 'in the first ten books Livy's freedom in adapting and inventing seems to have gone far beyond anything we find in the later books'.

[118] Ridley (1990), dealing with the conflict of orders in the first decade, came to the same conclusion.

'lies [. . .] in his own imaginative reconstruction of the past and his representation [. . .] of it to the reader', according to criteria that are functional to the message he wants to assign to history.

Works Cited

Auliard, C, 2006. *La diplomatie romaine, l'autre instrument de la conquête. De la fondation à la fin des guerres samnites (753–290 av. J-C)*. Rennes: Presses Universitaires de Rennes.

Barzanò, A, 1991. 'La morte di Turno Erdonio e il problema della localizzazione del *lucus* e del *caput aquae Ferentinae*.' *Aevum* 65.1:39–63.

Beard, M, J North, and S Price, 1998. *Religions of Rome. Vol. 2: A Sourcebook*. Cambridge: Cambridge University Press.

Bernard, J-E, 2000. *Le portrait chez Tite-Live*. Brussels: Latomus.

Bianchi, E, 2016. 'Augusto e l'utilizzazione carismatica delle istituzioni religiose. Una contestualizzazione frammentaria.' In *Studi su Augusto. In occasione del XX centenario della morte*, edited by G Negri and A Valvo, 7–54. Turin: Giappichelli.

Brizzi, G, 2008. *Il guerriero, l'oplita, il legionario. Gli eserciti nel mondo classico*. 2nd edn. Bologna: Il Mulino.

Brown, R, 1995. 'Livy's Sabine Women and the Ideal of *Concordia*.' *TAPA* 125:291–319.

Bujuklić, Z, 1998. 'Leges regiae: pro et contra.' *RIDA* 45.3:89–142.

Capogrossi Colognesi, L, 2009. *Storia di Roma tra diritto e potere*. Bologna: Il Mulino.

Carandini, A, L Argentieri, P Carafa, M Fiorentini, and U Fusco, eds, 2011. *La leggenda di Roma. Vol. 3: La costituzione*. Milan: Fondazione Lorenzo Valla, Arnoldo Mondadori Editore.

Champion, C B, 2017. *The Peace of the Gods. Elite Religious Practices in the Middle Roman Republic*. Princeton: Princeton University Press.

Cornell, T J, 1995. *The Beginnings of Rome: Italy and Rome from the Bronze Age to the Punic Wars (c. 1000–264 B.C.)*. London: Routledge.

Dangel, J, 1982. *La phrase oratoire chez Tite-Live*. Paris: Les Belles Lettres.

D'Ippolito, F M, 1998. 'Le origini del Senato e la prima età repubblicana.' In *Il Senato nella storia. Vol. 1: Il Senato nell'età romana*, 29–83. Rome: Istituto poligrafico e Zecca dello Stato, Libreria dello Stato.

Di Trolio, G, 2017. *Le leges regiae in Dionigi d'Alicarnasso. Vol. 1: La monarchia latino-sabina*. Naples: Jovene.

Dobson, M, 2008. *The Army of the Roman Republic. The Second Century BC, Polybius and the Camps at Numantia, Spain*. Oxford: Oxbow Books.

Fox, M, 2015. 'The Representation of the Regal Period in Livy.' In *A Companion to Livy*, edited by B Mineo, 286–97. Malden, MA: Wiley-Blackwell.

Franciosi, G, ed., 2003. *Leges regiae*. Naples: Jovene.

Fromentin, V, 2003. 'Fondements et crises de la royauté à Rome: les règnes de Servius Tullius et de Tarquin le Superbe chez Tite-Live et Denys d' Halicarnasse.' In *Fondements et crises du pouvoir*, edited by S Franchet d'Espèrey, V Fromentin, S Gotteland, and J-M Roddaz, 69–82. Bordeaux: Ausonius.
Gabba, E, 1996. *Dionigi e la storia di Roma arcaica*. Bari: Edipuglia.
———, 2000. *Roma arcaica. Storia e storiografia*. Rome: Edizioni di storia e letteratura.
Hickson, F V, 1993. *Roman Prayer Language. Livy and the Aeneid of Vergil*. Stuttgart: B G Teubner.
Kowalewski, B, 2002. *Frauengestalten im Geschichtswerk des T. Livius*. Munich: Saur.
Lanfranchi, T, 2012. 'Le leggi comiziali nella prima deca di Tito Livio.' In *Leges publicae. La legge nell'esperienza giuridica romana*, edited by J-L Ferrary, 341–403. Pavia: IUSS Press.
Latte, K, 1960. *Handbuch der Altertumswissenschaft*. Vol. 5.4: *Römische Religionsgeschichte*. Munich: Beck.
Liou-Gille, B, 1994. 'La *perduellio*: les procès d'Horace et de Rabirius.' *Latomus* 53.1:3–38.
Luce, T J, 1977. *Livy. The Composition of His History*. Princeton: Princeton University Press.
Mantovani, D, 2012. 'Le due serie di leges regiae.' In *Leges publicae. La legge nell'esperienza giuridica romana*, edited by J-L Ferrary, 283–92. Pavia: IUSS Press.
Marastoni, S, 2009. *Servio Tullio e l'ideologia sillana*. Rome: Bretschneider.
Martin, P M, 1982. *L'idée de royauté à Rome. Vol. 1: De la Rome royale au consensus républicain*. Clermont-Ferrand: Adosa.
de Martino, F, 1972. *Storia della costituzione romana*. Vol. 2. 2nd edn. Naples: Jovene.
McDonald, A H, 1957. 'The Style of Livy.' *JRS* 47:155–72.
Mineo, B, 2015. 'Livy's Historical Philosophy.' In *A Companion to Livy*, edited by B Mineo, 139–52. Malden, MA: Wiley-Blackwell.
Mora, F, 1995. *Il pensiero storico-religioso antico. Autori greci e Roma. Vol. 1: Dionigi d'Alicarnasso*. Roma: 'L'Erma' di Bretschneider.
Oakley, S P, 2005. *A Commentary on Livy: Books VI-X. Vol. 4: Book 10*. Oxford: Clarendon Press.
Ogilvie, R M, 1965. *A Commentary on Livy. Books 1–5*. Oxford: Clarendon Press.
Penella, R J, 2004. 'The *Ambitio* of Livy's Tarquinius Priscus.' *CQ* 54.2:630–5.
Poletti, S, 2013. 'Il Servio Tullio di Livio e le sue "contraddizioni." A proposito dell'elezione ritardata in Liv. I, 46, 1 e di altri stratagemmi liviani.' *SCO* 59:117–51.
Powell, J G F, 2011. 'Legal Latin.' In *A Companion to the Latin Language*, edited by J. Clackson, 464–84. Malden, MA: Wiley-Blackwell.
Rich, J, 2011. 'The Fetiales and Roman International Relations.' In *Priests and State in the Roman World*, edited by J H Richardson and F Santangelo, 187–242. Stuttgart: Steiner.

Ridley, R T, 1990. 'Patavinitas among the Patricians? Livy and the Conflict of the Orders.' In *Staat und Staatlichkeit in der frühen römischen Republik. Akten eines Symposiums 12.–15. Juli 1988, Freie Universität Berlin*, edited by W. Eder, 103–38. Stuttgart: Steiner.

——, 2014. 'The Enigma of Servius Tullius.' In *The Roman Historical Tradition. Regal and Republican Rome*, edited by J H Richardson and F Santangelo, 83–128. Oxford: Oxford University Press.

Rix, H, 2006. '*Ramnes, Tites* (sic), *Luceres*: noms étrusques ou latins?' MEFRA 118.1:167–75.

Santangelo, F, 2014. 'I feziali tra rituale, diplomazia e tradizioni inventate.' In *Sacerdos. Figure del sacro nella società romana: atti del convegno internazionale, Cividale del Friuli, 26–28 settembre 2012*, edited by G Urso, 83–103. Pisa: ETS.

Santoro, R, 1998. 'Sul *ius Papirianum.*' In *Mélanges de droit romain et d'histoire ancienne: hommage à la mémoire de André Magdelain*, edited by M Humbert and Y Thomas, 329–416. Paris: Éditions Pantheon-Assas.

Scapini, M, 2015. 'Literary Archetypes for the Regal Period.' In *A Companion to Livy*, edited by B Mineo, 274–85. Malden, MA: Wiley-Blackwell.

Solodow, J B, 1979. 'Livy and the Story of Horatius, 1.24–26.' TAPA 109:251–68.

Stem, R, 2007. 'The Exemplary Lessons of Livy's Romulus.' TAPA 137.2:435–71.

Thomsen, R, 1980. *King Servius Tullius*. Copenhagen: Gyldendal.

Tondo, S, 1971. 'Introduzione alle "leges regiae".' SDHI 37:1–73.

——, 1973. *Leges regiae e paricidas*. Florence: L S Olschki.

Turelli, G, 2011. *'Audi Iuppiter.' Il collegio dei feziali nell'esperienza giuridica romana*. Milan: Giuffrè.

——, 2014. '*Fetialis religio*. Una riflessione su religione e diritto nell'esperienza romana.' In *Religione e diritto romano. La cogenza del rito*, edited by S Randazzo, 449–91. Tricase: Libellula.

Vandiver, E, 1999. 'The Founding Mothers of Livy's Rome: The Sabine Women and Lucretia.' In *The Eye Expanded: Life and the Arts in Greco-Roman Antiquity*, edited by F B Titchener and R F Moorton, Jr, 206–32. Berkeley: University of California Press.

Vasaly, A, 1993. *Representations: Images of the World in Ciceronian Oratory*. Berkeley: University of California Press.

——, 2015. *Livy's Political Philosophy. Power and Personality in Early Rome*. New York: Cambridge University Press.

Chapter 6

The *leges regiae* through Tradition, Historicity and Invention: A Comparison of Historico-literary and Jurisprudential Sources

Rossella Laurendi

1. INTRODUCTION

Existing knowledge of the so-called *leges regiae* and of the political and institutional profiles of the *regnum* in general is based on information subjected to a complex literary tradition as well as pieced together from isolated references in Roman legal sources.[1] First-hand evidence is in fact rather limited. Although the *Cippus Antiquissimus* found in the Roman Forum, dating from between 575 and 565 BCE and considered by some to be a *lex regia*, is currently the object of some renewed scholarly interest, so far it has offered little clarification with regard to the substantive legal aspects of Rome during the period of the Monarchy.[2]

The collective examination of these sources must be undertaken through an interdisciplinary approach and a careful and critical reading of the information available.[3] In this way, the long and multilayered process of the formation and transmission of historical memory can be understood. In addition, the different forms and varying contents in which such information was received and sometimes reworked by historians, scholars, grammarians, writers, and jurists, from the late Republican Age onwards, can then be assessed.

This methodology also requires a re-examination of the relationship between royal laws and the *ius civile Papirianum*. The latter is represented as a collection of *leges*, and certain sources date the collection to the end of the sixth century BCE, having seemingly been created at the initiative of a member of the *gens Papiria*. On the other hand, the dissemination of the *ius civile Papirianum* in Roman

---

The author and editors are grateful to Carrie Booth (Edinburgh) for her translation of the text.

[1] *Status quaestionis* in Laurendi 2013, 9–18.
[2] On the dating and the content of the presumed *lex regia*, see most recently Tassi 2016, 73–90, according to whom a *decretum* of the *pontifices* would be engraved on the memorial stone with customary requirements 'relating to the worship to be given in the Shrine of the Comitium, requirements considered necessary to be set out in writing, given the particular importance of that sacred air to the ancient city community' (90), and not sanctions 'directed at individuals who find themselves in the state of *homines sacri*' (89).
[3] On problems of method, see Gabba 1993, 13–22.; Mantovani 2012, 283–4.

'cultural circles' is only evident from the first century BCE onwards, which raises the problem of its dating. From the verbatim quotes of royal laws, the only example available to us that seems to have a relationship with this collection and with its commentary, the *liber de iure Papiriano*, is the *lex* of the *paelex*, attributed to King Numa by Festus and Aulus Gellius. A philological analysis of the law suggests that it is substantially authentic, even if we are not able to assert that this was actually drawn up by the king to whom it has been ascribed by tradition.

2. THE *IUS PAPIRIANUM* ACCORDING TO DIONYSIUS AND POMPONIUS

In the third book of the Ῥωμαϊκή Ἀρχαιολογία, Dionysius reports that King Ancus Marcius had received the writings on the *sacra* from the pontiffs – writings that King Numa Pompilius had previously collected and transcribed on tablets to be exhibited publicly in the Forum.[4] Dionysius adds that, in such ancient times, the tablets used for the transcription of laws and ordinances on *sacra* were made not of bronze but of oak, which is why they were lost over time. Therefore, only after the expulsion of the kings did Gaius Papirius, ἀνήρ ἱεροφάντης,[5] make a transcription public again.[6]

Livy confirms the tradition with regard to Ancus' publication of Numa's transcriptions, but is silent on the publication edited by Gaius Papirius at an undefined moment after the end of the monarchy. Instead, Livy maintains that Ancus would have ordered the pontiffs to exhibit publicly the *sacra* contained in the *commentarii* of Numa after having the facts transcribed *in albo*.[7] The Dionysian news of the existence of a Papirius, the author of a collection of royal laws, is instead found in a known fragment of Pomponius' *liber singularis enchiridii*:

> D. 1.2.2.1: *et quidem initio ciuitatis nostrae populus sine lege certa, sine iure certo primum agere instituit omniaque manu a regibus gubernabatur. 2. Postea aucta ad aliquem modum ciuitate ipsum Romulum traditur in triginta partes diuisisse, quas partes curias appellauit*

---

[4] Dion. Hal. *Ant. Rom.* 3.36.4: συγκαλέσας τοὺς ἱεροφάντας καὶ τὰς περὶ τῶν ἱερῶν συγγραφάς, ἃς Πομπίλιος συνεστήσατο, παρ᾽ αὐτῶν λαβὼν ἀνέγραψεν εἰς δέλτους καὶ προὔθηκεν ἐν ἀγορᾷ πᾶσι τοῖς βουλομένοις σκοπεῖν, ἃς ἀφανισθῆναι συνέβη τῷ χρόνῳ· χαλκαῖ γὰρ οὔπω στῆλαι τότε ἦσαν, ἀλλ᾽ ἐν δρυΐναις ἐχαράττοντο σανίσιν οἵ τε νόμοι καὶ αἱ περὶ τῶν ἱερῶν διαγραφαί· μετὰ δὲ τὴν ἐκβολὴν τῶν βασιλέων εἰς ἀναγραφὴν δημοσίαν αὖθις ἤχθησαν ὑπ᾽ ἀνδρὸς ἱεροφάντου Γαίου Παπιρίου, τὴν ἁπάντων τῶν ἱερέων ἡγεμονίαν ἔχοντος.

[5] According to Tondo 1973, 32 n. 74, Gaius Papirius would have held the office of pontiff. In support of this, see Albanese 1998, 12–13 and Carandini 2011, 377, among others. By contrast, Pais 1915, 243 n. 4 and Bretone 1963, 386 n. 4 argue that Dionysius meant to refer to the position of *rex sacrorum* instead.

[6] A different but isolated reading of the passage is proposed by Di Trolio 2017, 255 n. 13, 257, 260, for whom the transcription of Numa's *sacra*, commissioned by Ancus Marcius, was carried out by Gaius Papirius, and therefore would not have occurred after the expulsion of the kings, but rather many years before.

[7] Liv. 1.32.2: *Antiqissimum ratus* (scil. *Ancus Marcius*) *sacra publica ut ab Numa instituta erant, facere, omnia ea ex commentariis regis pontificem in album relata proponere in publico iubet*.

propterea quod tunc reipublicae curam per sententias partium earum expediebat. Et ita leges quasdam et ipse curiatas ad populum tulit: tulerunt et sequentes reges. Quae omnes conscriptae exstant in libro Sexti Papirii, qui fuit illis temporibus, quibus Superbus Demarathi Corinthii filius, ex principalibus viris. Is liber, ut diximus, appellatur ius ciuile Papirianum, non quia Papirius de suo quicquam ibi adiecit, sed quod leges sine ordine latas in unum composuit. 3. Exactis deinde regibus lege tribunicia omnes leges haec exoleuerunt iterumque coepit populus Romanus incerto magis iure et consuetudine aliqua uti quam per latam legem, idque prope uiginti annis passus est.

In Pomponius' representation of this episode, the kings, from Romulus onwards, proposed certain *leges* to the people divided *per curias*,[8] then collected them in the book of Sextus Papirius *vir ex principalibus* during the time of King Tarquinius Superbus, the son of Demaratus of Corinth. Pomponius further explains that the book was called the *ius civile Papirianum*, not because Sextus Papirius had added something of his own, but simply because 'he compiled in unitary form laws passed piecemeal' (*leges sine ordine latas in unum composuit*). After the expulsion of the kings, due to a passing of a tribunician law, these royal laws fell into disuse and the people again began 'to work with vague ideas of right and with customs of a sort rather than with legislation' (*incerto magis iure et consuetudine aliqua uti quam per latam legem*), thus returning to a state of uncertainty with regard to origin.

The differences between the information handed down from Dionysius and later from Pomponius in the *Digest* of Justinian must, in my view, be partially interpreted by taking into account the content and the objectives of the Ῥωμαϊκή Ἀρχαιολογία and the *Enchiridion*,[9] specifically the sources and historiographical techniques used by the two authors.

The information that Dionysius provides about Papirius and his collection is in fact rather scant, since it is limited to the narration of a new edition of the writings on the *sacra* that was edited by him and followed the work of Ancus. There are no other references to the *ius Papirianum* in any of Dionysius' work, not even in the chapters on the Tarquinian monarchy. As such, we are unable to comprehend whether Gaius Papirius – according to the source upon which the historian drew – merely republished Numa's *sacra* or, if he was instead working after the expulsion of the kings, he also transcribed what Numa's successors had legislated on the *sacra*. Unlike Dionysius, Pomponius reports that the author of the work, which would have contained all the *leges curiatae* and not only Numa's *sacra*, was indeed *Sextus*, and not *Gaius Papirius*.[10] However, some uncertainty prevails, since Sextus

---

[8] On the word *curia* and its origins, see most recently Prosdocimi 2016, 256–430 and Pelloso 2018, 7–42.
[9] On the *Enchiridion*, see most recently Nasti 2012, 8–35.
[10] Dionysius discusses very briefly one Manius Papirius (Dion. Hal. 5.1.4); however, he does not connect him with Gaius, ἀνήρ ἱεροφάντης and author of the collection of *sacra*, and merely indicates the gentleness of his character. Von Glück 1780, 134, and most recently Manzo 2014, 104–5 and Fenocchio 2016, 30, are well aware of the diversity of offices held by Manius, *rex sacrorum*, and by Gaius, ἀνήρ ἱεροφάντης, respectively, and the distinction between the two persons.

Papirius becomes Publius Papirius in another part of the *Enchiridion*: 'yet a man in the first rank for skill was Publius Papirius, who compiled the *leges regiae* in a unitary form' (*fuit autem in primis peritus Publius Papirius, qui leges regiae in unum contulit*).[11] The tradition reported by Dionysius also indicates that Gaius Papirius had collected the *sacra* after the fall of the monarchy, but Pomponius, who dates Sextus or Publius Papirius to the reign of Tarquinius Superbus, reports that all laws collected in the *ius civile Papirianum*, just after the end of the monarchy, fell into disuse due to a *lex tribunicia*.

Beyond the many historical inaccuracies of the account of Pomponius,[12] it is nevertheless clear that the difficulties of interpretation, which result from the comparison of the information handed down from the Pomponian text and from that of Dionysius of Halicarnassus, are not based only on the *praenomen* of Papirius.[13] Dionysius says, in fact, that the compilation occurred after the kings were expelled from Rome, while Pomponius reports that then, 'when the kings were thrown out under a Tribunician enactment, these *leges* all fell too' (*exactis deinde regibus lege tribunicia omnes leges haec exoleverunt*).

The period during which the *ius civile Papirianum* was composed (according to Pomponius) is not vastly different from that in which Dionysius places the work of Gaius Papirius. Indeed, Pomponius reports that Papirius *fuit illis temporibus, quibus Superbus Demarathi Corinthii filius, ex principalibus viris*. This means that he lived at the time of Tarquinius Superbus, and not that he composed his work under his reign – work that could have been completed even after his expulsion. However, the ablative absolute, *exactis deinde regibus*, poses an obstacle to this interpretation. That said, if – in keeping with what has already been stated in the literature[14] – we consider Pomponius' passage to be a summary made by some epitomist inexperienced in Roman history, or manipulated by Justinian's compilers, one could reasonably assert that the Papirius of Pomponius, living under Tarquinius Superbus, carried out the work after the latter's expulsion and the end of the monarchy.

Tarquinius Superbus is consistently described by the sources as a despot. In addition, according to Dionysius, he not only repealed all the laws written by Servius – according to which the plebeians rendered and received justice – but also removed the tablet on which they were engraved from the Forum and destroyed it.[15] Therefore, it appears to be somewhat inconsistent with the recognised tradition of that king's tyrannical tendencies that he would have wanted or allowed the realisation of a work of codification of all royal laws – a codification which seems to allude to the word *componere*, used by Pomponius.[16]

---

[11] D. 1.2.2.36.
[12] See Laurendi 2013, 177.
[13] See Schulz 1968, 163–4; 1973, 32–3; Carandini 2011, 377.
[14] Albanese 1998, 12; Laurendi 2013, and now Fenocchio 2016, 28–30.
[15] Dion. Hal. *Ant. Rom.* 4.43.1
[16] On the use of *componere*, see the bibliography herein, Manzo 2014, 105.

3. THE *IUS PAPIRIANUM* ACCORDING TO PAULUS AND MACROBIUS

Information on the *ius Papirianum* can be traced not just through the works of Pomponius and Dionysius of Halicarnassus cited above. Setting aside the respective silences of Cicero, Festus, and many other authors, whose works mention the royal laws (silences which have led the doctrine to deny its existence or to date it to the Archaic Period[17]), it must be pointed out that references to the *ius Papirianum* are also present in some fragments of the work of the jurisconsult Paulus, the poet Macrobius, and the grammarian Servius.[18]

In particular, in *Saturnalia* 3, 11.5–6, an interesting theory is founded: 'The Papirian code plainly states that a consecrated table can serve as an altar. As in the temple of *Juno Populonia*, it says, there is a sanctified table' (*In Papiriano enim iure evidenter relatum est arae vicem praestare posse mensam dicatam. Ut in templo, inquit, Iunonis Populoniae augusta mensa est*).[19] The *ius Papirianum*, consulted by Macrobius, where there would be mention of a difference between a *mensa dicata* and an *ara*, would not have been Papirius' collection of *leges regiae* but instead a work addressing themes of a ritual nature, very similar – if not identical – to the *liber de iure Papiriano*, attributed by the jurist Paulus to Granius Flaccus (D. 50.16.144). These dealt with *paelex*; however, without mentioning any law concerning it: 'Granius Flaccus writes in book about the *ius Papirianum* that a *pellex* is now the usual name for someone who sleeps with someone who has a wife, but once upon a time someone who was in a household in place of a wife, but without being married, whom the Greeks call *pallaké*' (*Granius Flaccus in libro de iure Papiriano scribit pellicem nunc vulgo vocari, quae cum eo, cui uxor sit, corpus misceat: quosdam eam, quae uxoris loco sine nuptiis in domo sit, quam παλλακήν Graeci vocant*).

Therefore, it seems plausible to assume that two texts were circulating from the Republican Age: one containing the royal laws, perhaps in the form of an exact quotation, which Festus, and Verrius Flaccus before him, may have been drawn to; and the other containing instead a commentary on the royal laws by Granius Flaccus. This commentary, entitled *de iure Papiriano*, provided explanations for those that were thought to be archaic laws written in a language no longer comprehensible, and therefore in need of a structural modernisation and exegesis.

More recently, the theory of the existence of two sets of royal laws was put forward, which would have been considered notable during the late Republican Age.[20] One would have contained the *leges* of Numa and been entitled, or subtitled

---

[17] On this point, see Laurendi 2013, 171–3.
[18] Serv. auct. Aen. 12.836: *quod ait* (scil. *Vergilius*): *"morem ritusque sacrorum adiciam" ipso titulo legis Papiriae usus est, quam sciebat de ritu sacrorum publicatam*. See Santoro 1998, 403–8, and Mantovani 2012, 289 n. 25.
[19] Albanese 1998, 7–30. In contrast to what was claimed by D'Ippolito 1996, 75–7, according to whom the words '*Ut in templo, inquit, Iunonis Populoniae augusta mensa est*' would represent a textual ruin of a *lex regiae*.
[20] Mantovani 2012, 283–92.

(per the subject matter therein), '*de ritu sacrorum*'; the other would have contained statutes of civil law. The latter, approved in accordance with the tradition of the people convened *per curias*, would have constituted the *ius Papirianum*. Such a theory has the merit of taking into account that the discrepancies emerging from the comparison of the narratives of Dionysius and Pomponius are only apparent because it is a matter of information responding to two different realities. It also explains the problem of the debated question regarding the title of the *ius Papirianum*. In fact, Mantovani explains that the adjective *civile*, attributed to the *ius Papirianum* by Sextus Pomponius in the *Enchiridion*, refers to that text which compiled the *leges curiatae* on contracts. The adjective *civile*, therefore, would have served to distinguish the *ius Papirianum* to which was affixed 'from another *ius Papirianum*, constituted of Numaical norms (or norms presumed to be such) on *sacra*'.[21]

4. EXACT QUOTATIONS FROM THE *LEGES REGIAE*: THE LAW ON THE *PAELEX*

According to the tradition noted at the time of the jurist Paulus,[22] the *de iure Papiriano* of Granius Flaccus contained a reference to the *paelex*, the famous protagonist of a *lex regia*, the text of which was conveyed *litteris*, albeit with some variation, by two literary sources:

> Fest.- Paul. s.v. *Pelices* (L. 248.): *Pelex aram Iunonis ne tangito; si tanget, Iunoni crinibus demissis agnum feminam caedito.*
> Let no *paelex* touch the *ara* of Juno; if she touch it, let her, with hair unbound, offer up a ewe lamb to Juno.

> Gell., *Noct. Att.*, 4, 3.3: *Paelex aedem Iunonis ne tangito; si tangit, Iunoni crinibus demissis agnum feminam caedito.*
> Let no *paelex* touch the *aedes* of Juno; if she touch it, let her, with hair unbound, offer up a ewe lamb to Juno.

The arrangement, attributed by both authors to Numa, dictated the behaviour of the *paelex*, insofar as it circumvented the prohibition against them touching the altar (*tangere aram*, according Festus) or the *aedes* (*tangere aedem*, according Gellius) of Juno. In the event of an infringement, the *paelex* would be required to sacrifice a lamb to the goddess, making the sacrifice with her hair unbound or hanging loose (*crinibus demissis*).

The rule was repeatedly studied, especially by those who dealt with the issue of Roman concubinage, of which the Numan law is the oldest attestation.[23] In fact,

---

[21] Mantovani 2012, 289.
[22] See D.50.16.144.
[23] See, for example, Castello 1940, 10 ff.; Giunti 1990, 141–55; Arends Olsen 1999, 25–6; Bartocci 1999; Astolfi 2000, 1–4; Fayer 2005b, 15–20; Busacca 2012, 174. Further bibliographic references in Cristaldi 2014, 143–56 and Sanna 2016.

Pompeius Festus and Aulus Gellius cite the *lex Numae* when closing a discussion, the main theme of which was the *paelex* – and therefore, according to most, the 'concubine' – because both recognise that in that very primordial *lex* was contained, *in nuce*, the condition to which she was subjected in ancient times:

Fest.- Paul. s.v. Pelices (L. 248). *Pelices: nunc quidem appellantur alienis succumbentes non solum feminae, sed etiam mares. Antiqui proprie eam paelicem nominabant, quae uxorem habenti nubebat. Cui generi mulierum etiam poena constituta est a Numa Pompilio: 'Pelex aram Iunonis ne tangito; si tanget, Iunoni crinibus demissis agnum feminam caedito.'*
Now, it is true, we call not only women, but also men who indulge in the desires of others; but the ancients neatly named the woman who contracted with an already married man. A particular punishment was established for women of this species by Numa Pompilius: 'Let no concubine touch the *ara* of Juno; if she touch it, let her, with hair unbound, offer up a ewe lamb to Juno.'

Gell., Noct. Att., 4. 3.3. *'Paelicem' autem appellatam probrosamque habitam, quae iuncta consuetaque esset cum eo, in cuius manu mancipioque alia matrimonii causa foret, hac antiquissima lege ostenditur, quam Numae regis fuisse accepimus: 'Paelex aedem Iunonis ne tangito; si tangit, Iunoni crinibus demissis agnum feminam caedito.'*
Moreover, a woman was called *paelex* and regarded as infamous, if she lived on terms of intimacy with a man who had another woman under his legal control in a state of matrimony, as is evident from this very ancient law, which we are told was one of king Numa's: 'Let no Paelex touch the aedes of Juno; if she touch it, let her, with hair unbound, offer up a ewe lamb to Juno.'

The fortuitous dual transmission of law in the aforementioned contexts has not yet allowed the numerous controversies to be settled on its content, which is somewhat obscure, just like the protagonist: the *paelex*. First of all, it should be noted that the etymology and the original meaning of the word *paelex* remain unclear. Setting aside the proposal for an Etruscan linguistic-cultural mediation,[24] most scholars now believe that the term derives directly from the Greek παλλακή, in accordance with what the ancient sources refer to in this regard. The Greek origin of the term was in fact supported not only by the grammarian Granius Flaccus (cited by the jurist Paulus[25]) but also by Isidore of Seville[26] and Aulus Gellius,[27] for whom *"paelex' autem quasi πάλλαξ, id est quasi παλλακίς. Ut pleraque alia, ita hoc quoque vocabulum de Graeco flexum est.'*[28] However, one should not overlook the theory according to which the noun *paelex* derives not from the Greek *pallaké*, but from the verb *pellicio*, from

---

[24] Thus, but in an isolated manner, Cavazza 1987, 147.
[25] D. 50.16.144.
[26] Isid., *Orig.* 10, 229: *Pelex apud Graecos proprie dicitur, a Latinis concuba. Dicta autem a fallacia, id est uersutia, subdolositate uel mendacio.*
[27] Gell., *Noct. Att.* 4.3.3.
[28] On the contrary, one does not find the old etymological explanation from the Semitic '*pil(l)eges*', supported by Meyer 1895, 7.

which, according to Cato *apud* Festus, *pelliculatio*, i.e. the art of seduction,[29] would also have originated.

Upon closer inspection, whatever the origin of the word and its primary meaning, the term has certainly taken on different undertones, when not antithetical, in different social contexts and in different periods. In literary texts of the Republican and Imperial periods, the word is almost always used, albeit in various ways, to signify a woman who has an ongoing relationship with a married man, or a woman who entertains passing love affairs always with married men, or even a woman subject to rape or the rival of the wife. But in all cases, the sexual meaning of *paelex* does not appear to me to be absolutely paramount. In this regard it is enough to mention the epigraph placed on the tomb of Geneia Successa (CIL IX, 5771), dating from the second to third centuries CE, from Recina. The epitaph refers to an eleven-year-old girl who was thus dead before she could be considered, at least legally, to have reached puberty (*viripotens*[30]); her despondent mother, who placed the epigraph together with her father, called her *sua pellix*.

Returning to the *lex* and its content, we can see that this was known by reading two versions which are very similar to each other but not perfectly identical. Arguments of legal logic and palaeographical reasons have led me to prefer the version of Gellius because it is more congruent with the Archaic Period, the version which instead of the noun *ara* uses *aedes*, and instead of *pelex*, uses *paelex*[31]: '*Paelex aedem Iunonis ne tangito; si tangit, Iunoni crinibus demissis agnum feminam caedito.*'

Therefore, the text of the Numan law is made up of two parts: the precept and the sanction. The first is expressed through a rather linear grammatical construct and dictates the conduct reserved for the *paelex*: *Paelex aedem Iunonis ne tangito*. She is forbidden from touching the *aedes* consecrated to the goddess Juno. Not

---

[29] Fest. p. 280 L.: *Pelliculatio<nem Cato a pellicien>do, quod est inducendo dixit*. The derivation proposed by Cato is considered questionable by Castello 1940, 10, but see Zuccotti 1988, 90 with n. 9.

[30] See also Tramunto 2007, 182 and n. 16, for whom in order to exclude any sexual significance of *p(a)ellix* in this context, it is rightly observed that puberty was considered to have been reached at twelve years of age.

[31] If the sanction consists in prescribing a sacrifice, it would be truly paradoxical that the generating prohibition was precisely the disqualification from those sacrifices, in which *tangere aram* was necessary. If this were the case, then for having violated the requirement not to sacrifice – perhaps with a victim of little market value such as a dove, a winged animal also sacred to Juno, or with a simple libation of milk – a sanction would be imposed requiring the performance of an act of sacrifice of much greater economic value, and therefore even more solemn, such as killing a lamb. It is therefore clear, with regard to legal logic, that the prohibition, presupposed by the obligation *caedere agnum feminam crinibus demissis*, could not be that of performing an act of sacrifice. And so it was that of *tangere aedem*, as Gellius writes, whatever the meaning of this expression, that nonetheless, as we have seen, everything can mean less than 'sacrifice'. The shift should then be from the genuine '*aedem*' of the scholar Gellius to the faulty '*aram*' of the grammarian Festus, or rather his *excerptum* of the eighth century coming from the epitomator Paulus Diaconus. And this alteration of the text of the lex is probably explained by the 'logic of corruption' of the copyists in the manuscript tradition. On the Roman altars, see now Cavallero 2018.

touching the building fundamentally means not being allowed to enter, but also not being able to approach the outer walls of the cell. In the building – that is, in the *aedes* where the statue of worship resided – the faithful entered somewhat rarely and only under exceptional circumstances. Otherwise, the young could enter in the case of acts of worship, such as the transport of clothing with which to dress the statue of the goddess,[32] or the periodic washing of her, or to offer lavish 'personal' effects, so to speak. Acts of worship could also be performed on the external walls of the *aedes*, such as by decorating them with garlands and *bucrania*. The *pronaos* enclosed by a gate could serve the function of the *opistodomos* in the Greek *naós*, namely the collection of valuable and lasting offerings. It can, therefore, be understood that the prohibition of *tangere aedem* consisted in the absolute preclusion from the possibility not only of entering the cell but also of simply approaching it for secondary acts of worship.

The *paelex* was excluded from virtually everything, but she was not precluded from participating in the sacrifices that took place outside on the altars in front of the building of worship (*aedes*); only from those located inside the sacred enclosed area (*templum*). Indeed, the sanction imposed for the violation of the precept of touching the building of worship was precisely that of sacrificing a lamb, slaughtering it on the altar, but in an afflicted manner, requiring unbound hair. Apart from sacrifices, the *paelex* should not have officiated other rites in honour of the goddess Juno, the goddess of the Roman *Pantheon* and protector of marriage and childbirth,[33] she of *praeest coniugiis*[34] and *cui curae sunt nuptiae*.[35] The exclusion of a woman from the building of worship of the goddess, who presided over the two decisive moments of feminine life, suggests that the reasons are due primarily to these two spheres. This is, then, confirmed by what was discussed by Festus and Gellius, who insert the figure of the *paelex* into a complex framework of matrimonial relations, where the juridical and social role appears to be opposed to that of the 'legitimate' wife.

The fact that the condition of the *paelex* was negatively correlated to the worship of the goddess Juno is also attested by the following in the second part of the *lex*, which peremptorily inflicts the sanction in the case of the transgression of the regulatory precept: *si tangit, Iunoni crinibus demissis agnum feminam caedito*. Therefore, the penalty for the woman, even for simply approaching the building of worship of Juno, consisted in sacrificing a lamb[36] with her hair unbound or dishevelled. It is clear that the afflictive manifestation of the punishment shall be

---

[32] The *peplophoria*, the transport of the robe worn by the statue of the goddess, as in the case of *Athena Parthenos* in Athens or Persephone in *Locri Epizefiri*.
[33] Named Juno Licina, the protector of pregnant women.
[34] Seru. *ad Aen.* 4.45.
[35] Verg., *Aen.* 4.9.
[36] It is noted that the term *agnus* is normally used indifferently to the genus; the feminine *agna* is in fact later. To specify the sex of the animal, add *femina* (as in this case), or *mas*, as in the *lex* on *Opima spolia*. On this point, see Pavese 2013, 29.

recognised not in the market value, however high, of the sacrifice, but in the *form* imposed for carrying it out; that is, with unbound, dishevelled hair as would be worn in dire circumstances such as times of mourning, illness, or the atonement of guilt.

In the exegetical attempts proposed in modern scholarship, the manner of sacrifice – *crinibus demissis* – has been related to the *ornatus vetustissimus* of *seni crines*[37] (probably 'hair combed into six plaits'), of which Festus speaks once again:

> p. 454 L. *Senis crinibus nubentes ornantur, quod* [h]*is ornatus uetustissimus fuit. Quidam quod eo Vestales uirgines ornentur, quarum castitamen viris suis* . . .
> Women, when they get married, are adorned with six braids of hair, because this kind of ornament is the most ancient. According to others this comes from the fact that the Vestal virgins adorn themselves with this ornament, and that the new brides commit themselves to their husbands to preserve a chastity similar to that of the Vestals.

Thus, we learn from the grammarian that the hairstyle of the *seni crines*, considered a symbol of purity and chastity, was not just typical of future brides but also of the Vestal virgins devoted to the worship of the goddess Vesta. There is no shortage of dispute concerning the significance of this six-plait hairstyle. Riccardo Astolfi, in particular, considered it possible to identify in the *crines demissi* of Numa's *lex*, the *actus contrarius* 'in the gathering into six braids (*seni crines*) done in contracting into marriage'.[38] The reflection of the author is part of an interpretative proposal of the law as a whole, which consists of considering the concubine *paelex* of a married man, with whom, however, she contracts into marriage – a marriage that she would then put to an end through the *demissio* of *crines*. Astolfi believes that 'sacrifice is offered with unbound hair, to mean that not only does the woman repent and ask forgiveness for what she has done, she undoes what she has done: she is not deemed to be the bride and the marriage is considered to be invalid.'[39]

This interpretation is obviously open to criticism, and indeed there is plenty of it. In fact, it is argued that 'as *sex crines* is not characteristic of the *uxor*, but rather the *nubenda*, the outcome of the *actus contrarius* does not appear so stringent.'[40] But the most convincing, and certainly most precise, methodical criticism comes from Bernardo Albanese.[41] Focusing on the weak point of the contested exegesis, he observes the unproductiveness of the juridical effects of the *seni crines*, qualified by Festus simply as the hairstyle used by the *nubentes* (i.e. by women who were preparing themselves in this manner to contract into marriage and therefore to carry out the wedding ritual). Consequently, the *demissio* of the *crines* cannot

---

[37] On the hairstyle, see Fayer 2005a, 485–500.
[38] Astolfi 2000, 3.
[39] Astolfi 2000, 1.
[40] Carandini 2011, 339.
[41] Albanese 2006, 52–4.

be regarded as an 'independently relevant act'; one that could be considered in relation to the ceremony of the *diffarreatio* that Astolfi calls into question as an example of an *actus contrarius*. In addition, he argues that the *demissio* concerning the *seni crines*, specifically the hair combed into six braids, is a rather deductive approach, because in reality the hairstyles used in Rome were varied and different, and nothing leads us to believe that the *lex* in question referred to the ornate *nubendae*. If so, taking into account that the *seni crines* were reserved for the wedding day, should we then consider that the sacrifice of the lamb by the *paelex* also occurred on the wedding day? If so, at this point she would have touched the altar of Juno – and such a resulting conclusion is certainly not acceptable. In fact, given that the *lex Numae* does not mention the *seni crines*, I believe that the *demissio* should be extended to other types of *ornati* and also to *vetustissimi*.

From Varro (50.7.44) we learn that *id tutulus appellatus ab eo quod matres familias crines convolutos ad verticem capitis quos habent vit<t>a velatos dicebantur tutuli* ('The "tutulus" is named (in this way) by the fact that they were called "tutuli" the hairstyles of hair gathered at the top of the head, which the mothers of the family wear covered by a bandage') and from Festus (p. 484 L.) that *tutulum vocari aiunt flaminicarum capitis ornamentum, quod fiat vitta purpurea innexa crinibus, et exstructum in altitudinem* ('They say that is called "tutulus" the ornament of the head of the "flaminicae" (the wives of the priests), which is done with a purple bandage inserted into the hair and tying it in height'). Observing that 'in reality the *crines demissi* – in much the same way as unshaven beards or shabby clothes for men – forms part of a social code of clothing of mourning and humiliation, well attuned to a person about to make a reparatory sacrifice for the transgression of a ritual precept'[42] is acceptable, but it does not resolve the question completely. The legislator has, in fact, felt the need to prescribe the manner with which to proceed with regard to the slaughter (*caedere*) of the *agnus femina*. This is an outlandish requirement if the social code provided that during the sacrifices one should behave according to a well-known ritual by way of contrition. Therefore, the *demissio* of *crines* constituted an innovation because the prohibition of the *paelex* in relation to the *tangere aedem* did not even exist before the *lex Numae*. As such, the *demissio* of *crines* is typifying and clearly aims to bestow on the sacrifice a symbolic meaning of repentance for having touched the building of worship – a value closely related to the figure of Juno and her theological role in the feminine *kosmos*.

Through this rule, we can understand how the *paelex* usually wears her hair bound and that its dishevelment would occur by way of penance in the practice of the sacrifice. Moreover, we can see the complex hairstyle that would also characterise the *paelex* in the already-mentioned mask of Menander's *pallaké*. Indeed, the hairstyles found in some Liparesi terracotta[43] figures representing the *pallaké* are comprised of twelve (or sometimes ten) large braids, which from

---

[42] Carandini 2011, 339.
[43] Bernabò Brea 1981, 223–5; Bernabò Brea and Cavalier 2001, 253–4; Laurendi 2013, 87–8.

the forehead and temples converge towards a high diadem of bands at the top of the head. The sanction of the Numan law, therefore, does not seem to consist in the prohibition of sacrificing to Juno, nor even in the potentially significant value (in the Archaic economy) of the prescribed sacrifice – not a simple libation or a dove, but a lamb – but in the afflictive *modus* imposed for fulfilling the rite.

Moreover, the prohibition against touching the building of worship, the house of the goddess herself, was the first sign of social discrimination to the detriment of the *paelex*, who was differentiated from all other women. From this requirement, however, there clearly resulted a novelty – the lowering of the social status of *paelex*, who until then had not been considered *probrosa*. Numa does not forbid the fulfilment of sacrifices, however. On the contrary, he imposes an economically important one but conducted in such a way as to cancel out the typically festive, joyous, and celebratory nature of these acts, conferring in this case an atoning role and function. Furthermore, the *lex* does not absolutely prohibit the relationship between the *paelex* and Juno, thus revealing the original connection (and its persistence, despite everything, in the 'Numan') between the woman and the *nuptiae*, which, according to Festus, she entered (*nubebat*) even in the presence of another *uxor*. In fact, Juno is by antonomasia the goddess of fertility, marriage, and birth, while Venus is the goddess of extramarital *eros*.

5. CONCLUSION

In conclusion, there is no reason to doubt, beyond the formal linguistic adaptations suffered over the long process of transmission, the substantial authenticity of the *lex* and its dating back to an archaic, perhaps even royal, age. However, we cannot take for granted that this was actually developed by Numa Pompilius, nor that it was one of the *leges* collected by Papirius in the *ius Papirianum* and the subject of commentary in the *de iure Papiriano*, the *liber* developed by Granius Flaccus in the first century BCE.

In dealing with the study of the most archaic stage of Roman law, the starting assumption must always be that the tales of tradition 'unfolded in the framework of Roman historiography, from the end of the third century B.C.E. to the Augustan Age with a process of continuous enrichment, up to a point of arrival which for us is represented by the work literally constructed and proposed by Titus Livius and Dionysius of Halicarnassus [. . .] Therefore, they do not represent the final stage of a long reworking of many and varied traditional materials that [. . .] reassembled works of Greek historians [. . .] referring to strands of information orally transmitted, or obtained from documents or monuments, information which at times was not even Roman in origin.'[44]

---

[44] Gabba 1993, 13.

Works Cited

Albanese, B, 1998. 'Macrobio (Sat. 3,11,3 ss.) ed il *ius Papirianum.*' *AUPA* 45.2:5–30.
———, 2006. 'Sulla legge di Numa a riguardo della *Paelex.*' *MEP* 9 (11):52–8.
Arends Olsen, L, 1999. *La femme et l'enfant dans les unions illégitimes à Rome. L'évolution du droit jusqu'au début de l'Empire*. Bern: Lang.
Astolfi, R, 2000. *Il matrimonio nel diritto romano preclassico*. Padua: CEDAM.
Bartocci, U, 1999. *Le species nuptiarum nell'esperienza romana antica. Relazioni matrimoniali e sistemi di potere nella testimonianza delle fonti*. Rome: Galileo Galilei.
Bernabò Brea, L, 1981. *Menandro e il teatro greco nelle terrecotte liparesi*. Genoa: SAGEP.
Bernabò Brea, L and M Cavalier. 2001. *Maschere e personaggi del teatro greco nelle terrecotte liparesi*. Rome: 'L'Erma' di Bretschneider.
Bretone, M. 1963. '*Ius Papirianum.*' *NDI* 9:386.
Busacca, C, 2012. *Iustae nuptiae. L'evoluzione del matrimonio romano dalle fasi precittadine all'età classica*. Milan: Giuffrè.
Castello, C, 1940. *In tema di matrimonio e concubinato nel mondo romano*. Milan: Giuffrè.
Carandini, A, L Argentieri, P Carafa, M Fiorentini, and U Fusco, eds, 2011. *La leggenda di Roma*, III. *La costituzione*. Milan: Mondadori.
Cavallero, F G, 2018. *Arae Sacrae. Tipi, nomi, funzioni e rappresentazioni degli altari romani*. Rome: 'L'Erma' di Bretschneider.
Cavazza, F, 1987. *Aulo Gellio, Le notti attiche, Libri IV–V*. Bologna: Zanichelli.
Cristaldi, S, 2014. 'Unioni non matrimoniali a Roma.' In *Le relazioni affettive non matrimoniali*, edited by F. Romeo, 143–200. Milan: UTET.
D'Ippolito, F, 1996. 'I *memorialia* di Masurio Sabino.' In *Atti del Seminario 'per la storia del pensiero giuridico romano da Augusto agli Antonini'*, edited by D Mantovani, 71–85. Turin: Giappichelli.
Di Trolio, G, 2017. *Le leges regiae in Dionigi di Alicarnasso. Vol.1. La monarchia latino-sabina*. Rome: Jovene.
Fayer, C, 2005a. *La familia romana. Aspetti giuridici ed antiquari*, II. *Sponsalia, matrimonio, dote*. Rome: 'L'Erma' di Bretschneider.
———, 2005b. *La familia romana. Aspetti giuridici ed antiquari. Concubinato Divorzio Adulterio*, III. Rome: 'L'Erma' di Bretschneider.
Fenocchio, M A, 2016. '*Hallucinatus est Pomponius?*. Nota sull'identità del *superbus Demarati Corinthii filius* in D. 1.2.2.2.' *Index* 44:21–30.
Gabba, E, 1993. 'Problemi di metodo per la storia di Roma arcaica.' In *Convegno sul tema Bilancio critico su Roma arcaica fra monarchia e repubblica: in memoria di Ferdinando Castagnoli (Roma, 3–4 giugno 1991)*, edited by E Gabba, D Foraboschi, E Lo Cascio, and L Troiani, 13–24. Milan: Accademia Nazionale dei Lincei.
Glück, F von, 1780. = F. von Glück, *De jure civili Papiriano liber singularis*. Halae: Hemmerde.

Giunti, P, 1990. *Adulterio e leggi regie. Un reato fra storia e propaganda*. Milan: Giuffrè.

Laurendi, R, 2013. *Leges regiae e Ius Papirianum. Tradizione e storicità di un corpus normative*. Rome: 'L'Erma' di Bretschneider.

Mantovani, D, 2012. 'Le due serie di *leges regiae*.' In *Leges publicae. La legge nell'esperienza giuridica romana. Collegio di diritto romano 2010 Cedant*, edited by J-L Ferrary, 283–92. Pavia: CEDAM.

Manzo, A, 2014. 'Note sulla giurisprudenza arcaica.' *SDHI* 80:359–71.

Meyer, P, 1895. *Der Römische Konkubinat nach den Rechtsquellen und den Inschriften*. Leipzig: Teubner.

Nasti, F, 2012. *Studi sulla tradizione giurisprudenziale romana. Età degli Antonini e dei Severi*. Naples: Ed. Scientifica.

Pais, E, 1915. 'A proposito dell'*ius Papirianum*.' In *Ricerche sulla storia e sul diritto pubblico di Roma*, edited by E Pais, 241–70. Serie I. Rome: Ermanno Loescher & Co.

Pavese, M P, 2013. *Scire leges est verba tenere. Ricerche sulle competenze grammaticali dei giuristi romani*. Turin: Giappichelli.

Pelloso, C, 2018. *Ricerche sulle assemblee quiritarie*. Naples: Jovene.

Prosdocimi, A L, 2016. *Forme di lingua e contenuti istituzionali nella Roma delle origini. I*. Naples: Jovene.

Santoro, R, 1998. 'Sul *ius Papirianum*.' In *Mélanges de droit romain et d'histoire ancienne. Hommage à la mémoire de André Magdelain*, edited by M Humbert and Y Thomas, 399–416. Paris: Éditions Panthéon-Assas.

Sanna, M V, 2016. 'Adulterio, stuprum e concubinato nella *lex Iulia de adulteriis*.' In *El principio de igualdad desde un enfoque pluridisciplinar. Prevencion y represion de la violencia de genero*, edited by I C Iglesias Canle, J A Gonzalez-Ares Fernandez, M V Alvarez Bujan, 38–77. Valencia: Tirant lo Blanch.

Schulz, F, 1968. *Storia della giurisprudenza romana*. Italian trans. Florence: Sansoni.

Tassi, E, 2016. 'Sulla natura della *lex* del *Niger Lapis*. Alcune considerazioni preliminari.' *Index* 44: 73–90.

Tondo, S, 1973. *Leges regiae e paricidas*. Florence: Olschki.

Tramunto, M, 2007. '*Paelex aedem Iunonis ne tangito*: Gell. NT.A. 4.3.3.' In *Les exclus dans l'Antiquité. Actes du colloque*, edited by C Wolff, 179–86. Paris: De Boccard.

Zuccotti, F, 1988. '. . . *qui fruges excantassit*: il primigenio significato animistico-religioso del verbo "excanto" e la duplicità delle previsioni di XII Tab. VIII, 8.' In *Atti Seminario Romanistico Gardesano (22–25 ottobre 1985)*, 81–211. Milan: Giuffrè.

Chapter 7

The Laws of the Kings – A View from a Distance

Christopher Smith[1]

1. INTRODUCTION: THE PROBLEM

The problem in front of us is relatively simple to state but complex to solve. What can we say about the earliest legal system of Rome when the sources are so problematic?[2]

One answer to that conundrum, which is well explored in this volume, is to analyse the sources we do have with ever greater care and sophistication. Another answer is to offer a wider context, using comparison with other near-contemporary Mediterranean societies. Both these approaches have value, but both proceed in one form or another from a fundamental tendency to believe that the sources are correct in claiming that there was a law system of sorts prior to the Twelve Tables, and which is attributable to the kings.

This means that we wish to assume a historicity at some level but that we are picking and choosing what level, without any external means of justifying the decision. Very specifically, this refers to the concept of the king itself. In fact, one of the most problematic elements of our tradition is precisely the king. What sort of king the Romans had, and what their role was, can only be determined by the most roundabout of ways, and we often foist an image of a much later time onto the beginnings of Rome.[3]

Is there another way? What I want to try to do is to suggest an account of the emergence of Roman legislation which almost does away with both texts and any reference to the historical narrative. I am of course influenced by my

---

[1] I am grateful to the organisers of the conference and the participants for a stimulating occasion and to the Leverhulme Trust for supporting this research. Parts of this argument were also presented in the Max Weber Kolleg, Erfurt, and I drew much inspiration from colleagues there.
[2] On the *leges regiae*, there is only Pomponius' account in D.1.2.2.2 which would encourage any sense of a collection, and the *ius Papirianum* is potentially as much a fiction as the books on the regal period which were at some stage affixed, it would appear, to the beginning of the Annales Maximi. See Watson (1972) and Bujuklić (1998) for optimistic accounts, but Richardson (2010, 35–6 n. 45) for telling arguments against. On the problem of the Annales Maximi, see the account of Rich in FRHist 1. The best accounts of the way genuine information may have survived are in Mantovani (2012) and Laurendi (2013).
[3] I cherish Luigi Capogrossi Colognesi's comment on another occasion that my kings sometimes looked like British constitutional monarchs.

reading of the sources, but I have done my best to leave them to one side. In other words, I want to leave the *leges regiae* as traditionally understood and ask what sorts of legislation and what sorts of authority might we be able to hypothesise for archaic Rome?

Clearly one way of doing this would have been from a political philosophy point of view, to look at natural law or social contract theory.[4] There were indeed ancient writers who constructed similar models based on various forms of primitivism.[5] However, natural law is itself controversial, and it would be unusual nowadays to read archaic Rome through such a complex and debatable concept, in the manner of a Locke or a Rousseau.[6] In any case, one would need first to demonstrate that Rome was at some level a rule-based society before hunting for its natural law associations.

2. DIFFERENT MODELS AND QUESTIONS

So, to start somewhere else, what models might help to explain observable features of the Roman world in the first half of the first millennium BCE? What kinds of parallels exist for the emergence of law in archaic societies and early states, and might they help us? What features of Rome might such models encourage us to examine in more detail? Looking solely at the archaeology of Rome, as far as possible, do we have any evidence which might be taken to indicate the existence of regulations from the regal period, and if so, what models of authority exist to help us explain them? Finally, what might this have to do with the kings, or rather, what sorts of figures might the kings have been to have played a role in the sort of society we have ended up describing?

The first challenge is to decide what social models fit Rome from the eighth to the sixth centuries BCE. It is interesting to note that for many anthropologists, one of the challenges of their discipline is precisely to think away the classical. A good example is the way that evolutionary paradigms which have their origins in thinking about the classical world are then applied across very different case studies from Polynesia to North and South America.[7] Although classicists have used anthropological models, there is more work to be done in identifying the grounds of comparison; in other words, to say that another society operating under completely different social, economic, and geographical conditions is genuinely comparable, rather than being useful heuristic devices. If we stay closer

---

[4] See Pottage's contribution to this volume.
[5] Natural law is often associated with the Stoics, and especially Zeno of Citium; see for instance Brown 2009, Boeri 2013. See for Lucretius and his idea of 'hard primitivism' Blickman 1989; for Cicero Asmis 2008, and for Seneca Inwood 2003.
[6] On natural law and what it might look like in practice, see Waldron 2013. This paper situates early Rome somewhere between a state of nature and 'A world ruled by natural law is a world in which large numbers of us govern our actions and interactions according to forceful norms that exist independently of human institutions' (83).
[7] Yoffee 2004.

to home, the Mediterranean paradigm is now itself in some difficulty, partly from Mediterraneanists themselves.[8] The argument for diversity and adaptation shows that a single generalising account was abundantly problematic in its construction.[9]

This means that our choices are quite limited, between highly specific comparisons with other parts of the Mediterranean, or quite tricky comparisons with very different places and times. The former might therefore appear simply the most sensible, but when we put Rome alongside Athens, we are comparing two narratives which were produced in totally different ways, and where the apparent security of the Athenian narrative may itself be illusory.[10] It is impossible to insert a Solon into the historical tradition about Rome, and the tradition that the Twelve Tables was produced by comparison with Athens (implying its creation *ex nihilo*) is doubtful, even if it provoked fascinating debates.[11]

3. COERCION, COHESION, CITIES AND MARKETS

In this essay, for the purposes of thinking about the preconditions of law, I want to stay at quite a general level, and to think about the debates which would constrain and construct such an argument. The first is about coercive and cohesive societies.[12] A society based solely on arbitrary coercion without protection (if such a state could be imagined) would presumably have no need for law. The champion of cohesion was Durkheim, for whom religion as a sort of original ground for collective consciousness brought hunters and gatherers together. An understanding of society based on a more coercive approach was championed by his contemporary Weber, and Charles Tilly in modern times has made the situation in some ways even darker with his aphorism 'states make wars and wars make states'.[13]

However, cohesion and coercion have always been on a spectrum, and it is worth saying that Durkheim thought that society coerced cohesion, while Weber recognised that much authority was consensual. Out of this tension we can see the generation of some interesting sets of debates around urbanism and religion, which are emerging in state formation theory.[14] These argue for sequences of increasingly complex negotiation over time, in the context of the challenges of urban life.

---

[8] For arguments against Mediterraneanism, see Herzfeld 1984, 1985, 1991, and 2005, which is a response to the brilliant Mediterraneanist thesis Purcell and Horden 2000. See also Broodbank 2013.
[9] For an attempted recuperation of one of the greatest generalists, Fustel de Coulanges, see Yoffee and Terrenato 2015.
[10] On the Greek world, see Gagarin 1989; Woodruff and Gagarin 2007. It is worth remembering that our confidence in the narrative around Solon depends in part on the capacity of ancient writers to extract a reliable narrative from a corpus of poetry which we have only in fragments. For a series of essays on the development of the tradition around Solon, see Nagy and Noussia-Fantuzzi 2015; and see also Psilakis 2014.
[11] Liv. 3.31; Dion .Hal. *Ant. Rom.* 10.54; Steinberg 1982.
[12] Helpful summary of the debate in Smith 2011.
[13] Fournier 2013; Tilly 1993.
[14] Yoffee (2015) is more driven by urbanisation; the bibliography on state formation is usefully collected in Bliesemann de Guevara 2015. The strong argument for cooperative action is made by Blanton and Fargher 2016. Throughout what follows I use 'cities' in a very loose and inclusive sense.

If we start from the very earliest phase, the creation of a sedentary agricultural lifestyle, and later the early cities, are by no means obvious choices. James Scott's recent account emphasises the cost of the sedentary lifestyle; urban dwellers are often unhealthier and more stressed than nomadic pastoralists. And urban agglomerations are often short-lived trading arenas. It is the state that enslaved us, forcing more intensive agricultural practices, repression and inequality.[15] Yet Scott is also aware that his sharp dichotomies do not really work. As Anne Porter has shown in a very important book on early city-states in Mesopotamia, our adoption of a teleological evolutionary process has allowed us to draw too sharp a line between pastoralists giving way to urban dwellers—they were coterminous and co-dependent.[16]

The critical issues which emerge are: First, if urban life has significant drawbacks, for whom is it a good thing? Second, if urban life must be seen within the context of a flourishing and interdependent rural coexistence (which may be obvious but it also too often forgotten), what are the mechanisms which manage that coexistence? Third, in the context of a pronounced tendency to collapse, what are the mechanisms which promote continuity?

It is quite difficult to argue that the state, wherever we put it temporally, is a fundamentally democratic bottom-up creation. Coercion cannot be excluded from the picture, and while the skew in our evidence is obvious, on the whole, elite display is indissociable from other indicators of state formation and urban development – that is to say, it is highly unusual to find something we consider to be urban without also finding an elite present in grave goods, social differentiation, etc. A T Smith's emphasis on spectacle and recent work on feasting are examples of this.[17]

That is not really surprising, because what states are good at by necessity is control of population, taxation, surplus production, and resource management. That is why on most accounts, the state is inexorably linked to the development of bureaucracy, for instance in writing and record-keeping. However, coercion is never total, and bottom-up processes are critical even in periods of accelerated top-down development. One very specific issue is that states are highly segmented and retain group orientations at various levels. It follows that across areas such as legal violence, war, feud, and crime, there may have been a multiplicity of levels of law, an idea sometimes associated with the anthropologist of law, Leopold Pospisil.[18] One of the interesting problems which emerges from law operating at different levels is managing boundaries and conflicts. Rome has a strong notion of self-help, but this is inextricably linked to violence, and in any society in which feud existed, arbitration and peacemaking will be close at hand.[19]

---

[15] Scott 2017, very well reviewed by Richardson 2018. The claim for worse urban nutrition is counter to other influential accounts.
[16] Porter 2012; Wengrow and Graeber 2015.
[17] Smith 2011; cf. Hayden and Villeneuve 2011.
[18] French 1993.
[19] Lintott 1968, 1970, and 1982; Nippel 1995; on feuds, see Miller 1990.

Key to what states are good at, it seems to me, is the development of the practices of the market, and here we enter another interesting area of debate.[20] Karl Polanyi's brilliant notion of the embedded economy tended towards the idea that markets and the rationality required for them to work were a late phenomenon. Economic activities and institutions were enmeshed in social relations. The market of rational economic behaviour is a specific, late, and rather unnatural phenomenon according to Polanyi.[21] This is fascinating and in many ways very helpful, but it has also run into difficulties. We find ourselves fairly quickly in the argument over the ancient economy and the unsustainable arguments of Moses Finley as opposed to the strong push for a new institutional economics.[22]

Yet in ancient Mediterranean history and elsewhere, the importance of the market is being restated. The step which is needed is to embed the market itself within social relations, which means two things: first to break down the distinction between rational and non-rational economic behaviour to allow for elements of accumulation and planning at much earlier stages of human development; and second to permit a variety of kinds of value to operate.[23] In other words, if the economy is truly embedded in social relations, then some of the behaviours which we might consider irrational may in fact reflect specific social behaviours at a specific time, and relate to particular social formations which reflect dominant power groups and ideologies. If one looks at different expressions of value, as David Graeber has argued, then there may be rationality (whatever that means) to be found in archaic societies.[24]

That said, we do not need to make the archaic market too strange. In fact, there is good evidence for the recognition of a need for standardisation, and of fair exchange. The most relevant items for us perhaps are the inscription *hydrie metrie* at Gravisca,[25] items such as *tesserae hospitales*, and there is one of course at S. Omobono,[26] and arguments such as those of Greene, Lawall, and Polzer on mechanisms of developing the commercial environment of the archaic eastern Mediterranean through processes of establishing trust.[27] Both sides need to feel that value has been achieved in a process of repetitive exchange. The regulated market is a critical part of the answer as to why cities and their networks, given their peculiar challenges, are nevertheless deemed desirable and advantageous.[28] Moreover, it is clear that

---

[20] Feinman and Garraty 2010; Feinman 2013.
[21] Polanyi 1944; Dalton 1968. Polanyi's work has been superbly contextualised in Rogan (2017).
[22] Lie 1991; Krippner and Alvarez 2007 discuss the wider challenges of embeddedness.
[23] Riva (2017) for an example of this thinking in practice.
[24] Graeber 2001.
[25] Fiorini, Franceschi, and Luciano 2005, 181. For further developments in the archaeology of the port, see Fiorini 2015.
[26] Maggiani 2006.
[27] Greene, Lawall, and Polzer 2008.
[28] Blanton, Fargher 2008, 52–3, and passim; the market is an important place to develop cooperative as well as competitive mechanisms. It is important to give weight to the concept of the networks which form in the context of urban or urbanising nodes; see on this Malkin 2011; Knappett 2013; and Blake 2014.

the market was embedded in social practices and often surrounded by religious space and ritual forms.[29]

Are there archaeological indications that might give us grounds for seeing some of these processes at work? We can start by saying that Rome was large, though some earlier Mesopotamian cities were larger. Rome is about 250 hectares in size by the sixth century. Moreover, as far as we can make out, it started as a conglomeration of different groups, on the different hills. This is partly a conclusion drawn from literary evidence, but not wholly; the early city was not easy to traverse and at least in the nearest comparandum, Veii, we tend to the view that settlement was not spread over the whole plateau, but located in separate areas. One consequence we might be able to draw from this is that in the cohesion/coercion argument, one factor was that Rome comprised different groups which at some level may have been competitors.

The idea that early Iron Age Rome was a segmentary society of some size, which was able to exploit significant geographical resources from quite an early stage, and by the sixth century BCE had developed into a settlement which is comparable with a contemporary Greek *polis*, is now not surprising. In arguing that this then provided the conditions within which some sort of legal framework was likely and necessary, I want to draw on this archaeological record to pull out some salient features.

4. ARCHAEOLOGICAL INDICATORS

4.1 The Early Forum

One significant fact about the archaeology of Rome in the first quarter of the first millennium BCE may have been the closure of the Forum necropolis to adults.[30] There are no adult burials after about 800 BCE, except the burials in the area of the Vestals,[31] though the burial of children continues, as it does elsewhere in the context of *suggrundaria*.[32] Notably, this explicitly broke the capacity of the group to bury adults next to their ancestors. It places the Forum inside some definition of the community's space, and the prohibition against burial inside city limits is strong in antiquity.

Rome is not the only community where we see the movement of burials further away from the centre. The obvious parallel is Veii, where although we

---

[29] Kistler et al. 2015; further thoughts in Moser and Smith forthcoming.
[30] The necropolis was discovered by Giacomo Boni. I owe this point and much of what follows to a hugely helpful discussion with Nic Terrenato, though he is not to be held responsible for the direction in which I have taken it.
[31] This small group of burials has caused significant debate, on which see most recently Cirone and De Cristofaro 2018. If the whole of the area between the Palatine and Velia is closed to normal burials then this must be somehow anomalous. The alternative is to argue that they were in fact normal burials and to postdate the closure of the area to the end of the eighth century.
[32] The burials continue up into the Quirinal and Esquiline areas, which were formally outside the city. On *suggrundaria* see Gjerstad 1954.

cannot see burials in quite such a central space as at Rome, it does appear that the necropoleis move further out. The same shift is also visible at Pontecagnano, and it is a generally observed phenomenon.[33] There is clearly a highly pragmatic issue at stake, with growing populations demanding both more living space and more burial room. There are many other possible scenarios; competition between groups, lineages dying out and so forth, but I want to insist on the regulatory aspect of this decision. There is a choice here which is not only spatial but also historical. From some point in time, the Roman forum could no longer be used for burials of persons who have achieved adulthood, and the link between one group in the community and its ancestors is broken. That break with ancestors may be important. It remained permissible to bury 'incomplete' citizens, and their presence may indicate housing, since that is a pattern we find elsewhere, for instance in the new excavations at Gabii, and presumably family connections were sustained in burials in the extended necropolis, but the Forum was now no longer available.[34]

Of course, we do not know how the decision was arrived at, and it may have been a gentilicial rather than a community decision. However, we now have archaeological activity evidence from the late ninth century in the Comitium area and just beyond the Arch of Titus, in Tina Panella's excavations. If one draws a line between the two on many reconstructions of Roman topography, one is tracing the line of the Via Sacra.[35] Rome's sacred geography places a good deal of emphasis on the line from the Capitol to the Alban hills, the Via Sacra, which appears to have been a critical line for augury. On this we have no archaeological evidence but it is a contributory argument that this axis was significant from an early point.

The other now well-known and established feature of the area is the deliberate raising of the low-lying areas of the forum with 10,000 cubic metres or more of infill. This major work must have required substantial labour and cooperation, and it is relevant that the area created was then used for public gatherings.[36]

There is much that is speculative here but the elements that are not in dispute are the change in burial practice and the refocusing of attention on the forum area. The consistent use of the Forum for what would later be regarded as legal activity in the Republic, as well as the potentially legal aspect of the *Lapis Niger* inscription, and the absence of any suggestion of another legal space in Rome are by no means conclusive. But there is a logic to an evolution of the Forum as a space which was regulated, and from which regulation emerged, from its inception.

---

[33] On Veii, see Cascino, Di Giuseppe, and Patterson 2012; on Pontecagnano, see Pellegrino and Rossi 2011, and the series of publications of the necropoleis in the same series.

[34] The Gabii material is to be published shortly in Mogetta and Cohen forthcoming.

[35] On the *Lapis Niger* inscription and the notion of *sacer*, see Ter Beek 2011. On the concept of *sacer* more generally, see Fiori 1996; Lanfranchi 2017.

[36] Ammerman 1996, 2013.

4.2 Comitium

We have already mentioned the early evidence we now have for the Comitium.[37] There may be evidence of sortition practices here. The relationship between the Comitium and some definition of the community is probable even from its name. The *Lapis Niger* inscription shows an evident connection to both king and assembly. The complex hydrography of the whole area, with distinct and monumentalised springs by the sixth century, shows at the very least a continuing and indeed perhaps increasing sense of multiplicity even within a community we assume to be seeing the advantages of unity, as John Hopkins puts it.[38]

4.3 Jupiter, Castor and Pollux, Saturn

This multiplicity is also demonstrated by at least three major temples ringing the Forum area– the temples of Jupiter, Castor and Pollux, and Saturn. We should add perhaps an altar of Jupiter Stator, which must have been somewhere at the top end of the Forum (Peter Wiseman has recently argued for the area between the Palatine slope and the Atrium of the Vestals, suggesting that this area was dug out in the first century CE and the temple therefore lost).[39]

Saturn, a founding deity, Jupiter, another tutelary deity, Castor and Pollux who represented the cavalry, and Jupiter Stator whose association was with the infantry, constitute a cohesive definition of male community.[40] Only Jupiter Stator is weakly evidenced in this context; the other three are demonstrable from the late sixth and early fifth centuries. There are other deities and their temples and shrines which also reference elemental aspects of community, fire and water – Vulcan at the Comitium, Vesta by the Regia, Juturna and Janus, Mars and Ops Consiva in the so-called Regia. The religious imaginary of the archaic Roman community was clearly a significant part of the way the Romans saw themselves, as being under the eyes of the gods.[41]

4.4 Forum Boarium

We now have a much longer period of use of the Forum Boarium back into the later Bronze Age, and there has been some interesting recent work on the relevance of coastal sites in the later Bronze Age. Rome's riverine history is important

---

[37] See Fortini and Tassi Scandone's forthcoming publication on the Comitium area.
[38] Hopkins 2016.
[39] For details, see entries in the *LTUR*; on Jupiter Stator, Wiseman 2017.
[40] Locating the same for the female community is not so easy. Celia Schulz was right to reject the idea that female deities speak only to female concerns and presumably the reverse is also true; there is evidence of female participation in worship. Juno and Minerva in the Capitoline triad, Juno Sororia associated with the Tigillum Sororium, Mater Matuta and possibly Fortuna might help to redress the balance further. See Schulz 2006.
[41] Notwithstanding the methodological challenges which have been levelled against it, there is still much of value in Dumézil 1996; see also Capdeville 1995; Holland 1961. We are close to a new understanding also of the Regia complex, see Brocato and Terrenato 2016. On fire and water, Capdeville 2004; Di Giuseppe 2010; Haudry 2012; and De Martino 2017.

as we all know, and yet there are a series of consequences emerging from the work by Nic Terrenato's team at the Forum Boarium which imply management of water, and of the land/water interface, that may perhaps begin to encourage us to wonder if this was more structurally significant for the early city.[42]

There is now some seventh-century material from the Forum Boarium too; the excavators are rightly cautious but in a sense, given the nature of the site, they have been lucky to find anything.[43] The first temple is very early in the Etrusco-Italic sequence.[44] Coarelli's argument that this low-lying area which was also open to trade was outside the *Pomerium* still seems to me to be persuasive – it is a liminal area, and operated much as Pyrgi and Gravisca, but much closer to the city, no doubt owing to the problem of not controlling Veii.[45]

My argument will be becoming fairly evident I hope. In the period from the ninth to the end of the sixth century BCE, Rome becomes a very large settlement, it develops clear indications of the division and allocation of space, it makes significant normative decisions about the use of space, and while I cannot prove that these are of long duration, that would be a reasonable hypothesis. One major intervention produces a meeting place which is surrounded by temples, and another constructs an area with a specific trading function in the shadow of a further major temple, one of the earliest stone-built temples in central Italy. In short, two areas of complex assembly, both overseen by temples, both with deep histories. How might we arrive at a theory which explains this behaviour?

5. BIG GODS

At this stage I would like to bring in the debate around the influential book by Ara Norenzayan, *Big Gods: How Religion transformed Cooperation and Conflict*. Norenzayan works in the field of Cognitive Study of Religion and his book attracted a lot of attention, but has been largely set aside by classicists and indeed prehistorians owing to a number of factual and interpretative problems.[46]

The basic questions posed are how humans scaled up into cooperative societies, and why certain religions came to be so significant – especially the religions with 'watchful Big Gods'. Norenzayan argues that in the end the answer turns out to be the same – Big Gods are positively reinforcing for large-scale societies. Here are Norenzayan's basic theses:

1. Watched people are nice people.
2. Religion is more in the situation than in the person.

---

[42] Benjamin et al. 2017; Brock 2017; Brock and Terrenato 2016; Diffendale et al. 2016.
[43] Brocato and Terrenato 2017.
[44] Potts 2015.
[45] Coarelli 1988.
[46] Norenzayan 2013; see in response a series of essays led by Stausberg 2014. Coming at this from a different angle is the work of Bellah 2011. See also Norenzayan et al. 2016; Laurin 2017; Purzycki et al. 2017. For a striking combination of evolutionary biology and sociological method, see Turner and Abrutyn 2016.

3. Hell is stronger than heaven.
4. Trust people who trust God.
5. Religious actions speak louder than words.
6. Unworshipped Gods are impotent Gods.
7. Big Gods for Big Groups.
8. Religious groups cooperate in order to compete.

The process by which Norenzayan arrives at his conclusions is through a number of very cleverly constructed experiments on University of British Columbia students which purport to show deep-seated tendencies to behave better under scrutiny, or even under the mild suggestion of religion. There are some evident problems with the method, and Norenzayan is aware of many. Notably all the subjects are WEIRD – Western, Educated, Industrialised, Rich, and Democratic – and extrapolating from this group to more general and much more archaic populations is potentially misleading.

The Norenzayan response would be that these ideas are hard-wired into our cognition. The theses reveal that the sense of being under observation is a strong determinant of good behaviour, especially in interpersonal relationships, and that the threat of punishment is more powerful than the promise of reward. This set of reactions is recognised to encourage trust, so that we are likely to look favourably on people who express some level of religious belief and, more importantly, display some religious behaviour recognisably similar to that which is the norm in our own society. Scale drives up the need for powerful gods, but interestingly, Norenzayan argues that although religions clearly compete, they also often contain the capacity for managing competition.[47]

Amid the criticisms of the theory, however, Ann Taves effected a highly successful recasting of the strong Norenzayan thesis, suggesting that we should remain open to the possibility that groups develop 'watcher mechanisms' that do not rely on Big Gods; and that we should also look for 'commitment mechanisms' that internalise policing, i.e. generate an inner sense of commitment to the group that operates whether people are being monitored or not. The point made by another critic that ancestors can often play the same role as Big Gods are supposed to have played may prove relevant too.[48] First, the critical role of ancestors in customary law, as seen in the phrase the *mos maiorum*, or the identification of the senators as *patres* (fathers), is notable in Roman society, but second, there is an important tension between direct ancestors and state-level actors. The shift from showing respect to one's own ancestors to acknowledging the history of the group is a key one, perhaps reflected in the privileging of social space over family space in the Forum. This fits a hypothetical progression from ancestor worship to family

---

[47] This last point is more relevant to monotheistic competition, but it is worth bearing in mind when we reflect on the mechanisms of syncretism which appear to be in operation as Phoenicians, Greeks, Etruscans, Latins, and other inhabitants of Italy trade increasingly intensively with each other.
[48] Taves 2014; Geertz 2014.

solidarity to civic performance. Elements of each stage will be carried through (busts of ancestors on display in houses and so forth). The regulations relevant to each stage will then increasingly overlap and produce levels of custom and regulation, the tensions between which will require adjudication.

This nexus of ideas brings us to something like this:

1. The creation of large-scale settlements requires a degree of over-determination. It is not necessarily universally beneficial and it might be thought to be more societally stressful. It brings a multitude of cohesion/coercion problems. And it has to be explained in terms of active benefit, especially if we want to explain duration.
2. Religion – or at any rate ritualised behaviour – is a more or less universal concomitant of this process.
3. The concept of watchfulness, while it cannot be demonstrated to be universal, has attractions within the mechanisms of cognitive behaviour, and that may have evolutionary roots.
4. One specific area where this is most evidently marked out is in marketplace activities.

Returning to the archaeological evidence which we have reviewed, each case study raises issues of choice and decision, which are to a certain extent binding and of long duration. The eventual exclusion of burials from the Forum, the (partial) replacement of ancestors with other forms of authority, the prehistory of the augural activity we later see, the location of temples and the management of a market where we should be looking for the development of regulatory behaviour in the so-called regal period, whatever else we might be able to find, are all connected to concepts of regulation.

To what extent are we seeing coercion versus cohesion? Clearly, watchful mechanisms, and management of labour, point towards the coercive end. However, communal spaces and the logic of the embeddedness of both market and religious behaviour suggest that consensus was part of the deal as well. The city of Rome was a co-production of a number of competing factors, and for all the downsides of urban life it was beneficial not just to the elite. The curiate assembly, if it did anything at this period, operated at a community level as constraining elite behaviour.[49] This early period of regulation could be argued to have started in the orientalising period, which has often been thought to represent elite power at its height, and then continued into the Classical Period, when we tend to think that elite behaviour has been in some way managed and restrained.

In sum, the archaeological evidence clearly points towards the necessity for regulation and adjudication in such a complex society, and a modified model of Norenzayan's thesis suggests the existence of some watchful mechanisms, which include resources which are increasingly available through the resources of the

---

[49] See Armstrong, this volume.

city as it becomes increasingly monumentalised. This is not to reinstate an old polis religion model or to lapse into functionalism, but rather to argue for the intricately intertwined and sometimes mutually reinforcing development of mechanisms of power, practices of ritual, urban form, and economic behaviour across relatively large-scale urban settlements.

6. KINGS, ADJUDICATORS AND LAWS

Where does this leave the king? It seems to me that this leaves at least two possibilities (and various combinations of them).[50] One possibility is that there was the need for a fairly permanent figure tasked with this role. The other is that kings, or – better – rule-makers, people who make things right or straight, as Benveniste puts it, may have been more occasional necessities, somewhat like the rule-makers or *nomothetai* we see in the Greek tradition.[51] I am reminded of Karl Hölkeskamp's work on written law in archaic Greece, where he noted that both the literary accounts and the actual evidence tended to point away from codes: 'there is no hint whatever that these nomoi were dependent parts of general and systematic laws on inheritance, contract and penal law or fully-fledged comprehensive "law codes"'.

But this is not in any way to diminish the significance of the activity:

> Legislation, that is institutionalized procedure designed for the deliberation and making of universally binding decisions, became the very core of the peculiar 'statehood' of the polis: it was the most intensive kind of interaction of civic institutions within, and in the midst of, the polis – with itself, in the form of the citizen-body in assembly as the main subject, thus asserting and indeed realizing itself as a true polis.[52]

There is a tension between this model and, say, Seth Bernard's account of mass corvée labour, yet somehow both may be true, and I think we may revert to a highly heterarchic model of early Rome, and one which is poorly reflected in the dichotomies of the ancient sources and some modern reconstructions.[53]

It might be objected that the kind of law we see in early Rome does not fall directly into the relevant categories, and that Hölkeskamp's laws are far from the provisions of law envisaged for the regal period. The law which we can see clearly enough, the Twelve Tables, is customary, private, and city-based, though it is also fragmentary. Again the sources may not help us here. At a later stage, Roman lawyers had carefully demarcated the limits between kinds of law, but to return to Pospisil, it is likely that at an early stage there were different levels of law. The critical issue is whether we can see the capacity to think in legal ways, however vaguely that is described.[54] Here we have to go back to the sources.

---

[50] I have left to one side the issue of war and the king; on this area, see Armstrong 2016.
[51] Papakonstantinou 2008.
[52] Hölkeskamp 1992–3.
[53] Bernard 2018.
[54] See Smith (forthcoming) for a different kind of argument about the emergence of law as a form of abstract thinking.

There are hints of the sorts of thinking which is necessary for my case. Allusions to the complex rules over *mancipatio*, and the notion of fraud are there in the Twelve Tables.⁵⁵ The *ius commercii* has usually been thought to be of some antiquity as regulating relations between Romans and Latins. The regulation of title fits with the concepts of fair measure, trust, and reciprocity which are inherent in an effective marketplace. Roselaar's important article on *commercium* shows that the concept must have changed over time, and that there is no good evidence for it being particularly developed in the Archaic Period. Her suggestion is that at most there was an early right to trade in *res mancipi*, which was eventually overseen by the *praetor*.⁵⁶ The focus therefore is on the person or people permitted into the city and able to trade and hold the most significant items for agriculture, such as land and cattle. This is a good example of the sort of decision-making which was necessary, and the way that complexity will have grown over time.

It is notable that the first treaty between Rome and Carthage, dated to 509 BCE, stipulates that 'men coming to trade may conclude no business except in the presence of a [Carthaginian] herald or town-clerk, and the price of whatever is sold in the presence of such shall be secured to the vendor by the [Carthaginian] state, if the sale take place in Libya or Sardinia. If any Roman comes to the Carthaginian province in Sicily, he shall enjoy equal rights with the others.'⁵⁷ The absence of a similar clause for a Carthaginian trading in Rome is striking, especially since there is such a clause in the second treaty, usually dated to the mid-fourth century. However, the context of the treaty (and for that matter the reason it was being quoted) was about interventions in the territories of the respective parties. The first treaty says nothing about trade in Rome, but neither does it refer to trade in Carthage specifically, whereas the second treaty has the balancing clause, 'In the Carthaginian province of Sicily and in Carthage he may transact business and sell whatsoever it is lawful for a citizen to do. In like manner also may a Carthaginian at Rome.'⁵⁸ In short, Roselaar is surely right to be circumspect about the complexity of *commercium* rules in the sixth century BCE, and Rome may well have been less sophisticated than Carthage in its interstate trading arrangements, but we cannot deduce from the first treaty that the Romans had no notion of arbitration. Rather, an optimist might start from Roselaar's observation that 'this treaty does not constitute the right to trade per se, but grants certain privileges for trade which was already going on',⁵⁹ and suggest that the relevant rules for trade in Rome and in Carthage were implicit, but not relevant to a definition of behaviour in the territories of two expansionist states.⁶⁰

---

⁵⁵ See the provocative paper, Watson 2004.
⁵⁶ Roselaar 2012. Cf. Kremer 2005.
⁵⁷ Trans. Loeb.
⁵⁸ Trans. Loeb
⁵⁹ Roselaar 2012, 394.
⁶⁰ See Pol. 3.22–7. On the context of the treaties in Polybius' work, see Nörr 2005; Wiater 2018. The fact that Rome was in 509 BCE engaged in international law, as Wiater argues, is a strong argument in favour of other forms of law inside the city.

What happened when a crime was committed? Another interesting way of providing circumstantial support for the existence of arbitration and legal recourse in archaic Rome would be to look at regimes of punishment.[61] There have been suggestions that some anomalous burials at Rome reflect sacrifice or punishment.[62] For what it is worth, punishment does feature in the early accounts – the story of Horatius is predicated on explaining how to manage the tension between public glory and private violence.[63] One intriguing area where we know too little is around the issue of fines. Gellius tells us that fines were denominated in terms of sheep and cattle.[64] If this has any worth beyond a speculative antiquarian guess, it demonstrates a pre-monetary world, but that could be at almost any point before the third century BCE.

Ultimately, a notion of the grounds on which one interacts with others, and of arbitration when things go wrong, is absolutely basic to a functioning community. In his classic article on adjudication, Lon Fuller wrote:

> If, then, adjudication is a form of social ordering, to understand it fully we must view it in its relation to other forms of social ordering. It is submitted that there are two basic forms of social ordering: organization by common aims and organization by reciprocity. Without one or the other of these nothing resembling a society can exist.[65]

The argument of my paper holds that this is true of archaic society, even acknowledging the necessary caveats around the presence of violence, dispute, and factionalism. If these are to be contained, they must be adjudicated and this adjudication will needs be quasi-permanent (watcher-mechanisms) and occasional (brokerage). The Twelve Tables as a written document is the evolution from customary norms into a form of watcher-mechanism itself, but it would be extraordinary if it emerged from nowhere. Consequently, either the Twelve Tables are misdated and belong to a later period, or one must assume a prehistory in the Archaic Period.[66] The same argument will apply to the calendar, another document which crystallised regulatory behaviour, and which is highly relevant to the marketplace.

7. CONCLUSION

This argument is to a very large extent (but obviously not entirely) independent of the existence of any evidence for a law passed by a king, or for the traditional narrative of the kings in any shape or form. My account is based on the growing archaeological evidence for a society which had to grapple with

---

[61] Torelli and Guittard 1981.
[62] Carafa 2007/2008.
[63] Liv. 1.26; Dion. Hal. *Ant. Rom.* 3.22; cf. Watson 1979.
[64] Gell. NA 11.1.
[65] Fuller and Winston 1978, 357.
[66] For an interesting defence of the date on the basis of comparisons with Ionian practice, see Crawford 2011. On the Twelve Tables generally, see Humbert 2005.

size, fragmentation, and behaviours which required degrees of trust like market exchange, and therefore clear normative rules. This is coupled with some fairly well-founded theoretical arguments from state formation theory on the one hand and cognitive religious studies on the other in a dialectical relationship.

While I have clearly stated that the development of societies of this size are not likely to be products of democracy, once one steps away from a rigid progression from kings to Republic, as I think we have been doing in one way or another for some time, then we will end up with models which are both messier and in the end necessarily to some extent the product of widely held agreements between stakeholders.[67] Critically, watchful mechanisms and normative decision-making, while they may be rigged, cannot be applied arbitrarily for long. There has to be the assumption that they are being applied according to some pre-agreed formula, however odd that might appear to us. While the city offers an array of resources for the expression and enjoyment of power, it is also an arena in which competing interests are managed, in part through something which would in due course come to be recognisable as legislation.

Works Cited

Ammerman, A J, 1996. 'The Comitium in Rome from the Beginning.' *AJA* 100.1:121–36.

———, 2013. 'Looking at Early Rome with Fresh Eyes: Transforming the Landscape.' In *A Companion to the Archaeology of the Roman Republic*, edited by J DeRose Evans, 169–80. Malden: Wiley Blackwell.

Armstrong, J, 2016. *War and Society in Early Rome: From Warlords to Generals*. Cambridge: Cambridge University Press.

Asmis, E, 2008. 'Cicero on Natural Law and the Laws of the State.' *ClAnt* 27.1:1–33.

Bellah, R N, 2011. *Religion in Human Evolution: From the Paleolithic to the Axial Age*. Cambridge, MA: Harvard University Press.

Benjamin, J et al., 2017. 'Late Quaternary Sea-level Changes and Early Human Societies in the Central and Eastern Mediterranean Basin: An interdisciplinary Review.' *Quaternary International* 449:29–57.

Bernard, S, 2018. *Building Mid-Republican Rome: Labor, Architecture, and the Urban Economy*. New York: Oxford University Press.

Blake, E, 2014. *Social Networks and Regional Identity in Bronze Age Italy*. New York: Cambridge University Press.

Blanton, R and L Fargher. 2008. *Collective Action in the Formation of Pre-modern States*. New York: Springer.

———, 2016. *How Humans Cooperate: Confronting the Challenges of Collective Action*. Boulder: University of Colorado Press.

---

[67] For an admirable investigation of the complex development of aristocracy, see Bradley 2015.

Blickman, D, 1989. 'Lucretius, Epicurus, and Prehistory.' *HSCP* 92:157–91.
Bliesemann de Guevara, B, 2015. 'State Formation.' *Oxford Bibliographies in Political Science*. Oxford: Oxford University Press. DOI: 10.1093/OBO/9780199756223-0123.
Boeri, M, 2013. 'Natural Law and World Order in Stoicism.' In *Nature and the Best Life. Exploring the Natural Bases of Practical Normativity in Ancient Philosophy*, edited by G Rossi, 183–223. Hildesheim: Georg Olms Verlag.
Bradley, G, 2015. 'Investigating Aristocracy in Archaic Rome and Central Italy: Social Mobility, Ideology and Cultural Influences.' In *'Aristocracy' in Antiquity. Redefining Greek and Roman Elites*, edited by N Fisher and H Van Wees, 85–124. Swansea: Classical Press of Wales.
Brocato, P and N Terrenato, 2016. *Nuovi Studi Sulla Regia Di Roma*. Cosenza: Luigi Pellegrini Editore.
———, 2017. 'The Archaic Temple of S. Omobono: New Discoveries and Old Problems.' In *The Age of Tarquinius Superbus: Central Italy in the late 6th century BC; Proceedings of the Conference 'The age of Tarquinius Superbus a paradigm shift?', Rome, 7–9 November 2013*, edited by P S Lulof and C J Smith, 97–106. Leuven: Peeters.
Brock, A L, 2017. 'Floodplain Occupation and Landscape Modification in Early Rome.' *Quaternary International* 460:167–74.
Brock, A and N Terrenato, 2016. 'Rome in the Bronze Age: Late Second-millennium BC Radiocarbon Dates from the Forum Boarium.' *Antiquity* 90(351):654–64.
Broodbank, C, 2013. *The Making of the Middle Sea. A History of the Mediterranean from the Beginning to the Emergence of the Classical World*. London: Thames and Hudson.
Brown, E A, 2009. 'The Emergence of Natural Law and the Cosmopolis.' In *The Cambridge Companion to Ancient Greek Political Thought*, edited by S G Salkever, 331–64. Cambridge: Cambridge University Press.
Bujuklić, Z, 1988. 'Leges regiae: pro et contra.' *Revue Internationale des Droits de l'Antiquité* 3rd ser. 45:89–142.
Capdeville, G, 1995. *Volcanus: recherches comparatistes sur les origines du culte de Vulcain*. Rome: École française de Rome.
———, ed., 2004. *L'eau et le feu dans les religions antiques: actes du premier Colloque international d'histoire des religions, Paris, 18–20 mai 1995, Université de Paris IV-Sorbonne, École normale supérieure*. Paris: De Boccard.
Carafa, P, 2007/8. 'Uccisioni rituali e sacrifici umani nella topografia di Roma.' *ScAnt* 14.2: 667–704.
Cascino, R, H Di Giuseppe, and H Patterson, 2012. *Veii, the Historical Topography of the Ancient City: A Restudy of John Ward-Perkins's Survey*. London: British School at Rome.
Cirone, D and A De Cristofaro. 2018. 'Ancora sulla nova via vecchie ipotesi, nuove proposte.' *ArchCl* 69:113–66.
Coarelli, F, 1988. *Il Foro Boario*. Rome: Quasar.

Crawford, M H, 2011. 'From Ionia to the Twelve Tables.' In *Römische Jurisprudenz: Dogmatik, Überlieferung, Rezeption: Festschrift für Detlef Liebs zum 75. Geburtstag*, edited by K Muscheler, 153–9. Freiburger Rechtsgeschichtliche Abhandlungen. Neue Folge 63. Berlin: Duncker und Humblot.
Dalton, G, ed., 1968. *Primitive, Archaic, and Modern Economies: Essays of Karl Polanyi*. New York: Anchor Books.
De Martino, M, 2017. *Le divine gemelle celesti: sacertà del fuoco centrale e semantica dell'aurora nella religione indoeuropea*. Lugano: Agorà and Co.
Di Giuseppe, H, ed., 2010. *I riti del costruire nelle acque violate: atti del convegno internazionale, Roma, Palazzo Massimo, 12–14 giugno 2008*. Rome: Scienze e Lettere.
Diffendale, D, P. Brocato, N. Terrenato, and A Brock, 2016. 'Sant'Omobono: An Interim status quaestionis.' *JRA* 29:7–42.
Dumézil, G, 1996. *Archaic Roman Religion*. Baltimore, MD: Johns Hopkins University Press.
Feinman, G M, 2013. 'Crafts, Specialists, and Markets in Mycenaean Greece. Reenvisioning Ancient Economies: Beyond Typological Constructs.' *AJA* 117:3:453–9.
Feinman, G M and C P Garraty, 2010. 'Preindustrial Markets and Marketing: Archaeological Perspectives.' *Annual Review of Anthropology* 39:1:167–91.
Fiori, R, 1996. *Homo sacer: dinamica politico-costituzionale di una sanzione giuridico-religiosa*. Napoli: Jovene.
Fiorini, L, 2015. 'The Sacred Area of Gravisca: Ethnic and Religious Interactions in Comparison.' In *Sanctuaries and the Power of Consumption: Networking and the Formation of Elites in the Archaic Western Mediterranean World: Proceedings of the International Conference in Innsbruck, 20th–23rd March 2012*, edited by E Kistler, B Öhlinger, M Mohr, and M Hoernes, 205–19. Wiesbaden: Harrassowitz Verlag.
Fiorini, L, E Franceschi, and G Luciano. 2005. *Topografia Generale e Storia del Santuario: Analisi dei Contesti e delle Stratigrafie*. Bari: Edipuglia.
Fournier, M, 2013. *Émile Durkheim. A Biography*. Oxford: Polity Press.
French, R R, 1993. 'Leopold J. Pospisil and the Anthropology of Law.' *Political and Legal Anthropology Review* 16.2:1–8.
Fuller, L L and K I Winston, 1978. 'The Forms and Limits of Adjudication.' *Harvard Law Review* 92.2:353–409.
Gagarin, M, 1989. *Early Greek Law*. Berkeley: University of California Press.
Geertz, A W, 2014. 'Do Big Gods cause Anything?' *Religion* 44.4:609–13.
Gjerstad, E, 1954. 'Suggrundaria.' In *Neue Beiträge zur klassischen Altertumswissenschaft. Festschrift zum 60. Geburtstag von B. Schweitzer*, edited by R Lullies, 291–6. Stuttgart: Kohlhammer.
Graeber, D, 2001. *Toward an Anthropological Theory of Value: The False Coin of Our Own Dreams*. New York: Palgrave.
Greene, E S, M L Lawall, and M S Polzer, 2008. 'Inconspicuous Consumption: The Sixth-Century B.C.E. Shipwreck at Pabuç Burnu, Turkey.' *AJA* 112.4:685–711.

Haudry, J, 2012. 'Les feux de Rome.' *RÉL* 90:57–82.
Hayden, B and S Villeneuve, 2011. 'A Century of Feasting Studies.' *Annual Review of Anthropology* 40:433–49.
Herzfeld, M, 1984. 'The Horns of the Mediterraneanist Dilemma.' *American Ethnologist* 11:439–54.
——, 1985. 'Of Horns and History: The Mediterraneanist Dilemma Again.' *American Ethnologist* 12:778–80.
——, 1991. 'On Mediterraneanist Performances.' *Journal of Mediterranean Studies* 1:141–7.
——, 2005. 'Practical Mediterraneanism: Excuses for Everything, from Epistemology to Eating.' In *Rethinking the Mediterranean*, edited by W V Harris, 45–63. Oxford: Oxford University Press.
Hölkeskamp, K-J, 1992–3. 'Written Law in Archaic Greece.' *PCPS* 38:87–117.
Holland, L A, 1961. *Janus and the Bridge*. Papers and Monographs of the American Academy in Rome XXI. Rome: American Academy in Rome.
Hopkins J N, 2016. *The Genesis of Roman Architecture*. New Haven and London: Yale University Press.
Humbert, M, ed., 2005. *Le Dodici Tavole: dai decemviri agli umanisti*. Pavia: IUSS Pr.
Inwood, B, 2003. 'Natural Law in Seneca.' In B Inwood, *Reading Seneca: Stoic Philosophy at Rome*, 224–48. Oxford: Oxford University Press. Originally published in *The Studia Philonica Annual*, edited by D T Runia, G E Sterling and H Najman, 81–99. Providence, RI: Brown University Press.
Kistler, E, B Öhlinger, M Mohr, and M Hoernes, eds, 2015. *Sanctuaries and the Power of Consumption: Networking and the Formation of Elites in the Archaic Western Mediterranean World: Proceedings of the International Conference in Innsbruck, 20th–23rd March 2012*. Wiesbaden: Harrassowitz Verlag.
Knappett, C, 2013. *Network Analysis in Archaeology: New Approaches to Regional Interaction*. Oxford: Oxford University Press.
Kremer, D. 2005. 'Trattato internazionale e legge delle Dodici Tavole.' In *Le Dodici Tavole. Dai Decemviri agli Umanisti*, edited by M Humbert, 191–207. Pavia: IUSS Press.
Krippner, G R and A S Alvarez, 2007. 'Embeddedness and the Intellectual Projects of Economic Sociology.' *Annual Review of Sociology* 33.1:219–40.
Lanfranchi, T, 2017. *Autour de la notion de sacer*. Rome: École française de Rome.
Laurendi, R, 2013. *"Leges regiae" e "ius Papirianum." Tradizione e storicità di un "corpus" normative*. Rome: 'L'Erma' di Bretschneider.
Laurin, K, 2017. 'Belief in God: A Cultural Adaptation with Important Side Effects.' *Current Directions in Psychological Science* 26.5:458–63.
Lie, J, 1991. 'Embedding Polanyi's Market Society.' *Sociological Perspectives* 34.2:219–35.
Lintott, A, 1968. *Violence in Republican Rome*. Oxford: Oxford University Press.
——, 1970. 'The Tradition of Violence in the Annals of the Early Roman Republic.' *Historia* 19:12–29.

———, 1982. *Violence, Civil Strife, and Revolution in the Classical City, 750–330* B.C. Baltimore: Johns Hopkins University Press.
Maggiani, A, 2006. 'Dinamiche del commercio arcaico: le tesserae hospitales.' In *Gli etruschi e il Mediterraneo: commerci e politica: atti del XIII Convegno internazionale di studi sulla storia e l'archeologia dell'Etruria*, edited by G M della Fina, 317–50. Orvieto: Fondazione per il Museo Claudio Faina.
Malkin, I, 2011. *A Small Greek World: Networks in the Ancient Mediterranean*. New York: Oxford University Press.
Mantovani, D, 2012. 'Le due serie di leges regiae.' In *Leges publicae: la legge nell'esperienza giuridica romana*, edited by J-L Ferrary, 283–92. Pavia: IUSS.
Miller, W I, 1990. *Bloodtaking and Peacemaking: Feud, Law, and Society in Saga Iceland*. Chicago: University of Chicago Press.
Mogetta, M and S Cohen, forthcoming. 'Infant Burial Practices from an Élite Domestic Compound at Early Iron Age and Orientalising Gabii.' In *From Invisible to Visible. New Data and Methods for the Archaeology of Infant and Child Burials in Pre-Roman Italy*, edited by J Tabolli. Uppsala: Studies in Mediterranean Archaeology.
Moser, C and C Smith, eds, forthcoming. *Transformations of Value: Lived Religion and the Economy*. Special issue of *Religion in the Roman Empire*.
Nagy, G and M Noussia-Fantuzzi, eds, 2015. *Solon in the Making: The Early Reception in the Fifth and Fourth Centuries*. Berlin: De Guyter.
Nippel, W, 1995. *Public Order in Ancient Rome*. Cambridge: Cambridge University Press.
Norenzayan, A, A F Shariff, W M Gervais, A Willard, R McNamara, E Slingerland, and J Henrich, 2016. 'The Cultural Evolution of Prosocial Religions.' *Behavioral & Brain Sciences* 39:1–65.
Norenzayan, A, 2013. *Big Gods: How Religion transformed Cooperation and Conflict*. Princeton: Princeton University Press.
Nörr, D, 2005. 'Osservazioni in tema di terminologia giuridica predecemvirale e di ius mercatorum mediterraneo: il primo trattato cartaginese-romano.' In *Le Dodici Tavole dai Decemviri agli Umanisti*, edited by M Humbert, 147–90. Pavia: IUSS Press.
Papakonstantinou, Z, 2008. *Lawmaking and Adjudication in Archaic Greece*. London: Routledge.
Pellegrino, C and A Rossi, 2011. *Pontecagnano. I.1. Città e campagna nell'Agro Picentino (Gli scavi dell'autostrada 2001–2006)*. Chiusi: Edizioni Luì.
Polanyi, K, 1944. *The Great Transformation: The Political and Economic Origins of Our Time*. New York: Farrar and Rinehart.
Porter, A, 2012. *Mobile Pastoralism and the Formation of Near Eastern Civilizations: Weaving Together Society*. Cambridge: Cambridge University Press.
Potts, C R, 2015. *Religious Architecture in Latium and Etruria, c. 900–500* BC. Oxford: Oxford University Press.
Psilakis, C, 2014. *Dynamiques et mutations d'une figure d'autorité: la réception de Solon aux Ve et IVe siècles avant J.C.* PhD thesis, Université Charles de Gaulle–Lille III.

Purcell, N and P Horden, 2000. *The Corrupting Sea: A Study of Mediterranean History*. Oxford: Blackwell.

Purzycki, B G et al., 2017. 'The Evolution of Religion and Morality: A Synthesis of Ethnographic and Experimental Evidence from Eight Societies.' *Religion, Brain & Behavior* 8:101–32.

Richardson, J, 2010. 'The Oath per Iovem lapidem and the Community in Archaic Rome.' *RhM* 153:25–42.

Richardson, S, 2018. 'Review of James Scott, *Against the Grain*.' *JNES* 77.2:307–11.

Riva, C, 2017. 'Wine Production and Exchange and the Value of Wine Consumption in Sixth-century BC Etruria.' *JMA* 30.2:237–61.

Rogan, T, 2017. *The Moral Economists: R. H. Tawney, Karl Polanyi, E. P. Thompson and the Critique of Capitalism*. Princeton: Princeton University Press.

Roselaar, S T, 2012. 'The Concept of Commercium in the Roman Republic.' *Phoenix* 66.3/4:381–413.

Schulz, C, 2006. *Women's Religious Activity in the Roman Republic*. Chapel Hill: University of North Carolina Press.

Scott, J C, 2017. *Against the Grain: A Deep History of the Early States*. New Haven: Yale University Press.

Smith, A T, 2011. 'Archaeologies of Sovereignty.' *Annual Review of Anthropology* 40:1:415–32.

Smith, C J, forthcoming. 'The Gift of Sovereignty: Kings from Mauss to Sahlins and Graeber.' *Politica Antica*.

Stausberg M, 2014. 'Big Gods in Review: Introducing Ara Norenzayan and his Critics.' *Religion* 44:4:592–608.

Steinberg, M, 1982. 'The Twelve Tables and Their Origins: An Eighteenth-Century Debate.' *Journal of the History of Ideas* 43.3:379–96.

Taves, A, 2014. 'Big Gods and Other Watcher Mechanisms in the Formation of Large Groups.' *Religion* 44.4:658–66.

Ter Beek, L J, 2011. 'Divine Law and the Penalty of "sacer esto" in Early Rome.' In *Law and Religion in the Roman Republic*, edited by O E Tellegen-Couperus, 11–29. Mnemosyne Supplements 336. Leiden and Boston: Brill.

Tilly, C, 1993. *Coercion, Capital, and European States, AD 990–1992*. Oxford: Blackwell.

Torelli, M, and C Guittard, eds, 1981. *Le Délit religieux dans la cité antique. Actes de la table ronde de Rome (6–7 avril 1978)*. Collection de l'École française de Rome 48. Rome: École française de Rome.

Turner, J H and S Abrutyn, 2016. 'Returning the "Social" to Evolutionary Sociology: Reconsidering Spencer, Durkheim, and Marx's Models of "Natural" Selection.' *Sociological Perspectives* 60.3:529–56.

Waldron, J, 2013. 'What is Natural Law Like?' In *Reason, Morality, and Law: The Philosophy of John Finnis*, edited by J Keown and R P George, 73–89. Oxford: Oxford University Press.

Watson, A, 1972. 'Roman Private Law and the Leges Regiae.' *JRS* 62:100–5.

——, 1979. 'The Death of Horatia.' *CQ* 29.2:436–47.

——, 2004. 'Two Early Codes, The Ten Commandments and the Twelve Tables: Causes and Consequences.' *The Journal of Legal History* 25.2:129–49.

Wengrow, D and D Graeber, 2015. 'Farewell to the "Childhood of Man": Ritual, Seasonality, and the Origins of Inequality.' *JRAI* 21:597–619.

Wiater, N, 2018. 'Documents and Narrative: Reading the Roman Carthaginian Treaties in Polybius' Histories.' In *Polybius and His Legacy*, edited by N Miltsios and M Tamiolaki, 131–65. Berlin: De Gruyter.

Wiseman, T P, 2017. 'Iuppiter Stator in Palatio. A New Solution to an Old Puzzle.' *MDAI(R)* 123:13–45.

Woodruff, P and M Gagarin, 2007. 'Early Greek Legal Thought.' In *A History of the Philosophy of Law from the Ancient Greeks to the Scholastics.* [=A Treatise of Legal Philosophy and General Jurisprudence, vol. 6], edited by F D Miller, Jr, with C-A Biondi, 7–34. Dordrecht: Springer.

Yoffee, N, 2004. *Myths of the Archaic State: Evolution of the Earliest Cities, States and Civilizations*. Cambridge: Cambridge University Press.

——, ed., 2015. *The Cambridge World History 3: Early Cities in Comparative Perspective, 4000 BCE–1200 CE*. Cambridge: Cambridge University Press.

Yoffee, N and N Terrenato, 2015. 'Introduction: A History of the Study of Early Cities.' In *The Cambridge World History 3: Early Cities in Comparative Perspective, 4000 BCE–1200 CE*, edited by N Yoffee, 1–24. Cambridge: Cambridge University Press.

Chapter 8

Beyond the *Pomerium*: Expansion and Legislative Authority in Archaic Rome

Jeremy Armstrong

1. INTRODUCTION

The story of early Rome can be summed up in many ways, but perhaps the most obvious is as a story of expansion. From its humble origins as 'Romulus' asylum', the literature records that each of Rome's *reges* expanded the city in some way. Even Numa Pompilius, the famously religious and non-violent *rex*, was credited by Livy with 'enlarging the community' through peace, just as Romulus had by war (*ita duo deinceps reges, alius alia via, ille bello, hic pace, civitatem auxerunt*).[1] Expansion seems to have been written into Rome's DNA from the start.

Rome continued to expand during the early Republic, supposedly subjugating Veii at the turn of the fourth century and ultimately incorporating all of Latium by 338, before moving on to realise even greater ambitions.[2] By the start of the second century, when Rome's first native historians sat down to write the history of the city, Rome was already master of the western Mediterranean and within another two centuries would control the entirety of the basin. And whether or not one believes the details of the literature as it relates to early Rome – and certainly a range of positions exists – most scholars generally agree on the broad outline of this expansion narrative. We know Rome expanded. The real questions are the when, why, and how.

Frustratingly, of course, the explicit literary narrative for expansion in the regal and early Republican periods is difficult to trust, having been written so many years after the fact. While the exploits of Rome's *reges* and early consuls, including the conquest and incorporation of various areas, communities, and populations, are related in detail in the surviving literary accounts, this sort of evidence is notoriously problematic. Although at least some Romans do seem to have been literate in the early period, with epigraphic evidence and a tradition of record-keeping going back to (perhaps?) the regal period, Roman historical writing only began

---

[1] Liv. 1.26.6. Indeed, Numa was associated with new (possibly foreign) cults and priesthoods, including introducing the god Terminus and organising the exploitation and defence of the *pagi* (Plut. *Numa.* 16).

[2] All dates are BCE unless otherwise noted.

c. 200.³ The Romans' first written narrative of their expansion therefore represented the view from 'the top of the mountain', not the journal of the climb.

Some scholars have adopted a reasonably optimistic view of the early material, arguing that, in the absence of definitive proof to the contrary, the narrative for the early period should generally be trusted. Most, however, have assumed a more cautious stance.⁴ While there is some reason to believe that Rome's historians had access to records which stretched back to at least the late fifth century, with for instance the reference to an eclipse from c. 400 supposedly found in Ennius and preserved in Cicero,⁵ the nature of the evidence for the period before the third century is highly suspect to say the least – and particularly the accounts of battles and conquest.⁶ Although some of this material may have been preserved through festivals (for instance, with specific reference to Rome's expansion, the *Septimontium* and *Ambarvalia*), 'ballads', or family histories, it is likely that all of it would have been subject to the vagaries and issues of the oral tradition.⁷ Even the Romans of the late Republic were sceptical of its value and often accused rivals of manipulating it, or indeed adding to it through outright fabrication.

On the issue of early Roman expansion, archaeology has yet to offer anything particularly conclusive either. While ongoing excavations in and around Rome have revealed a wealthy and well-connected community from at least the sixth century, they have not been able to reveal the extent of Roman dominion.⁸ Given the patchy nature of excavation outside of the Palatine-Forum-Capitoline area, even our understanding of the extent of the archaic urban area is still incomplete, and the relationship of the urban zone to both the *ager Romanus antiquus* and the community's wider hinterland in the Archaic Period is almost entirely unknown.⁹ Indeed, the more we delve into the question of Roman power and influence, the more questions and problems seem to arise – most notably with identifying and defining a distinctive 'Roman' culture early on. The first concrete archaeological evidence for an identifiably 'Roman' influence beyond the *Pomerium* arguably dates to the period c. 300, when the first Roman 'coins' appear in central Italy with ΡΩΜΑΙΩΝ/ROMANO inscribed on them. Before this everything is quite

---

³ At least forty-two Latin inscriptions survive from the sixth and fifth centuries, five on stone and thirty-seven on other materials – generally pottery (see Solin 1999). On the origins of Roman historical writing, the bibliography is obviously extensive. For an excellent recent overview of the current state of scholarship, however, see Sandberg and Smith 2018.
⁴ Famously, see the contrasting positions of Cornell 2005, 58–9 (cf. Cornell 1995, 17–18) and Raaflaub 2005, 24–31. See also Armstrong and Richardson 2017 for discussion.
⁵ On the eclipse, see Cic. *Rep.* 1.16.
⁶ See Ampolo (1980, 15–30 and 168–75) for discussion and historiography of the size of Rome's early population, territory, and urban area.
⁷ Most recently, see Smith 2017. Cf. Cornell 1995, 204–8. More generally, see Wiseman 1995 and also Rich 2018.
⁸ See Hopkins 2016 for a recent summary of the evidence and a discussion of Rome's connectedness with other centres and cultures.
⁹ Fulminante 2014, particularly 104–70, offers one of the better and more recent analyses, although the results are still highly speculative.

hazy, with 'Roman' identity muddled together with the wider, and seemingly quite fluid, populations and dynamics of archaic central Italian society.[10] Consequently, while there is a clear memory of early expansion preserved in our sources, and archaeological evidence for a rich and vibrant city (with a relatively large population) existing from an early period, many modern scholars continue to find it easier to present Rome's empire as if it sprang – like Minerva from the head of Jupiter – fully formed onto the Mediterranean stage at the start of the third century, the early years being too difficult to decipher.

This is not to say various attempts have not been made to work around this impasse. In the early twentieth century, Beloch attempted to estimate Roman territory based on census figures and estimated carrying capacity of the land – an approach also attempted by De Martino.[11] However, such a method is predicated on the fundamental reliability of the early census data, which is by no means certain.[12] Approaching the same issue from the other side, Fulminante has attempted to use the landscape – with Thiessen polygons, carrying capacity, and viewsheds – to make suggestions about archaic Rome's footprint.[13] But while this work has shed tremendous light on various aspects of Rome's relationship with the land, for every question which is answered, two more questions emerge. The extent of 'Roman territory' in practical terms is still as murky as ever.

Taking a more symbolic approach, Bourdin, following Alföldi, has used shrines to try to define Rome's power and influence.[14] And in recent years, even more unconventional paradigms have also been applied to the problem. Fred Drogula's recent study of the concept of *provincia* outlined how changes in the definition of this term, and its seeming shift from 'task' to 'region', may help us understand both the growth of empire and the evolution of Roman command in the early and middle Republic.[15] Rome may not necessarily have had a geographic mindset when considering the extent of her early power.[16] Alternatively, Stek and Pelgrom's volume on colonisation in the Republic worked to redefine what 'expansion' may have meant in the first place, blurring the lines between state and private.[17]

In the present chapter, and in this more unorthodox vein, I would like to approach the issue of early Roman expansion by exploring what early Roman law might be able to suggest about the limits of the community. In particular, it will investigate what we can learn from the nature of, and changes in, early Roman legislative authority.

---

[10] Benelli 2017, 89–104.
[11] Beloch 1926 and De Martino 1979.
[12] See, most notably, Brunt 1971, 27.
[13] Fulminante 2006 and 2014.
[14] Bourdin 2012 and Alföldi 1962.
[15] Drogula 2015. This is also in line with Richardson's study of the word *imperium*. Richardson (1991) identified a change in meaning in the late Republic which plausibly coincides with a changing understanding of 'empire' during the period.
[16] See also Elden 2013 on this concept being an anachronism.
[17] Stek and Pelgrom 2014.

2. LEGISLATIVE AUTHORITY

Thinkers, ranging from Plato to Aristotle, Thomas Aquinas, Locke, Kant, Derrida, and Foucault, have commented on the fundamental importance of legislative authority – the power to create laws – and the insights it can provide into society. While those with superior strength or military might can enforce their will physically, and those with social or economic clout can use various tools and methods to influence or get their way, those imbued with formal legislative authority – which I define here as one entity's ability to evaluate and propose normative principles for the group – have a special position and can be seen to be both speaking for the group and helping to delineate and define it. Like laws themselves, legislative authority is a formal recognition of power.[18] By granting or accepting an entity's legislative authority, an individual explicitly accepts their definition of the group, places themselves under that power (albeit often in a limited way), and within a group alongside others also bound by that authority's laws. Alternatively, if an individual refuses to accept a legislative authority or attempts to create a new one, that is also illustrative of their view of society. It is, in short, a vitally important expression of community and corporate identity. It can offer at least an indication of the perceived extent, and negotiations of, power at various points in time.

With this in mind, the nature of legislative authority in archaic Rome is incredibly revealing. Most notably, in contrast to the very clear Roman/non-Roman divide that we encounter in the literary narrative, the picture of early Rome's legislative authority which emerges is both complex and arguably contradictory. Our sources suggest that archaic Rome featured a number of 'layers' of legislative authority which functioned concurrently, and indeed seem to have overlapped. For example, within a Roman family the 'word' of the *paterfamilias* was akin to law (the enigmatic *patria potestas*), but in the wider community behaviour was also controlled by laws and edicts issued by a number of different institutions. The Roman *reges* supposedly had legislative powers of some sort, although these were evidently moderated and/or authorised in some way by both the Senate and the *comitia curiata*. And in the early Republic, our sources suggest three distinct assemblies could legislate – the *comitia centuriata*, the *comitia curiata*, and the *comitia tributa* – as well as the boards of the *decemviri* c. 450, in addition to the *consulta* of the Senate and the *edicta* of the magistrates. This is not a simple or straightforward model. Even our late Republican sources were confused about what it all meant.[19]

It must be noted that some of this complexity and confusion is likely a product of the nature of our evidence. Our vision of early Rome's legislative situation comes to us via what was (at best) a cryptic and fragmentary set of early

---

[18] This principle goes back to at least the Enlightenment, and forms much of the basis of modern law. See Waite 1889 for a historical overview. More recently, see Caron (1993), discussing similar principles surrounding the legitimacy and authority of the UN Security Council.

[19] Robinson 1997, 19–58.

inscriptions, interpreted through the cloudy lens of Rome's middle republican 'historical consciousness', and ultimately set down in our surviving late republican sources.[20] Given the centuries which separate the Archaic Period from the first written histories of Rome (let alone our first extant ones), an accurate and detailed picture of early Roman legislative authority was arguably inaccessible for even late republican historians and is undoubtedly beyond us. However, although the evidence for Rome's early laws suffers from many of the same issues as the rest of the narrative, there are some reasons to think it might offer a slightly more reliable data set. Many laws, and most famously the Twelve Tables, were apparently inscribed and posted publicly, with some evidently surviving down into the historical period.[21] Archaic laws often also had strong religious associations, offering further sets of institutions, (pontifical) archives, and traditions which may have preserved them.[22] Furthermore, archaic laws were deployed and continued to resonate, even in the late Republic, in both law courts and the political realm. While this usage obviously would not have stopped laws from being manipulated and reinterpreted, and indeed it may have encouraged it, it suggests that a record of legislation existed which lawyers and jurists were working from. While the details may have been altered and the context assuredly lost, the principle of a law, or at least its basic wording, may have been preserved, provided it was still useful. Rome's early laws therefore represent a data set which arguably had the greatest chance of being 'remembered authentically'. Within the highly problematic collection of evidence relating to Rome's early history, they are on the more reliable end of the spectrum.

Consequently, taking a broad view of the entities involved, some general inferences may well be possible. In particular, the present chapter will suggest that, although complex, the picture of legislative authority visible in the laws, and the spheres of power they seem to indicate, may very well be accurate – at least in their broad outline. Indeed, as will be demonstrated, the picture which emerges from the literature, although complex and seemingly contradictory, actually matches up reasonably well with what the archaeology is increasingly suggesting about the development of the early community. In particular, the evidence for Rome's legislative authority hints at a population which may have been more fluid and diverse than traditionally thought (and suggested by the overt literary narrative) and that the sixth and fifth centuries in particular were an important period of negotiation and tension between groups within the community – particularly among the region's more rural *gentes* and the emerging urban centre of Rome. In this context, each of the legislative authorities visible in the archaic city may be seen to be indicative of a different facet, understanding, or reimagining of Rome's

---

[20] See Oakley (1997, 23) on Rome's 'historical consciousness'.
[21] The laws were quoted from Cicero, Varro, Festus, Gaius, Ulpian, Gellius, Pliny, and others. See Watson (1992, 14–30) and Robinson (1997, 19–40) for discussion.
[22] Watson 1992, 30–8.

archaic community, and their evolving relationships may help to unlock (at least part of) the nature of early Roman society.

3. LEGISLATIVE AUTHORITY IN REGAL ROME

Beginning with the regal period, any discussion of legislative authority must always begin with, or at least account for, the *rex*. The power of the *rex*, as with everything else for the regal period, is uncertain and a tremendously wide range of positions have been argued for. These range from the *rex* having effectively unrestricted power in all matters, as originally argued by Mommsen and more recently by Magdelain, to a more limited military command, as argued by Huess and others.[23] The evidence is so problematic for this period that it is highly unlikely that a definitive answer will ever be possible. This being noted, it is clear that the Romans of the late Republic and early Empire certainly saw the *rex* as a focal point for Roman power and legislative authority, at the very least. Indeed, as discussed by Pomponius (D. 1.2.2.1-3), Tacitus (*Ann.* 3.26), Livy (1.8, 1.26, etc.), and Cicero (*Rep.* 2.14.26; 5.2.3), among others, the laws of the regal period, whether they were formally introduced by the *reges* or not, were traditionally associated with individual *reges* and thought to be backed by, and imbued with, their power. As Dionysius suggested, since the time of Romulus the *rex* was commonly thought to have had 'the guardianship of the laws and customs of the country and the general oversight of justice in all cases, whether founded on the law of nature or the civil law; he was also the judge in person of the greatest crimes, leaving the lesser to the senators, but seeing to it that no error was made in their decisions'.[24]

Despite this association with the *reges*, or indeed perhaps because of it, the true character of the *leges regiae* themselves is hard to identify. While Dionysius records that Servius Tullius sanctioned roughly fifty laws,[25] and a full set of *leges regiae* was supposedly compiled in the reign of Tarquinius Superbus by a certain Papirius (variously called Gaius, Sextus, and Publius), they have only been preserved for us today through citations and asides in the wider narratives of later writers.[26] As a result, although modern scholars (including Dirksen, Riccobono, Girard, and Pugliese, among others) have attempted to assemble them, their definition and listing is far from technical or secure. Most modern lists typically just chronicle each time a *rex* is described as establishing or 'legislating' (taken in the broadest of terms) anything in our sources. Effectively, any act associated with the *reges* could be, and has been, seen as a *lex*. As a result, one cannot reliably separate 'actual laws',[27] which may have been compiled by Papirius, from other less secure aspects of the narrative, including etymologies and even rhetorical inventions.

---

[23] Mommsen 1887; Heuss 1944; Magdelain 1968.
[24] Dion. Hal. *Ant. Rom.* 2.14. Trans. Cary.
[25] Dion. Hal. *Ant. Rom.* 4.13.
[26] A fact commented on by both Livy (6.1) and Gaius Flaccus (D. 50.16.144) in the late Republic.
[27] It must be admitted that even the concept of a *lex* may be anachronistic in a regal context.

This indefiniteness being noted, it is interesting that the focus of almost all of our extant *leges regiae* seems to have been local, and aimed at regulating behaviour and institutions in and around the urban area of Rome. *Leges regiae* explicitly relating to areas outside of the *Pomerium* are rare and often quite problematic.[28] The most notable of these are Numa's laws on landed property and the creation of *pagi*,[29] as well as Servius Tullius' expansion of this system as part of the establishment of the so-called 'Servian Constitution', both of which will be returned to later.[30] Additionally, there is Numa's edict on spoils, although this may relate more to the subsequent dedication than any extramural activity,[31] and Tullus Hostilius' prosecution of deserters, although, again, this may relate more to the institution of the court than the action.[32] Indeed, in general, the preserved *leges regiae* are focused on activity and relationships within the city.[33] And this is in many ways in contrast to the provisions of later laws; for instance, those laws traditionally associated with Table VII of the Twelve Tables on property.

It is not entirely certain how far these laws extended, although it is likely that they were in some way defined by the *Pomerium* (as will be discussed). That being said, evidence does exist for a slightly wider interpretation of Roman territory at least, which extended to between the fourth and sixth milestones: that is, the traditional *ager Romanus Antiquus*.[34] For instance, Strabo (5.3.2) suggests that, from the time of Romulus, Roman territory extended 30 stadia and 'between the fifth and the sixth of those stones which indicate the miles from Rome there is a place called "Festi", and this, it is declared, is a boundary of what was then the Roman territory; and, further, the priests celebrate sacrificial festivals, called "Ambarvia" on the same day, both there and at several other places, as being boundaries'. Alternatively, Ovid (F. 2.679-84) comments on the celebration of the *Terminalia* at the sixth milestone on the Via Laurentina, Livy discussed Coriolanus meeting with his mother at the sanctuary of Fortuna Muliebris at the fourth milestone, and there are various other traditions for boundaries and 'frontier sanctuaries' at roughly this distance.[35] So it is possible that Roman law may have extended this far.

However, as Smith has argued, 'there is a tension between a border and a place of interaction', and it is increasingly likely that this zone between the *Pomerium* and these sanctuaries should be considered, at best, a liminal space – or, as Guzzo argued, part of a negotiation between different productive zones.[36] Indeed, as

---

[28] On the *Pomerium*, see Cornell (1995, 202–4) for general discussion. This discussion does not include treaties, which also seem to have been concluded by the *rex*, but which seem to fall into a different category. See Richardson 2010.
[29] Dion. Hal. *Ant. Rom.* 2.74–76.
[30] Liv, 1.42–43; Dion. 4.13–21; Cic. *Rep.* 2.20.
[31] Fest., L. 189, *opima*; cf. Serv. in Verg. *Aen.* 6, 860; Plut., *Marc.* 8.
[32] Dion. Hal. *Ant. Rom.* 3.30.
[33] See Watson (1972) for more complete discussion.
[34] See Fulminante 2006 and Smith 2017 for discussion.
[35] Bourdin 2012, 429–513.
[36] Guzzo 1987.

Smith concludes in his recent article on the topic, we should 'dispel the notion of some clearly defined archaic entity, the *ager Romanus antiquus*'.[37] Even if it did exist, the sort of uncertainty which seems to have prevailed in this area, as well as its indefiniteness, would have been unhelpful in legal terms. This is particularly true when a much more established and suitable boundary (at least for our extant *leges regiae*) existed in the form of the *Pomerium*, which the evidence is unanimous in considering as a legal division in at least one sphere during this period: the power of the *rex*.

When considering the wider narrative, the focus of regal legislation on the urban community is revealing for many reasons, but particularly for the way it relates to our understanding of regal power. While there is very little agreement on anything related to the *rex*, most will concede that a *rex*'s *imperium* seemed to give him immense power to act for the community outside of the *Pomerium*. This included the expected military authority, but also the ability to make treaties and other facets of what might be called 'foreign policy'.[38] The area outside of the *Pomerium* seems to have been the area where the *rex* exercised his greatest authority. And yet this is the area where he seems to have left the lightest legislative footprint. The extent of a *rex*'s power within the *Pomerium* is more vigorously debated. For instance, Drogula argued that it is unlikely that republican *imperium* existed within the *Pomerium*, except in incredibly specific and highly circumscribed situations, such as with a triumph.[39] It is hard to say whether this holds true for the regal period, although it should give us pause. Additionally, within the *Pomerium* there also existed the *curiae*, Rome's other great, archaic legislative body. Thus the area where the *rex* seems to have been the most legislatively active may have been a contested zone, and indeed, these points may be related.

The archaic *curiae* are arguably just as enigmatic as the *rex*, despite the fact that the *comitia curiata* survived (albeit in a vestigial form) down to at least the late Republic.[40] Despite their largely religious function in later periods, associated with the *lictores* and auspices, the *comitia curiata* seems to have been the major (and indeed only) civic assembly for most of the regal period and was also intimately associated with early Roman law. While it is possible that they merely confirmed the decisions of the *rex*, the *curiae* do seem to have played an at least symbolic role in the passage of *leges*. Indeed, as Watson has argued, Pomponius seemed to blur the perceived line between the *leges regiae* and *leges curiatae*.[41] And while the exact relationship between the archaic *curiae* and the *Pomerium* will likely always remain a mystery, the *curiae* do seem to have been intimately associated with it as well. The site of *Curiae Veteres* was connected to the Palatine *Pomerium* even in

---

[37] Smith 2017, 21–2.
[38] Richardson 2010.
[39] Drogula 2007.
[40] See Palmer 1970, 67–287, Carandini 1997, and Smith 2006, particularly 184–234 and 356–62, for detailed discussion.
[41] Watson 1972, 105.

the imperial period (Tac. *Ann.* 12.24), all of the *curiae* seem to have been inside the limits of the *Pomerium*, the power of the *curiae* outside the *Pomerium* seems to have been non-existent (or at least subsumed with the *imperium* of the *rex*), and – most importantly of all in our present context – the extant *leges curiatae* either relate to the *Pomerium* or activities inside it.[42] Thus, looking at the regal period, Rome's *leges* (both *regiae* and *curiatae*) seem to relate almost entirely to the domestic sphere, within the *Pomerium*, as opposed to the military sphere, outside it. Some of this may relate to their negotiated aspect. *Leges*, as clearly defined and agreed regulations, were not needed outside the *Pomerium*, where the power of the *rex* seems to have reigned supreme. But inside the *Pomerium*, in a contested and negotiated space, formal rules were required. So, in the great conceptualisation of Roman power defined by *domi* and *militiae*, archaic laws and early legislative authority seem to have been circumscribed by the *Pomerium* and within the sphere of the *domus*.[43]

The *Pomerium* was, of course, not necessarily a rigid geographical line, but rather a conceptual one, which divided the *urbs* from the *agri* as well as the spheres *domus* and *militiae*.[44] As such, it seems to have been both a vitally important boundary, and one which was fluid and flexible – although, seemingly, much more definite than that which existed for the wider *ager Romanus*. In the early period the Romans recorded that the *Pomerium* was extended at various times to incorporate more territory, and by the later Republic, when Romans (and indeed even just the inhabitants of Rome) lived well beyond the *Pomerium*, it fundamentally changed its meaning.[45] But throughout the Republic, and particularly in the earliest periods, it seems to have held a strong legislative and religious meaning. As Gellius (*NA* 13.14) noted, the *Pomerium* marked the 'limit of the city auspices' (*finem urbani auspicii*) and also, it seems, the limits of legal authority.

We should also mention, at least in passing, the power of the Senate and the *patresfamiliae*. Although neither entity technically had the power to 'legislate,' in the context of early Rome their authority was seemingly immense in certain spheres. Interestingly though, both the power of the *paterfamilias* and the Senate seems to have been subservient to that of the *rex* and the *curiae* within the *Pomerium*. Many of the *leges regiae* curtail aspects of *patria potestas*, such as those concerning marriage and control of children, which are two of the main traditional facets of this power.[46] The relationship between *patres*, both of the Senate and not, and the *rex* and *curiae* outside of the *Pomerium* is entirely unknown, although power is likely to have operated in a far less institutionalised fashion. Thus, we seem to have two major legislative spheres of authority functioning in Rome,

---

[42] Smith 2006, 202–4.
[43] Koortbojian 2010, 247.
[44] Gell. *NA.* 13.14.1; Varr. *LL.* 5.143; Catalano 1960, 302–3. Cf. Giovannini 1983 and Liou-Gille 1993.
[45] Koortbojian 2010, 247–9.
[46] For instance, Dion. Hal. *Ant. Rom.* 2.19 and 2.25–26.

those of the *rex* and the *curiae*, and several smaller ones, all of which are at least partially defined in relation to the *Pomerium*.

The Rise of the Comitia Tributa

Entering the early Republic, one could argue that, on the surface, much seems to have remained the same. The *comitia curiata* seems to have retained its position as the primary legislative assembly in the community and the magistrates, be they *praetores* or consuls, seem to have taken over the legislative prerogatives of the *rex* by also taking on the power of *imperium*.[47] The Senate and the power of the *patresfamiliae* also seem to have continued to function in negotiation with the magistrates and the *curiae* within their various spheres. While the *comitia tributa* and *comitia centuriata* were both supposedly instituted by Servius Tullius, Rome's sixth *rex*, neither seems to have been particularly active in the early period. Although our sources clearly assume they are in place from the regal period, the first clear actions of the *comitia centuriata* relate to the middle of the fifth century, when they are most notably linked to the creation of the censorship. The *comitia tributa* is also not recorded as being active until the early Republic and only assumes real importance with the Lex Publilia Voleronis de tribunis plebis of 471 (Liv. 2.56–58), which transferred the election of the tribunes of the plebs from the *comitia curiata* to this assembly.

There is the possibility that the *comitia tributa* was active earlier though, and indeed the gradual development of this body in the early Republic may provide some tantalising hints as to the wider currents of change in Rome. Most notably, there is a series of problematic *rogationes* in the record for the 480s: land laws which are associated with either the *comitia tributa* or the *consilium plebis* (there is some confusion on the matter, given that they are often thought to have been synonymous in later periods). These include: in 484 the *Rogatio agraria* (Livy 2.42), in 482 the *Rogatio Licinia agraria* (Livy 2.43), in 481 the *Rogatio Pontificia agraria* (Livy 2.44), in 477 the *Rogatio Fabia agraria* (Livy 2.48), and in 476 the *Rogatio Considia Genucia agraria* (Livy 2.52). None of these legislative attempts seem to have been successful and many scholars discount them as anachronistic and a product of Rome's late republican land debates.[48] While this may in fact be the case, there is no specific reason to doubt their historicity more than any other law, and indeed they make some sense in this period and context, as will be discussed.[49]

---

[47] Livy suggests this explicitly, at least from the perspective of the plebeians, having the tribune Gaius Terentilius Harsa argue 'against the authority of the consuls as excessive and intolerable in a free commonwealth, for whilst in name it was less invidious, in reality it was almost more harsh and oppressive than that of the kings had been, for now, he said, they had two masters instead of one, with uncontrolled, unlimited powers, who, with nothing to curb their license, directed all the threats and penalties of the laws against the plebeians' (Liv. 3.9.3–4, trans. Roberts).

[48] For instance, Beloch 1926 and Ogilvie 1965. See Cornell 1995, 269–71 for discussion.

[49] See De Martino 1979, 15 and Cornell 1995, 270.

While very little can be said for certain about the Servian *tribus*, most scholars agree that they seem to have had geographic associations. The four urban tribes were traditionally associated with the regions of *Suburana*, *Palatina*, *Esquilina*, and *Collina*, while most of the rural tribes seem to have been associated with areas controlled by various *gentes*, based on their gentilicial names.[50] These geographic associations seem to have become blurred by the mid-Republic, with various populations being added to tribes irrespective of where they lived (most notably after 241 when new citizens were simply added to existing *tribus*). However, even as late as the mid-fourth century, with the creation of the tribes of *Pomptina* and *Publilia* in 358 in Volscian territory, and of course the four tribes (*Arniensis*, *Sabatina*, *Stellatina*, and *Tromentina*) created in 387 after the conquest of Veii, there seems to have been a connection between the political entities of the *tribus* and distinct pieces of land – almost all of which (with the notable exception of the four urban tribes) were outside of Rome's *Pomerium*. Thus, the early *tribus* of Rome can be thought to represent, at least roughly, the geographic extent of membership in the Roman community, and this extended far beyond the *Pomerium*.

Returning again to the failed *rogationes* of the 480s and 470s then, what we may have is a tension around what it meant to be 'Roman', at least as it related to law and legislative authority.[51] Rome's traditional legislative body (the *comitia curiata*), and most Roman law, was related to the area and population inside the *Pomerium*. Together they embodied the archaic conception of the Roman community.[52] However, entering the fifth century, such a limited conception of 'Rome' seems to have been no longer appropriate. On the wider, demographic level, from the sixth century Rome seems to have experienced a massive increase in the number of *gentes*, and presumably smaller families, settling permanently in the city's hinterland and seen in the rise of 'villas'.[53] These entities, although evidently choosing to base themselves outside the community for what was likely a wide range of reasons (economic, political, social, etc.), seem to have increasingly focused on Rome as a nexus point for communication and interaction. Indeed, the rising power of some of these newly settled *gentes* may have led to not only the development of Rome's urban landscape during the period, but also the increasing tension between the last Roman *reges* and the local elites in the final decades of the sixth century, and ultimately the introduction of the new 'power-sharing' arrangement which the *res publica* represented c. 509.[54] While the geographically limited *curiae* were unsuited to accommodating this new extramural population,

---

[50] Lintott 1999, 50–1.
[51] The actual concept of *Romanitas* and Roman citizenship may very well be an anachronistic concept to apply to this period, and is almost certainly beyond the limitations of our available evidence.
[52] As Smith noted, 'the *curiae* were taken to represent Rome as it was, an image of the earliest community' (Smith 2006, 233).
[53] See Fulminante 2014 and Terrenato 2001.
[54] See Terrenato 2011, 231–44 and Armstrong 2016, 74–128 for discussion.

the *tribus* and *comitia tributa* may have emerged as a way to organise, formalise, and integrate this new population into a community structure. It represented a regional population which seems to have extended out many miles from Rome, and yet the focal point of the tribal organisation was the community of Rome, as demonstrated by the traditional meeting place of the *comitia* within the *Pomerium* (in contrast to the *comitia centuriata*).

From the somewhat erratic history of the early *comitia tributa*, however, it is likely that this integration was not an entirely smooth process. As noted, if it was indeed created in the sixth century, the *comitia tributa* took a while to initiate any actions, and once it did, it was often initially unsuccessful. So its function, and power, may have been somewhat uncertain. It is also uncertain what membership in the *tribus* entailed. The extent and limits of tribes seem to have been flexible even in later periods, and also contained a strong social element where inclusion depended not only on location but also affiliation. As a result, the *tribus* of Rome may have been a liminal population where the power and identities of the *gentes* and community overlapped. And, of relevance to the present discussion, where legislative authority did not seem to align neatly with socio-political identity. There may have been 'Romans' who were not subject to 'Roman' – or at least curiate – law. Outside the *Pomerium*, the *rex* likely enforced the power of the community through his *imperium*, but in his absence (or neglect) the power of the *paterfamilias* presumably held sway. This liminal zone, represented by the tribes, seems to have sat uneasily between the various legislative spheres.

However, over the course of the first half of the fifth century, things slowly developed, and it seems that the gravitational pull of Rome on the populations of the *tribus*, and the tribes' desire to exert power through a community structure, may have ultimately won out. What may indeed have been instituted in the regal period as an assembly representing the wider population of Rome, both inside and outside of the *Pomerium*, slowly formed a discrete identity. Evidently aligning itself alongside the archaic *curiae* as the representation of the wider community of Rome, defined at least partly geographically (and perhaps ideologically in opposition to the gentilicial elite, or at least their power), the *comitia tributa* slowly assumed the political functions of the *comitia curiata*. Indeed, in addition to the clear signal sent by the *tribus* taking over the election of the tribunes from the *curiae* in 471, we also have the *rogatio Terentilia* of 462 (Liv. 3.9-10), which proposed a panel of five men to write laws which regulated the power of the consuls. This is an extraordinary law, and although it is commonly seen as a precursor to the *decemviri* and the Twelve Tables a decade later,[55] it really lacks a direct parallel given that it seems to represent an attempt to redefine *imperium*, or at least the prerogatives of *imperium*-wielding

---

[55] Urso 2011, 59.

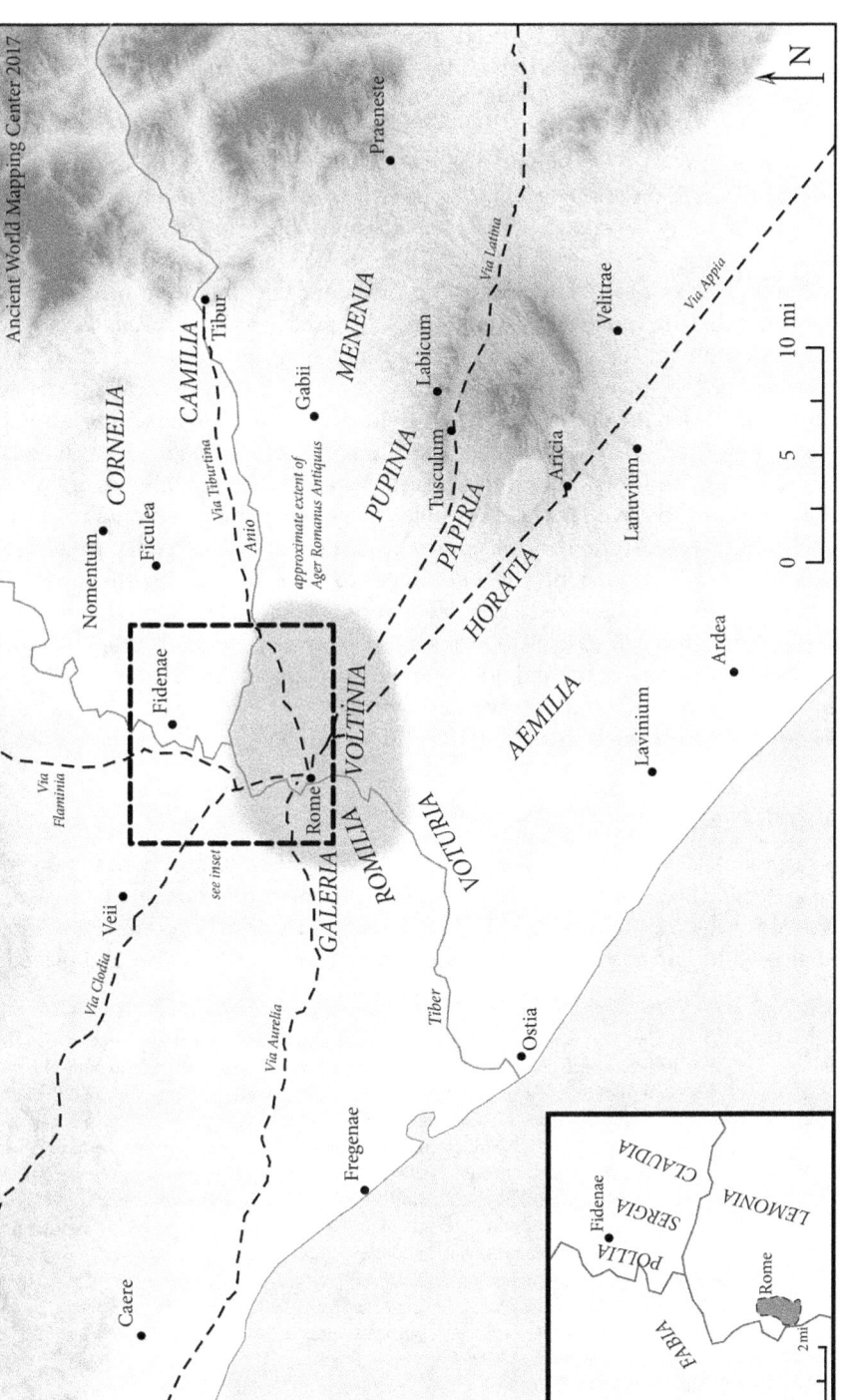

Figure 8.1 Rome's early rural tribes. Source: After Armstrong and Becker (forthcoming). Used with permission.

magistrates.⁵⁶ While it can be read in myriad different ways, one of these is as yet another way in which the *comitia tributa* was assuming the roles normally associated with the *curiae*, this time in mediating the relationship with magistrates.

So returning to the attempted *rogationes* of the 480s and early 470s, these may have represented an initial attempt by the *tribus* to extend the legislative power of the community beyond the *Pomerium*. It is possible that they represented an attempt to align the geographic extent of Rome's emerging population with the geographic extent of the laws, following the principles that seem to have been established by the *comitia tributa*'s immediate predecessor, the *comitia curiata*. Indeed, these *rogationes* represent some of the first measures attempted by a Roman assembly which attempted to do this – the most notable earlier instances being 'laws' which set up *pagi* and *tribus* themselves. But, of course, this attempt to exert power beyond the *Pomerium* was ultimately unsuccessful. And the ways in which the *tribus* were limited, and indeed thwarted, are also interesting. While the *tribus* seem to have had little trouble in assuming the traditional roles and duties of the *curiae* within the *Pomerium*, the vast majority of the attempts to push legislative power outside the *Pomerium* seem to have failed. The radical *rogatio Terentilia* of 462 was defeated, as indeed were later agrarian laws attempted in the 470s and 460s.⁵⁷ If the *comitia tributa* did represent a reimagining of Rome's population, it is clear that it did not have the full support of the local elite, which makes some sense, given that it was attempting to eat into their traditional sovereignty outside of the Roman *Pomerium*.

Shifting boundaries and new identities

As suggested, although a range of other boundaries likely existed, both within and outside of it, the *Pomerium* seems to have represented the most important legal division for the community. Inside the *Pomerium*, the community (as represented initially by the *curiae*) moderated behaviour, mediated interactions, and played a

---

⁵⁶ Livy's (3.9.3–5) wording seems to imply that he viewed this as a legal issue and related to consular edicts, and so possibly relating to consular power within the *Pomerium*. 'For it was only in name, he said, that it was less hateful than that of a king; in reality it was almost crueler, since in place of one master they had now got two, who possessed an unregulated and unlimited power, and while free themselves and without restraint, brought to bear all the terrors of the law and all its punishments upon the plebs. That they might not for ever have this license, he was about to propose a law providing for the appointment of five men to write out the statutes pertaining to the consular power; such authority over them as the people had granted the consuls they should enjoy, but they should not make a law of their own whims and caprices' (*Nomine enim tantum minus invidiosum, re ipsa prope atrocius quam regium esse; quippe duos pro uno dominos acceptos, immoderata, infinita potestate, qui soluti atque effrenati ipsi omnis metus legum omniaque supplicia verterent in plebem. Quae ne aeterna illis licentia sit, legem se promulgaturum ut quinque viri creentur legibus de imperio consulari scribendis; quod populus in se ius dederit, eo consulem usurum; non ipsos libidinem ac licentiam suam pro lege habituros*) (trans. Foster).

⁵⁷ The only real exception being the colonisation of Antium (Liv. 3.1), which is complicated by occurring after warfare and so plausibly falling under the distribution of spoils.

major role in defining laws and social norms. Outside of the *Pomerium*, the voice of the community was muted, if not silent. In the hinterland of Rome, the power of the *paterfamilias* was likely the dominant legal paradigm. Whether it was in control of their own *gentes*, or commanding a community-based military force via a grant of *imperium*, outside of the *Pomerium* the power of the gentilicial leaders was largely unfettered by formal laws and only restrained by custom and social constructs, and perhaps open conflict with other *gentes* or groups.

This being said, the line of the *Pomerium* was unlikely to be absolute or uncontested. Indeed, the power of *imperium* seems to have crossed it in some ways, most notably through the figures of the *lictores*, the institution of the triumph, and likely men and women crossed it every day when going about their lives. Further, we must consider liminal zones, like that of the *forum boarium*, which likely played on their location as both outside Rome's ritual boundary and also a vital part of Roman society. Or indeed, perhaps, the wider *ager Romanus Antiquus*, which may have acted as a wider buffer to the community in various ways. The *Pomerium*, though, seems to have offered an important legal, and obviously ritual, construct which Roman law related to and which offered vitally important limits and definition.

As Roman society developed during the course of the sixth and fifth centuries, this definition of the community was increasingly ill-suited and unable to accommodate Rome's evolving population. With the settling down of *gentes* and other groups in Rome's hinterland, the community's population was no longer easily defined by the *curiae* and the urban area of Rome within the *Pomerium*. Populations and identities were increasingly blurred in the expanding liminal zone around the urban core of Rome. There was now an ever-increasing population outside of the *Pomerium* which associated itself with the community and which, it seems, desired to create a set of agreed laws and norms which applied to it as well. The *tribus*, and the *comitia tributa*, emerged as the entities seemingly best equipped to accomplish this. Like the *curiae* before them, the *tribus* seem to have been largely geographic divisions (although often dominated or identified by a particular *gens* or grouping), and offered a voice to the population residing outside of Rome which may have mirrored the existing community structures within the *Pomerium*. And so, within the literary narrative for the 480s and 470s, we can arguably detect a gradual attempt to shift and expand Rome's legislative authority. During this period, we see an assembly associated with the community attempting to exert legislative control beyond the *Pomerium* for the first time (on its own at least). The emergence of the *comitia tributa* may have therefore been an attempt to reimagine Rome's boundaries and identity to include what was increasingly its *de facto* population, and not just the traditional, archaic core.

It is clear, however, from both the wider narrative of the Struggle of the Orders and later legal developments, that this attempted shift was not successful. Or at least not initially, as it took several centuries for the *comitia tributa* to assume a true position of dominance in Roman politics, and by that time it represented a very different population in a very different social and political context. In the mid-fifth century, the emerging power of the *comitia tributa* was initially thwarted, and then circumvented, by the local aristocracy. Possibly because the power of the *tribus* and *comitia tributa* mirrored the more 'egalitarian' system of the *curiae*, or simply because it attempted to exert some control over traditional gentilicial areas, its rising power is consistently presented (and probably quite rightly) as an attack on aristocratic privilege.[58] The *tribus* and *comitia tributa* offered a new, community-based organisation, identity, and legal structure for a population which had previously been subject to gentilicial control outside the *Pomerium*. Indeed, one could plausibly see the two boards of the *decemviri*, which together represented nineteen of Rome's *gentes*, as an attempt by gentilicial leaders to pre-empt the legislative power-grab of the wider population of the *tribus*. The laws of the Twelve Tables seem to have covered the area of the *tribus*, but were not established by the *comitia tributa*.[59] They therefore may have represented a compromise between the gentilicial elite and this wider, tribal population which gave them the formal legal structure they seem to have desired, while still affirming the authority of the gentilicial elite to grant it. The emergence of the *comitia centuriata* in the 440s, with its socio-economic weighting towards the top of Roman society, could also be seen in this light: as an attempt by Rome's existing elites to control the community's emerging legal and political apparatus (although in this instance, perhaps, weighting things towards the urban elite).

4. CONCLUSIONS

In sum then, although it is incredibly difficult to pinpoint anything for certain in the convoluted evidence for early Rome, in the early development and legal forays of the *comitia tributa* it may be possible to see one of the first instances of Rome's urban identity tentatively extending beyond the confines of the *Pomerium*. And, in so doing, working to redefine all of Roman society in a particular way. Although Rome's *reges* had likely extended Roman power and influence beyond the local area of Rome in the seventh and sixth centuries, 'being Roman' and following Roman law seems to have been more tightly

---

[58] One should not push this 'egalitarianism' too far though. While each vote in the *curiae* was supposed equal, it is still virtually certain that the system was controlled by local elites – through the mechanism of the *curiones* and *curio maximus* (who was supposed to be 'patrician') if not by more subtle socio-political and economic mechanisms. However, it clearly represented a different power dynamic from that which existed within the *gentes*, with different routes to power, which may have been the only threat required.

[59] The initial set of laws in 451 were supposedly ratified by the *comitia centuriata* (Liv. 3.34). This is problematic for a number of reasons, most notably because it seems as if the involvement of the centuries is based on their supposed election of the *decemviri* in the first place, although it is noteworthy that the *comitia tributa* were not involved. The second set of laws are slightly more problematic, as Livy suggests that they may have been published by the command of the tribunes (*sunt qui iussu tribunorum aediles functos eo ministerio scribant*, Liv. 3.57.10), although there is no indication that the *comitia tributa* were involved in their passage or ratification either.

circumscribed. Both archaic Roman identity and Roman law seem to have been oriented, and likely only consistently functioned, within the *Pomerium* of the early city.

In the emergence of the *comitia tributa* and its attempts to control land and legislate beyond the *Pomerium*, we seem to have some of the first clear evidence for the (at least attempted) expansion and redefinition of what it meant to be 'Roman'. In these *rogationes*, there is the implicit assumption that the wider population and territory of the *tribus* are sufficiently cohesive that they could, and possibly should, be regulated corporately by an assembly operating from within the community. As a result, while it is possible, and indeed I would suggest likely, that these early *rogationes* merely represented attempts to align legal authority with the existing social reality on the ground – perhaps protecting some form of 'plebeian' landholding from gentilicial predation, as much as redistribution – the underlying change in the social and legal power structures was revolutionary. This was nothing less than an attempt to redefine the power and identity of both the community and the *gentes* who resided in the *tribus* in a more inclusive manner.

Of equal interest in this discussion is the fact that these measures all seem to have been failures. Although the tribal assembly seems to have been able to assume many of the roles and prerogatives of the *comitia curiata* within the *Pomerium*, it seems to have been consistently blocked by powerful gentilicial leaders when it attempted to push that power into the hinterland. Although they may simply have been attempting to align laws with the existing social and economic situation, the traditional, pre-existing gentilicial power in the *tribus* was not so easily overcome. Indeed, Roman law was seemingly only extended into these regions by what amounted to gentilicial decree and agreement through the powerful family leaders who made up the two boards of the *decemviri* which promulgated the Twelve Tables.

In this tension between the evolving population associated with the urban centre of Rome and the traditional, gentilicial leadership, we can also arguably see the seeds of Rome's later expansion and her republican government. In the early *tribus* and their attempts to establish the power of community over an ever-larger population and geographical expanse, we have the beginnings of a new conception of political and legal identity which was infinitely expandable. And indeed, when Rome did begin to expand territorially in the fourth century, it is noteworthy that she did this through the mechanism of the *tribus* – despite the tensions which existed between the elites and this structure. The *tribus* and *comitia tributa*, from a very early date then, seem to have offered the Romans a conceptual framework for the community which was suited for incorporating new groups and individuals. The Roman *tribus*, perhaps even more than the *populi Romani*, gave a name, identity, and structure to corporate (and expansionist) Rome.

But this framework was not without problems, as its fundamental organisation and power dynamic seems to have put it in opposition to the interests of

Rome's elite families.[60] Although it is entirely possible that some of the tension we have seen around the tribal assembly is the result of anachronistic elaboration/fabrication by our later sources, given what we know about the *tribus* it is not unthinkable that it is authentic. With its more inclusive and egalitarian principles, it was, almost by nature, always in tension with the traditional, conservative, more hierarchical gentilicial power dynamic in the region. Thus, even in the muddled narrative of early Rome and a series of failed *rogationes*, we may actually detect resonances of Polybius' emphasis on Rome's mixed constitution at the core of her expansionist success. Although Rome's expansion may have been led by powerful, elite generals, in many ways it was secured through the easily expanded, egalitarian structure of the *tribus*. Rome's great success, as Polybius notes, was in how the community balanced these opposing forces.

Works Cited

Alföldi, A, 1962. 'Ager Romanus Antiquus.' *Hermes* 90:187–213.
Ampolo, C et al., eds, 1980. *La formazione della città nel Lazio. Seminario tenuto a Roma, 24–26 giugno 1977.* DdA ns 2. Rome: Alphaprint.
Armstrong, J, 2016. *War and Society in Early Rome: From Warlords to Generals.* Cambridge: Cambridge University Press.
Armstrong, J and J Becker, forthcoming. *The Archaeology of Archaic Central Italy.* Oxford: Oxford University Press.
Armstrong, J and J H Richardson, 2017. 'Authors, Archaeology, and Arguments: Evidence and Models for Early Roman Politics.' *Antichthon* 51:1–20.
Beloch, J, 1926. *Romische Geschichte bis zum Beginn der punischen Kriege.* Berlin: De Gruyter.
Benelli, E, 2017. 'Problems in Identifying Central Italic Ethnic Groups.' In *The Peoples of Ancient Italy*, edited by G Farney and G Bradley, 89–104. Berlin: De Gruyter.
Bourdin, S, 2012. *Les Peuples de l'Italie préromaine: identités, territoires et relations inter-ethniques en Italie Centrale et Septentrionale (VIIIe–Ier S.av. J.-C.).* BÉFAR 350. Rome: École française de Rome.
Brunt, P A, 1971. *Italian Manpower, 225 BC–AD 14.* Oxford: Oxford University Press.
Carandini, A, 1997. *La nascita di Roma: Dei, lari, eroi, uomini all'alba di una civilta.* Turin: Einaudi.
Catalano, P, 1960. *Contributi allo studio del diritto augurale.* Turin: G. Giappichelli.
Cornell, T J, 1995. *The Beginnings of Rome: Italy and Rome from the Bronze Age to the Punic Wars (c. 1000–264 BC).* London: Routledge.

---

[60] It is therefore, perhaps, not surprising that the Romans seem to have twinned the tribal assembly with the hierarchical and timocratic centuriate assembly, likely as both a check on this character and a reinforcement of its power.

———, 2005. 'The Value of the Literary Tradition Concerning Archaic Rome.' In *Social Struggles in Archaic Rome: New Perspectives on the Conflict of the Orders*, edited by K A Raaflaub, 47–74. 2nd edn. Malden, MA: Blackwell.
De Martino, F, 1979. *Diritto e societa nell'antica Roma*. Rome: Editori Riuniti.
Drogula, F, 2007. '*Imperium*, *potestas*, and the *pomerium* in the Roman Republic.' *Historia* 56:419–52.
———, 2015. *Commanders and Command in the Roman Republic and Early Empire*. Chapel Hill: University of North Carolina Press.
Elden, S, 2013. *The Birth of Territory*. Chicago: University of Chicago Press.
Fulminante, F, 2006. 'The *ager Romanus antiquus*: Defining the Most Ancient Territory of Rome with a Theoretical Approach.' In *Studi di Protostoria in onore di Renato Peroni*, 513–20. Florence: All'Insegna dell Giglio.
———, 2014. *The Urbanisation of Rome and Latium Vetus: From the Bronze Age to the Archaic Era*. Cambridge: Cambridge University Press.
Giovannini, A, 1983. *Consulare imperium*. Basel: F. Reinhardt.
Hopkins, J, 2016. *The Genesis of Roman Architecture*. New Haven: Yale University Press.
Heuss, A, 1944. 'Zur Entwicklung des Imperiums des romischer Oberbeamter.' *ZSav* 64:57–133.
Koortbojian, M, 2010. 'Crossing the *Pomerium*: The Armed Ruler at Rome.' In *The Emperor and Rome: Space, Representation, and Ritual*, edited by B Ewald and C Norena, 247–74. Cambridge: Cambridge University Press.
Lintott, A, 1999. *The Constitution of the Roman Republic*. Oxford: Oxford University Press.
Liou-Gille, B, 1993. 'Le pomerium.' *MusHelv* 50:94–106.
Magdelain, A, 1968. *Recherches sur l'imperium*. Paris: Presses universitaires de France.
Mommsen, T, 1887. *Romisches Staatsrecht*. 3 vols. 3rd edn. Leipzig.
Oakley, S, 1997. *Commentary on Livy Books VI–X, I: Introduction and Book VI*. Oxford: Oxford University Press.
Ogilvie, R M, 1965. *A Commentary on Livy Books I–V*. Oxford: Oxford University Press.
Palmer, R E A, 1970. *The Archaic Community of the Romans*. Cambridge: Cambridge University Press.
Raaflaub, K A, 2005. 'From Protection and Defense to Offense and Participation: Stages in the Conflict of the Orders.' In *Social Struggles in Archaic Rome: New Perspectives on the Conflict of the Orders*, edited by K A Raaflaub, 47–74. 2nd edn. Malden, MA: Blackwell.
Rich, J, 2018. 'Fabius Pictor, Ennius and the Origins of Roman Annalistic Historiography.' In *Omnium Annalium Monumenta: Historical Writing and Historical Evidence in Republican Rome*, edited by K Sandberg and C Smith, 15–65. Leiden: Brill.
Richardson, J, 1991. '*Imperium Romanum*: Empire and the Language of Power.' *JRS* 81:1–9.

———, 2010. 'The Oath *per Iovem lapidem* and the Community in Archaic Rome.' *Rheinisches Museum für Philologie* 153:25–42.

Robinson, O, 1997. *The Sources of Roman Law: Problems and Methods for Ancient Historians*. London: Routledge.

Sandberg, K and C Smith. 2018. Omnium Annalium Monumenta: *Historical Writing and Historical Evidence in Republican Rome*. Leiden: Brill.

Smith, C, 2006. *The Roman Clan: The Gens from Ancient Ideology to Modern Anthropology*. Cambridge: Cambridge University Press.

———, 2017. 'Ager Romanus Antiquus.' *ArchCl* 68:1–26.

Solin, H, 1999. 'Epigrafia repubblicana. Bilancio, Novità, prospettive.' In *XI Congresso Internazionale di Epigrafia Greca e Latina. Roma, 18–24 settembre 1997*, 1:379–404. Rome: Quasar.

Terrenato, N, 2001. 'The Auditorium Site in Rome and the Origins of the Villa.' *JRA* 14:5–32.

———, 2011. 'The Versatile Clans: Archaic Rome and the Nature of Early City-States in Central Italy.' In *State Formation in Italy and Greece: Questioning the Neoevolutionist Paradigm*, edited by N Terrenato and D Haggis, 231–44. Oxford: Oxbow.

Urso, G, 2011. 'The Origin of the Consulship in Cassius Dio's Roman History.' In *Consuls and* Res Publica: *Holding High Office in the Roman Republic*, edited by H Beck, A Duplá, M Jehne, and F Pina Polo, 41–60. Cambridge: Cambridge University Press.

Watson, A, 1972. 'Roman Private Law and the *Leges Regiae*.' *JRS* 62:100–5.

Wiseman, T P, 1995. *Remus: A Roman Myth*. Cambridge: Cambridge University Press.

Part III

Roman Law in Historiography and Theory

Chapter 9

Niebuhr and Bachofen: New Forms of Evidence on Roman History[1]

Luigi Capogrossi Colognesi

When Barthold Georg Niebuhr was appointed ambassador by the King of Prussia to the papal court in Rome in 1816, in charge of negotiating a new Concordat with the Holy See, he was already a prominent figure, both politically and culturally. Not only had he served in the upper reaches of the Prussian administration, but he was also a member of the Prussian Academy of Sciences and was at the centre of intellectual life in Berlin, now the German cultural capital. Here he had formed a dense network of relationships, which included, among other luminaries, Savigny and Schlachermeyer, who in those years had played an important role in the establishment of the Prussian capital's new university. Indeed, starting in 1810, Niebuhr had given a series of lectures on Roman history at the University of Berlin, and these formed the basis for the first two volumes of his *History of Rome*, published between 1811 and 1812. The importance of his relationship with Savigny, and with the world of German philologists more generally, became especially evident when he travelled to Rome in 1816 to assume his new post.[2] This proved to be a fortunate journey, because during a stop in Verona, Niebuhr discovered a manuscript of Gaius' *Institutiones* in his visit to the cathedral library. Despite not having the time to realise fully its significance, he immediately informed Savigny of his discovery.[3] It was an epochal event in the history of Roman law, a field in which Savigny was recognised as indisputably the highest European authority.

---

[1] Translated from Italian by Laura Kopp.
[2] We can find Niebuhr's personal acknowledgement of the importance of his relationship with Savigny (together with Buttmann and Heindorff) at the start of his *Geschichte*. He writes that, without their help, he 'certainly never would have had the courage to undertake this work' (Niebuhr 1811, xiv; 1837, xiv). But on his scholarly cooperation with Savigny in his research on the Roman *ager publicus* and its relationship with the origin of the interdict *Uti possidetis*, see Niebuhr 1827, 172 (=Niebuhr 1838, 152). Cf. Bonacina 1991, 31–3.
[3] The first announcement of that discovery was in his letter from Venice dated September 4: cf. Niebuhr 1839, 237 (=Niebuhr 1852, 319).

In contrast to this auspicious start, Niebuhr's time in Rome turned out to be far from pleasant: to the objective difficulty of his mission[4] must be added the bad weather and the terrible conditions in which he found the city, made all the worse by the papal government's poor administration. Niebuhr's letters from Rome dwelled repeatedly on these aspects, allowing us to grasp, albeit indirectly, how utterly alien he found papal Rome's 'spiritual environment' – to use perhaps too charitable a term for the city's degradation – but also how little he shared those visions of Rome's greatness that the city still evoked for the elite travellers who almost always made it the final stop on their Grand Tour. Furthermore, for this tireless and often lucky explorer of libraries, the attractiveness of a city that housed vast quantities of ancient manuscripts was tempered by the poor working conditions he had to endure and by his mistrust of the curators of these collections, foremost among them Cardinal Angelo Mai himself, the Vatican's chief librarian.

What is even more striking in reading the letters, however, is how unmoved Niebuhr was by the extraordinary wealth of archaeological evidence of Rome's ancient past that surrounded him on all sides. It sheds light on the peculiar nature of his interest in the history of Rome, which seemed to privilege its two endpoints: the origins, on the one hand, and the later centuries, on the other.[5] We need only recall, in this regard, that the completed part of his masterpiece did not go beyond the first Punic War, stopping before the great watershed moment of Rome's defeat of Hannibal and its expansion to the East.

Niebuhr was, in fact, principally interested in Rome's early history, in the struggle between patricians and plebeians over land distribution, a struggle waged in a rural context that would endure throughout the Republic. If, before his lectures in Berlin, he had planned to draw up a 'treatise on Roman Domains',[6] in the lectures themselves he later concentrated on the 'primitive state of Italy, and . . . the ancient races, not only from the narrow point of view of their subjugation, but also as they were in themselves, and as they had been in their earlier stages'.[7] What drew him

---

[4] The new Concordat was intended to address the ecclesiastical situation of the new German territories (whose population was Catholic) that Prussia had acquired after the Congress of Vienna. Niebuhr's difficulties stemmed from the fact that he lacked political guidance from his sovereign to orient him in the negotiations with the Roman authorities.

[5] Letter to Savigny, 17 October 1816, in Niebuhr 1852, 326–7 (= Niebuhr, 1939, 249–51): 'The aspect of Florence and Venice appeared to me grand and pleasing; in both the images and the monuments of the times of their greatness still remain visible and tangible. Venice has been the greatest thing I have ever seen, Rome has no right to its name, at most it should be called "New Rome" (as New York).' But his lack of admiration also extended to the remains of Roman times: 'the ruins all date from the times of the Emperors, and he who can get up an enthusiasm about them must at least rank together Martial with Sophocles'. He sadly concludes: 'this, then, is the place and the country in which my life is to be passed!', for which 'it is only a poor amends that I can get from libraries, and yet my only hope is from the Vatican [Library]'. In fact, he was to discover that the Vatican Library was closed until 5 November, and for all the other 'innumerable Catholic festivals', and open 'only three days a week', and then only for three hours each day.

[6] Niebuhr 1852, 210.

[7] Letter to Madame Hensler, 1 September 1810, quoted in Niebuhr 1852, 213.

to Rome's origins and to the world of farmers so typical of the early history of Rome and of Italy more generally, was the deep structure of his personality, formed in direct contact with the rural lands of the Danish provinces, governed by a strict Protestant ethic that left a lasting mark on his character. It is hardly surprising, therefore, that he should have felt little affinity for the reality he found in Rome, where the pomp of the Catholic Church contrasted strangely with the miserable condition of a brutalised people subjected to the heaviest police repression.[8]

Niebuhr had little appreciation for the marble ruins of Imperial Rome, or the traces of a great past now reduced to humiliating decadence – things that have inspired, then as now, so many foreign visitors' scientific interest or moralising reflections. What interested Niebuhr most were the traces of ancient life that could be found primarily outside of Rome. In his letters we find numerous references to his stays in Tivoli, Albano, Frascati, or at Genzano, and even as far as Terni.[9] Of course, conditions were no better there than in Rome, owing to the climate and the threat of fevers in summer, along with the pervasive presence of 'banditti' (sic), which forced visitors to seek shelter behind the towns' walls. But that is where his real interests lay: in the remains of ancient dwellings; the traces of ancient land divisions that might shed light on the origins of private land ownership; the survival of agricultural practices dating back to the Romans;[10] and the Cyclopean stone walls that defended archaic cities. This interest was imbued with

---

[8] His letters are full of references to the wretched living conditions and the *sauvagerie* of Rome's population, and also reveal his lack of aesthetic interest in the city, including its splendid Renaissance and Baroque past. Cf. Eyssenhardt 1886, 201–4.

[9] However, the threat of bandits was such that he was prevented from travelling even to Palestrina or Cori, as he wrote to Nicolovius in a letter of 22 January 1817: Niebuhr 1852, 339 (=Niebuhr 1839, 274), and had to remain within the secure perimeter of the walls of Frascati or Albano, as he told D Hensler in a letter of 7 February 1817: Niebuhr 1852, 340 (=Niebuhr 1839, 281). In addition, Rome's terrible summer climate inevitably drove him to flee to the Castelli, but not before September – at least in 1818, according to his letters to D Hensler of 1 September of that year, and to Savigny of 1 October: Niebuhr 1852, 372, 373 (=Niebuhr 1839, 375, 384). Especially in his letter to Savigny, there is an important reference to the habit of the Roman nobility, and of those bourgeois who could afford it, of leaving for the Castelli only towards the end of the summer, for the months of September and October, a fact confirmed just a few years later by Massimo d'Azeglio in his memoirs. Because of this, 'it is a very expensive affair to stay in the country during October, for all who have contrived to remain in Rome during the unhealthy months when you are condemned to utter idleness by the heat and the weight of the air, spread into the country as soon as the atmosphere begins to cool and the vegetation to revive'.

[10] Letter to Savigny, 17 October 1816, in Niebuhr 1852, 327: 'Of living antiquities I can expect none at Rome, as all estates are "latifundia" without peasants. At Terni I found the old art of land surveying still extant; I rode along what was probably an ancient "limes", found the "rigor" and the "V pedes", and the coals and bricks under the "termini". Unfortunately there was no "acclimensore" in the town (as the people now call the occupation)', while there are at least 'fifty houses in the town ... from the Roman times', and 'several of the churches are Roman private houses'. He enthusiastically concludes, 'everything is ancient in Terni and its neighbourhood, even the mode of preparing the wine'. Cf. also Niebuhr 1838, 636: the modern scholar, in Italy, he suggests 'should go into the country: he should diligently observe and study to understand the slightest particularities: everything is a relic in this sacred ground.'

a deeply romantic sense of the continuity of the present with a past that was to be recovered with loving patience – an interest he would continue to pursue in the years to come, well beyond this first deeply moving journey, and which would lead him to new and sometimes unexpected discoveries.

In the letters written during his repeated stays in the Castelli Romani, he expresses the conviction that, beneath the squalor and the abject poverty of a population oppressed by the great landowners of the Roman aristocracy and squeezed by moneylenders, could still be found evidence not only of the ancient virtue of the Quirites, but also of the Romans' actual use of the land.[11] And this is why he strove to glean, from the agricultural practices and landholding structure of the Lazio of his day, an original structural core dating back to ancient Rome.[12] The links between the past and the present that he had already drawn in his Berlin lectures and in the first edition of his *History* thus became all the more significant. This is forcefully reiterated in a fascinating appendix to the second volume of the *History* published in 1812, well before he first travelled to Italy. Here he had already proposed the idea that in those lands and in Lazio was still hidden a trace of the first land divisions dating from the earliest history of Rome.[13]

Most importantly, however, in this appendix the great German historian called attention to the pressing need for a critical edition of the writings of the Roman surveyors, to establish a better foundation of knowledge than that offered by the two old and unsatisfactory editions of Rigault and van der Goes then in use, in addition to the *editio princeps* by Turnebe.[14] This appeal, in effect, broke a silence that demonstrated the near total lack of interest in these writings on the part of philologists and historians since the mid-seventeenth century.[15] Niebuhr's call seemed all the more authoritative as it arose from a deep appreciation of the value of such evidence for gaining a proper understanding of the Romans' methods of land organisation, together with their legal and practical implications.[16] And it was all the more significant given the total stagnation of such studies that

---

[11] Cf. the letter to D Hensler of 21 May 1819, in Niebuhr 1852, 378 (=Niebuhr 1839, 398): 'if one could penetrate further into the retreats of the agricultural population! It is only among them that any addition to our knowledge of antiquity could be obtained.'

[12] Niebuhr makes this point explicitly and often in his correspondence: cf. the letter to D Hensler of 1 September 1818, in Niebuhr 1852, 373 (=Niebuhr 1839, 375), where, in preparation for his trip to Genzano, he wrote: 'in the country I shall occupy myself with agriculture, in order fully to understand that of the Romans'.

[13] In Capogrossi Colognesi 1997, 403–8; 2008, 45–8. There I discuss how this hypothesis seems to anticipate the discovery of traces of centuriation in the Italian peninsula that took place in the second half of the nineteenth century, a discovery whose central importance grew even more apparent in the course of the twentieth century.

[14] Toneatto 1994, 64–75.

[15] Toneatto 1994, 74.

[16] Niebuhr 1830, 538–62. These pages formed part of an 'Appendix über die Agrimensoren' (Niebuhr 1830, 532–62) that the author omitted from the second edition of the second volume of his *Geschichte*, published in 1830. Only the first part of it – thus excluding the one I mentioned above – was included in the English translation of the work: cf. Niebuhr 1838, 634–44.

followed after the sixteenth century, in stark contrast therefore with the humanistic fervour that had accompanied the rediscovery and editing of these manuscripts. Niebuhr's remarks were informed by an understanding equal to his knowledge, evident on every page (and in his extensive use of the gromatic texts throughout the volume), of the difficult diplomatic and philological problems that this manuscript tradition posed for his contemporaries – and for us as well.

Niebuhr concluded with a passionate appeal which sought 'to excite others to take the same interest' in this documentation, hoping that it 'could excite some philological scholar possessing the spirit of our age, along with the learning and the industry of the French school of the sixteenth century, to devote them to these venerable ruins, so interesting from the recollections they awaken, and even in the disfigured state in which we find them!'.[17] We know this plea was heeded, since as early as the next edition of this second volume of the *History*, Niebuhr omitted the appendix on the Gromatici, considering it outdated in view of the results his 'friend' Blume was already obtaining from his research on the land surveyors' manuscripts.[18]

A remarkable genealogy of knowledge was thus taking shape, which linked the great historian of the origins of Rome to the first generation of philologists who began to transform and broaden our understanding of the ancient world. It would be many years before Niebuhr's aspirations were fulfilled, however, and by then he was unfortunately no longer present to witness the event. For it was not until 1848 that the great critical edition of the Gromatici was published, giving a powerful impetus to scholarship through to the end of the century. It was compiled by Blume (the scholar who, a few years earlier, had helped to decipher the Verona Gaius) together with Lachmann and Rudorff.[19] And Blume himself, at the start of his extensive essay on the land surveyors' manuscript tradition, repeatedly cited the pages written by Niebuhr forty years earlier, not as a mere homage to one whose stature had grown immeasurably in the memory of his contemporaries, but as confirmation of the joint project that united these historians in an extraordinary process of knowledge-gathering.[20]

Equally important, if less obvious, was another element of continuity, relating to geography. Here Niebuhr's insights would both be confirmed and to some extent disproved, in a more specifically Italian context, by topographic discoveries that, in the second half of the nineteenth century, started to find traces of the ancient *limites* in geographical areas different from those Niebuhr had identified as offering the likeliest sites for their survival. The plan had already been outlined perfectly in 1812: the historian, whom Niebuhr ideally addressed, should employ not only the techniques of modern philology to publish the land surveyors' writings. He also 'should go into the country: he should diligently observe and study to

---

[17] Niebuhr 1838, 641.
[18] Niebuhr 1830, 694 n. 1.
[19] Blume, Lachmann, and Rudorff 1848.
[20] Blume 1852, 3.

understand the slightest particularities: everything is a relic on the sacred ground: in some place or other he will find a key to those difficulties, which we . . . should vainly exercise our ingenuity in solving.'[21]

Here we see Niebuhr already describing the kind of detailed investigation of the territory he would later seek to put into practice in his explorations of the Lazio countryside. The romantic sensibility that permeates this plan is unmistakable, given the continuous line it draws between the past and the present. But equally undeniable is its modernity, insofar as it broadens the research interests of the historian of antiquity. Not only did it move beyond the traditional confines of contemporary scholarship, still largely reliant on literary sources, by recovering technical texts, such as the land surveyors' writings, that had been almost totally neglected. It also insisted that such new sources of information be directly confirmed and complemented by the knowledge and interpretation of physical evidence: whether this be the ancient monuments, long the subject of mere antiquarian curiosity or aesthetic appreciation, or the land itself, now conceived as a historical document in its own right. This is exactly what historians and scholars of topography began to pursue in the second half of the nineteenth century, studying the traces of ancient *limites* in the modern maps of northern and central Italy. These were the first steps of a new science, and can be considered a development of Niebuhr's original intuition.

Nor were there any geographical boundaries to the daring juxtapositions Niebuhr sometimes resorted to in his attempt to find evidence from the present for the reconstruction of ancient history. We might recall how, to illustrate a central point of his interpretation of early Roman history, he unhesitatingly referred to contemporary India's land system to clarify the nature of the forms of exploitation and appropriation of public lands in ancient Rome.[22]

Not all of Niebuhr's explorations have stood the test of time. But there is no question that by casting such a wide net, he made possible the great efflorescence of scholarship that resulted once the various branches of knowledge that he had pursued simultaneously were separated and developed individually. A new foundation for historical studies had been established, allowing the study of the ancient world to reach a level, in nineteenth-century Germany, that has perhaps never been surpassed.

About twenty years after Niebuhr's post as ambassador to the Holy See had ended, and he had left Rome and Italy, the 27-year-old Jakob Bachofen began his own *Italienische Reise*, in 1842. The previous year, having completed his university studies in Germany, and obtained a doctorate in Roman law under the supervision of Savigny, Bachofen had been awarded a professorship in Roman law at the University of Basel. But he did not hold the position for long: within three years, he left first the professorship, then all university teaching, to retire to a life of

---

[21] Niebuhr 1852, 642.
[22] On these points, see Momigliano 1980 (also published as Momigliano 1984, 155–67).

independent study.[23] At that time[24] Bachofen had already begun to publish his most important works on Roman law, which would assure him unquestioned scientific and academic respectability.[25] A respectability that would be equally short-lived, however, as he soon embarked on a new intellectual adventure epitomised by those works of his maturity that brought him fame, and which continue to be most interesting to us today.

We are, of course, referring to Bachofen's *Mutterrecht*, which for the first time in European culture put forward the hypothesis of a different organisational structure of ancient societies, one based on matriarchy, which would have preceded the patriarchal system so central to scholarly debates about the origins of civil society since the eighteenth century. It is also well known how his first public lectures,[26] and then the publication of his most important works – the *Gräbersymbolik*, followed by *Mutterrecht* and *Das Lykische Volk*, between 1859 and 1862[27] – caused such bewilderment among German and European scholars as to lead, from the late 1850s, to his total isolation from the scholarly community.[28]

We will not follow these developments further, to avoid straying too far from the subject at hand. For rather than attempting to delineate the complete intellectual history of these two scholars, we should in a more limited way try to grasp their specific contributions—so different, if not diametrically opposed—to the innovative use of ancient sources and the development of new interpretative

---

[23] At the University of Berlin he had attended, among others, the lectures of Boeckh, Ranke, Rudorff and Lachmann, while Savigny's teachings confirmed his vocation to study Roman law; later, in Göttingen, he attended the courses of Gustav Hugo and Carl O Müller. After receiving his doctorate in 1838, he travelled to England and then to France, spending two years familiarising himself with those widely divergent legal systems. In 1841 he finally became Professor of Roman law at the University of Basel, a position from which he resigned almost immediately in response to political opposition to his appointment and a curtailment of his teaching. In 1843 he ceased teaching at the university altogether, and also declined offers from other universities. See the still valuable biography by Meuli (in Bachofen 1948, 3: 1024–46), and the excellent research of Garré (1999, 13–51).

[24] The journey to Italy, begun in September 1842, ended in the spring of the following year. Bachofen visited Turin and Pisa, and also travelled to Naples, Campania, and even Sicily. But, of course, most of his time was spent in Rome: cf. Meuli in Bachofen 1948, 1058–63.

[25] I am referring principally to Bachofen 1843a on a key mechanism in Roman law, especially as regards the status of women, and which had garnered the appreciation of Mommsen (1907, 513–19), as well as to Bachofen 1843b. Finally, 1847 saw the publication of Bachofen 1847, his last work that still adhered to the 'orthodox' Roman scholarly tradition. Cf. Momigliano 1988, now in Momigliano 1992, 103.

[26] In 1856, at the annual congress of German philologists held in Stuttgart, Bachofen delivered a lecture on 'the nature of the rights of women' which anticipated the first part of the *Mutterrecht*, and which was received with interest by the audience, rather than the hostility he would later encounter.

[27] The first to be published was Bachofen 1859, now in Bachofen 1954; next came *Das Mutterrecht. Eine Untersuchung über die Gynaikokratie der alten Welt nach ihrer religiösen und rechtlichen Natur* (now in Bachofen 1948) in 1861, followed by Bachofen 1862.

[28] Jesi 1988 aptly compares the work to 'a brick thrown by a child or a half-wit into a gathering of scholars' and which, after a moment of perplexity, is quickly removed and forgotten.

methods that began to be applied to the study of the history of ancient Rome and the Italian world in the first half of the nineteenth century.

We know that as a result of his first trip to Italy and then a second one, in 1848–9, Bachofen's attitude towards the ancient world changed radically. He modified the 'predominantly esthetic basis' of Winckelmann's view of classical antiquity into a 'predominantly religious one',[29] without however losing sight of the central importance of the world of images that the archaeological evidence gave access to. Indeed, as he would later write, it was 'the discovery of the graves of Rome and of the Roman Campagna or Etruria' that transformed Bachofen's outlook.[30] He discusses this in his autobiography, written at Savigny's suggestion and sent to him a few years later as a letter.[31] Its importance cannot be overstated, given the detailed information he provides that allows us to reconstruct the overall intellectual journey of its author, particularly between the late 1840s and his even more momentous trip to Greece, begun in March 1851 and concluded over a year later, after another stop in Italy.

It has often been remarked that, just when this autobiography seemed to confirm the closeness of the ties linking Bachofen to Savigny, it simultaneously marked the definitive distancing of the forty-year-old scholar from the path traced by the great Berlin professor. Indeed, until the mid-1840s Bachofen had adhered to the scholarly precepts established by Savigny, as witnessed by his vigorous affirmation of them in his inaugural address at the University of Basel,[32] and his later works on Roman law, with their remarkable scientific rigour and high quality of research. But one might suspect that, already at that time, the young Bachofen was decidedly at variance with that substantial group of scholars of Roman law – although inspired by Savigny and belonging to the 'Historical School' – who subordinated disinterested historical investigation to contemporary concerns. For we must not forget that a fair number of German-language Romanists were especially intent on deriving from the study of Roman legal forms a body of concepts and categories applicable to contemporary society.

Bachofen argued against this practical application of the study of Roman law in his autobiographical letter to Savigny, citing as his authority Savigny himself, and thus without realising, or, more likely, pretending not to realise, that the approach he criticised had been initiated and sanctioned by his professor. Furthermore, when in another passage Bachofen described legal historiography as a mere

---

[29] Gossman 1983, 21.
[30] Momigliano 1992, 775.
[31] Bachofen 1916, 358: 'In my wanderings through Italy's museums, my attention was quickly drawn to one aspect of those immense treasures: funerary art ... The ancient tombs have disclosed to us an almost inexhaustible treasure-trove. We may at first consider the study of tombs a specialist branch of archaeology; but we ultimately find ourselves at *the heart of a veritable universal doctrine*' ('in mitten einer wahren Universaldoctrin': the italics are mine).
[32] Bachofen 1841.

branch of philology – which he identified, *tout court*, with *Altertumwissenschaft* – he was only outwardly respectful of the historicist approach established by the great historian. In fact, his position rejected at its very roots Savigny's assertion of the primacy of Roman law, and its ambivalent relevance both to *Altertumwissenschaft* and to German legal science and its practical outlook. In truth, well before 1854, when he wrote his autobiographical letter to Savigny, Bachofen had started on his own, solitary journey.[33]

We can see the first signs of this shift in the two essays he wrote in the early 1850s, one addressing current political upheavals, including in the Papal states,[34] and the other, undoubtedly more significant, consisting of his contribution to the *History of Rome* – a larger project undertaken together with his old professor, Gerlach, that was published in 1850–1. Both texts assume that the foundation of a state's sovereignty lies not in the will of the people but in divine authority.[35] This was about as far as one could get from the political and institutional principles of modern states or from the rational underpinnings of historical-legal studies and classical philology.

Even more important, however, are the further developments of his intellectual shift in those years, since he was also distancing himself from the rigorous philological foundations and attention to textual evidence and 'facts' that, ever since Niebuhr, had undergirded the work of German historians. Indeed, while expressing his sincere admiration for him, Bachofen dismissed Niebuhr's critical method, claiming that 'Livy, Cicero and Dionysius knew much more about the character and history of their people than did Niebuhr'.[36] Based on these premises, in his later works he went so far as to make use of all kinds of ancient sources – indiscriminately and 'uncritically', by the scholarly standards of the time – to create indisputable historical events out of the most ancient tales, from Evander to the coming of Aeneas from Troy and his founding of Lavinium, to Amulius and Numitor.

Though so far removed from Niebuhr intellectually and methodologically, there remained a consonance, however, if we recall the Prussian ambassador's wanderings in the hills and towns surrounding Rome in search of the traces of ancient history. For it was in much the same spirit that Bachofen contemplated the desolate Campagna and the ruins of the distant past scattered over the landscape. As Momigliano has noted, no other historian of the time expressed 'such

---

[33] However, it would be quite wrong to assume that Bachofen's lengthy epistle was poorly received by Savigny. On the contrary, in thanking him for the letter, Savigny encouraged Bachofen to publish it: cf. his letter to Savigny of 18 May 1855, in Bachofen 1967, 142. See Arrigoni 1988.

[34] Cf. Bachofen 1850: a 'not very compelling work, but a striking demonstration of his reactionary ideas', as accurately noted by Cesana 1988, 96. See also Arrigoni 1988.

[35] Momigliano 1988, 104.

[36] As Bachofen wrote to his loyal old friend H Meyer-Ochsner in a letter of January 1851, now in Bachofen 1967, 114.

a fine appreciation of the simultaneously rustic and aristocratic character of the Roman Campagna' where, around 1848, he could still find 'the spirit of patrician Rome in the tragic atmosphere of religious devotion and malaria'.[37] These two great but utterly different explorers of the Lazio landscape were shaped in a common matrix, one shared by so many of their contemporaries as well: we need only think of the fascinating image of early nineteenth-century Rome portrayed in German romantic literature. But the outcomes were very different: in the case of Niebuhr, the experience stimulated his interest in the physical traces of the Romans' use and subdivision of the land; in the case of Bachofen, instead, it intensified his tendency to focus exclusively on ideas related to the world of ancient myths and symbols.

What prevented his approach from becoming a reductive schoolroom conversion of legends into false history was Bachofen's immense knowledge of the literary sources and his exceptional interpretative and associative capacities, allowing him to produce new connections that were sometimes extraordinarily compelling. Hence the unexpected forays into unknown or neglected aspects of ancient societies that we find in Bachofen's works, together with sharp insights and arresting hypotheses, albeit mixed in with occasional naiveties or ideas verging on mysticism. All of which contributes to making his pages difficult to read, and at times frankly quite obscure, although often powerfully suggestive.

We certainly cannot follow him all the way in his 'commitment to see things from the point of view of the ancients' and to assign 'a truth value to symbolic connections', an approach essentially based on an 'actual rather than purely instrumental faith ... in the belief system that he is describing'.[38] But although modern scholars may need to distance ourselves from him, it is with an awareness that he addressed some real problems that remain unresolved. Despite recognising that we neither want to nor can go so far as to identify the history of human societies with their myths, we must nevertheless acknowledge that, as yet, we do not have an adequate way to account for the formative processes of ancient societies, which cannot be addressed solely in terms of a rational philological approach. And this is because we do not have direct sources, nor, unlike Bachofen, are we willing to attribute the same value to mythical narratives as to other sources. And at the same time, we are also barred from engaging in the kind of à rébours reconstructions favoured by those nineteenth-century scholars who relied on a predetermined evolutionary framework. But perhaps even more serious is the fact that the whole heritage of myths about Rome's origins was generally dismissed or ignored by nineteenth- and twentieth-century scholars of antiquity, and even today this legacy endures, explaining why it is still largely unexplored. Except, it must be said, by those who, some convincingly, others less so, have tried to follow in Bachofen's footsteps.

---

[37] Momigliano 1988, 105.
[38] Jesi 2005, 80.

An altogether different order of problems arises for us when Bachofen denies that scholarly approaches based on rationality alone can give us adequate historical knowledge even for less remote periods, and for which we have richer sources. We might recall his well-known reaction to Mommsen's *History*, when he went so far as to assert it a 'duty' to protest publicly against this:

> reduction of Rome to the cliché of the most insipid Prussian salon liberalism . . . particularly nauseating . . . so that everything is embraced by the most miserable concepts and completely stood on its head. The only moving force of ancient life, it seems, is trade, speculation, competition, free ports, navigation acts, factories, emporia, as if these provide the principal, indeed the only, point of view from which the lives of peoples can be considered and judged.[39]

Obviously, this attack against Mommsen is excessive and, almost completely, misdirected. However, the concerns on which it is based are in some ways legitimate, in so far as they relate to the problem – now as relevant as ever – of the presence of irrational forces in history: it is no coincidence that Bachofen's outlook should reflect the fundamental turning point of nineteenth-century pessimism represented by Nietzsche, who read Bachofen and drew ideas from him. Indeed, it seems to me that it is no longer possible, when studying the political events, the institutions, and the social and economic processes that have shaped the history of Rome, to rely solely on the rational framework established during Europe's golden age of reason. We would be overlooking, for example, the mixture of *ius* and *fas* underlying the mechanisms of self-legitimation and consolidation that drove Rome's elemental and inexhaustible power policy, at least until the imperial conquest of the East. A policy that, as it was radically transforming the entire structure of the ancient world, could not but appear frightening and qualitatively new to those who lay in its path.

The relationship between law and religion, as administered by the college of pontiffs and their rules, is one of the things that Bachofen has helped us to reflect on, together with their actual intertwined presence in Roman history. Likewise, he was before his time in expanding the range of evidence to be used in comparing different social and legal systems. The latter interest became more important to him over time, as the emerging discipline of anthropology gave him opportunities for dialogue and exchange which he had not found in his own field of specialised studies. And indeed, there was a clear connection between Bachofen's thesis on matriarchy and the debate on primitive social and family organisation that was taking place in the social and anthropological sciences. It is hardly surprising therefore that he should have received praise from the likes

---

[39] Bachofen 1862, 252.

of John Lubbock and John McLennan, and, most notably, Lewis H Morgan in the United States.[40]

But it was not because he was seeking scientific recognition that Bachofen turned increasingly to this field of inquiry, and away from the ancient world and Roman law, to which he had devoted his undivided attention until the 1870s. This turn is evidenced in the *Antiquarische Briefe*, published in 1880 and 1886, but it was already inherent in the conceptual premises on which his entire oeuvre was based, even before his *Mutterrecht*.[41] Momigliano captures this very well when he reminds us how Bachofen remained:

> a Roman lawyer and a historian who discovered that he could not understand Roman law and politics without turning to religion, and yet when he had settled on religion he was compelled to pass from classical religion to comparative religion, from comparative religion to comparative sociology, and finally from comparative sociology to the study of patterns of political and intellectual life.[42]

This is a very important remark: it provides us with a valuable interpretative key for understanding the direction anthropological studies was taking during the early years of the discipline, especially in that peculiar configuration imbued with evolutionary ideas that was ambiguously termed 'comparative sociology'. As I have already had occasion to observe elsewhere, it is striking how many legal scholars were involved in the first fundamental findings of this new field of study in the second half of the nineteenth century.[43] And never, before or since, did Roman law play such an important role, not least in the great debate on patriarchal society that was one of the central themes of this new science. In another passage, Momigliano states that Bachofen was 'the first of the giants who in the sixties and seventies of the last century created the new anthropology', and places his name next to those of Numa Denis Fustel de Coulanges, Henry S Maine, John F McLennan, Edward B Tylor, Lewis H Morgan, and later James Frazer, a list to which we might add the name of John Lubbock.[44]

---

[40] On Bachofen's relation with Morgan, see the correspondence in Bachofen 1967, 468–9, 479–503; cf. also Momigliano 1988, 781. When McLennan wrote his most important work, on *Primitive Marriage*, published in 1865, he was still unaware of Bachofen's *Mutterrecht*. He obtained it only the following year, in 1866, but we do not know if he read the whole work: cf. McLennan 1886, xiv (intr. to the first edn of 1876), and 319–25 ('Bachofen's "Das Mutterrecht"'), where (319 n. 1) McLennan fully acknowledged Bachofen's prior discovery, while rightly noting how 'no two routes . . . could be more widely apart than those by which Bachofen and I arrived at this conclusion'. He also took the occasion to express his admiration for the way Bachofen had developed his hypotheses, by studying the traditions 'and especially the mythologies, of antiquity which his prodigious learning comprehended in all their vast details' (319 n. 1). In 1888, together with the many acknowledgements on behalf of English scholars, he did receive that of Tylor: cf. Stocking 1987, 319 n. 1.

[41] Bachofen 1880.

[42] Momigliano 1992, 595.

[43] Capogrossi Colognesi 2008.

[44] Momigliano 1985, now in Momigliano 1987a, 410. On Lubbock, see Momigliano 1987b, 93.

Of these, three – Maine, McLennan, and Morgan – were legal scholars, and the first two, also and above all, had a good knowledge of Roman law, while Fustel, throughout his career as a historian, consistently made reference to the legal and institutional aspects of ancient and medieval history. It is true that modern historians of nineteenth-century anthropology might not cheerfully consent to include these names among the founders of the discipline. However, Momigliano's list is far from random, if we consider the broader perspective of cultural history. It also allows us to raise an interesting and hitherto neglected question: that of the fundamental contribution of legal categories, and in particular the abstract models provided by Roman law, to the comparative methods that were so important to nineteenth-century anthropology, and which it borrowed directly from the scholarship of the previous century, merely developing them further. But this would lead us to a new investigation that would have little to do with the theme of this volume.

Works Cited

Arrigoni, G, 1988. 'Autobiografia, religione e politica in Johann Jakob Bachofen.' In *L'Antichitá nell'Ottocento in Italia e in Germania*, edited by K Christ and A Momigliano, 119–44. Berlin: Duncker & Humblot.

——, 1996. *La Fidatissima corrispondenza: un ignoto reportage di Johann Jakob Bachofen da Roma nel periodo della rivoluzione romana (1848–1849)*. Milan: La Nuova Italia Editrice.

Bachofen, J J, 1841. *Das Naturrecht und das geschichtliche Recht in ihren Gegensätzen*. Basel: Neukirch.

——, 1843a. *Die lex Voconia und die mit zusammenhängenden Rechtsinstitute*. Basel: Schweighauser.

——, 1843b. *Das nexum, die nexi und die lex Poetelia*. Basel: Neukirch.

——, 1847. *Das römische Pfandrecht*. Basel: Schweighauser.

——, 1850. *Politische Betrachtungen uber das Staatsleben des romischen Volkes*. In J J Bachofen 1943, 27–75.

——, 1859. *Versuch über die Gräbersymbolik der Alten*. Basel: Bahnmaier.

——, 1861. *Das Mutterrecht. Eine Untersuchung über die Gynaikokratie der alten Welt nach ihrer religiösen und rechtlichen Natur*. Stuttgart: Krais & Hoffmann.

——, 1862. *Das Lykische Volk und seine Bedeutung für die Entwicklung des Altertums*. Freiburg im Breisgau: Herder.

——, 1916. 'Eine Selbstbiographie, zugleich ein Gedenkblatt zu seinem hundersten Geburtags (22. Dezember 1915).' *Zeitschrift für vergleichende Rechtswissenschaft* 34:337–80.

——, 1943. *Gesammelte Werke*, vol. I. Basel: Schwabe.

——, 1948. *Gesammelte Werke*, vols II–III. Basel: Schwabe.

——, 1954. *Gesammelte Werke*, vol. IV. Basel: Schwabe.

——, 1966. *Antiquarische Briefe*. In J J Bachofen, *Gesammelte Werke*, VIII. Basel: Schwabe.

——, 1967. *Gesammelte Werke*, vol. X. Basel: Schwabe.
Blume, F, 1852. 'Ueber die Handschriften und Ausgaben der Agrimensoren.' In *Die Schriften der Römischen Feldmesser, Vol. II: Erläuterungen und Indices*, edited by F Blume, K Lachmann, and A Rudorff, 36–9 with 473–4. Berlin: Reimer.
Blume, F, K Lachmann, and A Rudorff. 1848. *Die Schriften der Römischen Feldmesser*, vol. I. Berlin: Reimer.
Bonacina, G, 1991. *Hegel il mondo romano e la storiografia. Rapporti agrari diritto cristianesimo e tardo antico*. Florence: La Nuova Italia.
Capogrossi Colognesi, L, 1997. *Modelli di stato e di famiglia nella storiografia dell'800*. 3rd edn. Rome: La Sapienza.
——, 2008. *Dalla storia di Roma alle origini della società civile. Un dibattito ottocentesco*. Bologna: il Mulino.
Cesana, X, 1988. 'L'antico e nuovo stato. La critica del moderno e la sua motivazione storico-universale in J.J. Bachofen.' *Quaderni di Storia* 28:87–105.
Eyssenhardt, F B, 1886. *B.G. Niebuhr. Eine biographischer Versuch*. Gotha: Perthes.
Garré, R, 1999. *Fra diritto romano e giustizia popolare. Il ruolo dell'attività giudiziaria nella vita e nell'opera di Johann Jakob Bachofen (1815–1887)*. (Ius Commune. Studien zur europäischen Rechtsgeschichte 126.) Frankfurt am Main: Klostermann.
Gossman, L, 1983. *Orpheus Philologus. Bachofen versus Mommsen and the Study of Antiquity*. TAPS 73.5. Philadelphia: American Philosophical Society.
Hare, J C and C Thirwall, 1837. *The History of Rome*, vol. I. London: Taylor and Walton.
Jesi, F, 1988. 'I recessi infiniti del 'Mutterrecht.' In J J Bachofen, *Il Matriarcato*, xiii–xxxv. Turin: Einaudi.
Jesi, F, 2005. *Bachofen*. Turin: Einaudi.
McLennan, J F, 1886. *Studies in Ancient History Comprising a Reprint of Primitive Marriage*. 2nd edn. London: Macmillan.
Meuli, K, 1948. 'Nachwort.' In *Bachofens Leben*, in J J Bachofen, *Gesammelte Werke*, vol. III:1024–46. Basel: Schwabe.
Momigliano, A, 1980. 'Alle origini dell'interesse su Roma arcaica: Niebuhr e l'India.' *Rivista Storica Italiana* 92:561–71.
——, 1984. *Settimo contributo allo studio degli studi classici e del mondo antico*. Rome: Edizioni di Storia e Letteratura.
——, 1988. 'Bachofen tra misticismo e antropologia.' *Annali della Scuola Normale Superiore di Pisa – Classe di Lettere e Filosofia* 18:601–20,
——, 1987a. Review of L Gossmann, *Orpheus Philologus* (1983). In A Momigliano, *Ottavo contributo alla storia degli studi classici e del mondo antico*, 410–13. Rome: Edizioni di Storia e Letteratura.
——, 1987b. 'Johann Jakob Bachofen: From Roman History to Matriarchy.' In A Momigliano, *Ottavo contributo alla storia degli studi classici e del mondo antico*, 91–107. Rome: Edizioni di Storia e Letteratura.

——, 1992. 'From Bachofen to Cumont.' In A Momigliano, *Nono contributo alla storia degli studi classici e del mondo antico*, 595–607. Rome: Edizioni di Storia e Letteratura.

Mommsen, T, 1907. Review of J J Bachofen, *Die lex Voconia* (1845). In *Gesammelte Schriften*. III: *Juristischen Schriften*. III: 513–19. Berlin: Weidmannsche Verlagsbuchhandlung.

Niebuhr, B G, 1811. *Römische Geschichte*, vol. I. Berlin: Reimer. (=*The History of Rome*, I. Trans. J C Hare and C Thirwall. London: Taylor and Walton, 1837.)

——, 1812 *Römische Geschichte*, II. Berlin: Realschulbuchandlung. (=*The History of Rome*, II. Trans. J C Hare and C Thirwall. London: Taylor and Walton, 1838.)

——, 1830. *Römische Geschichte*, II. 2nd edn. Berlin: Reimer.

——, 1839. *Lebensnachrichtenüber Barthold Georg Niebuhr aus Briefen desselben und aus Erinnerungen einiger seiner nächsten Freunde*, vol. II, edited by F Perthes and D Hensler. Hamburg: Perthes.

——, 1852. *The Life and Letters of Barthold Georg Niebuhr, with an Essay on his Character and Influence*, vol. II, edited by K J Bunsen, C A Brandis and J W Loebell. New York: Harper & Brothers.

Stocking, Jr, G W, 1987. *Victorian Anthropology*. New York: Free Press.

Toneatto, L, 1994. *Codices artis mensoriae. I manoscritti degli antichi opuscoli latini d'agrimensura (V–XIX sec.)*, vol. I. Spoleto: Centro Italiano di Studi sull'Alto Medioevo.

Chapter 10

Finding Melanesia in Ancient Rome: Mauss' Anthropology of *nexum*

Alain Pottage

1. INTRODUCTION

Marcel Mauss' *The Gift* is an original and unique anthropology of law.[1] Law is the object and medium of the analysis, and the conceptual and political strategies of the text are closely adapted to the symptomatic tensions that Mauss elicits from law. And for Mauss these tensions were concentrated in one particular legal institution – the archaic Roman institution of *nexum*. In the early twentieth century, the legal-historical debate about the technicalities of *nexum* was sufficiently intense as to be described as 'volcanic'.[2] Events that qualify as seismic in the field of legal history may not have such effects elsewhere, so it is interesting that the question of *nexum* became a central concern of sociology and ethnography in early twentieth-century France. Ludwig Mitteis had set off the legal-historical debate in a text published in 1901, which was followed in the next decade or so by a number of responses and syntheses. Many of these accounts of *nexum* were noticed in *L'Année sociologique*, the house journal of the Durkheimians, and the journal in which the text of *The Gift* first appeared. Most of these notices were written by Mauss' collaborator Paul Huvelin,[3] who also published his own brief essay on *nexum*; these, together with the studies of Georges Davy, had familiarised Mauss with the intricacies of *nexum*. The interest of Mauss and his collaborators emerged from a broader comparative investigation of the institution of contract, which drew together the study of law, magic, and religion. In *The Gift*, Mauss reframed the terms of this

---

[1] The characterisation is obviously anachronistic. In the terms of his day, Mauss might be better described as a sociologist, but the future of *The Gift* lay in twentieth-century anthropology, and I suggest that the political and epistemic strategy of the work is most fully realised in anthropological scholarship. It is obviously also true that law or legal form is only one part of the story. For Mauss the gift brings into view 'a multiplicity of social things in motion [*cette multiplicié de choses sociales en mouvement*]', and the form and sense of the gift is at once juridical, political, economic, and philosophical: '*Tous ces phénomènes sont à la fois juridiques, économiques, religieux, et même esthétiques, morphologiques, etc.*' My reading of *The Gift* is one that partially (in two senses of the term) honours Mauss' concluding observation that he was proposing a set of 'objects of study' rather than a 'definitive answer' (2012, 234). All translations from the French are my own.
[2] De Zulueta 1913, 140.
[3] See Audren 2001.

investigation quite radically: first, by hybridising history and ethnography to generate a novel apprehension of 'the archaic'; second, and more importantly, by turning this relation to the archaic into the medium of a critical political project, which held European society up to a still vital legacy of its own past.

Nexum was originally the form taken by a loan made by patrician to plebeian. A quantity of bronze bullion representing the sum borrowed was weighed out in the presence of a *libripens* and five witnesses, and this ritual, together with the verbal formulae uttered by the parties, created a bond under which the borrower effectively pledged himself as security for the loan. Even to say this is to decide between the competing positions in the old legal-historical debate, which turned on the question of whether the subjection of the body or its *operae* was an integral part of the original transaction or the result of a supervening operation. In any case, if the borrower defaulted on the terms of the loan, the creditor could immediately proceed to enforcement, which at that time meant imprisoning the debtor and forcing him to work until he had repaid his debt. In theory, the *nexus* could absolve himself by replaying the original transaction in reverse – by handing over the sum owed in the presence of a *libripens* and the original five witnesses – but we have no accounts of this happening. Instead, the annalistic sources emphasise the abject and hopeless condition of the *nexus* as the victim of debt bondage. The question for legal historians was how to construe – in technical legal terms – this condition of servitude: 'what were the legal institutions underlying that situation, in particular what was the legal form of the contract of loan, and by what steps or stages did the debtor pass from borrowing to bondage?'[4] Despite the flurry of activity that was prompted by Mitteis' critique of Huschke and Niebuhr, we do not exactly know what words were uttered and what ritual gestures were performed in the act of *nexum*, let alone what those words and gestures signified to the participants and how they actually took effect.

Remaining with geological metaphors, one contemporary historian suggests that the legal-historical debate concerning *nexum* has now congealed into 'bibliographical permafrost'.[5] By contrast, historians and archaeologists continue to engage with the underlying phenomenon of debt bondage in early Rome, notably by way of speculation as to the relations between external warfare and internal social-structural conflict, or between the economies of land and labour, in the period between (roughly speaking) the sixth and fourth centuries. From this perspective, *nexum* is construed as a form of servitude that allowed patricians to compensate for a shortage of (servile) agricultural labour that lasted until the end of the fifth century, when the Italian campaigns met with greater success and the supply of foreign slaves was resumed. In a sophisticated and expansive historical analysis, Lerouxel suggests that the whole point of *nexum* was not to make a debt more readily enforceable, but rather to force plebeians either to submit to

---

[4] De Zulueta 1913, 137.
[5] Lerouxel 2014, 110.

servitude as soon as the transaction was made, or to undertake a loan at a rate of interest that would inevitably lead to default and debt servitude.

> The elevated rate of interest allowed creditors to realise the full economic potential of the legal institution of *nexum*, which authorised execution on the person of the insolvent debtor. The object that was loaned, weighed bronze, was imposed upon plebeians by the patricians, and it was chosen because of its novelty and rarity, so as to create a debt that was as difficult as possible to repay. From the very inception of the contractual relation, the object of the debt was to create a state of dependence that allowed the labour of debtors to be exacted. From the point of view of the creditor, default on payment was not an accident that required compensation but a projected phase of the contractual relation.[6]

From this perspective, the technicalities of the legal institution of *nexum* – however they are now recollected – should be seen as largely subordinate to the social-structural and economic forces that shaped ancient Roman society. And this approach might in turn lead to a set of questions that Mauss would have found entirely pertinent, as to what *nexum* might tell us about the genealogy or deep infrastructure of debt and precarity in contemporary societies.

2. REINVENTING THE ARCHAIC

Before engaging with the technicalities of *nexum*, it is necessary to ask: Why was a close, reciprocal engagement with those technicalities so central to Mauss' project? In *The Gift*, Mauss frames his 'provisional' enquiry in terms that will be familiar: 'What is the rule of law and interest that, in backward or archaic societies, means that a present that is received is obligatorily returned? What force is there in the thing that causes the recipient to return it?'[7] In understanding the strategy of Mauss' engagement with law, the reference to a 'rule of law and interest' is less significant than the proposition that there is a 'force' in the thing given. Notice that Mauss begins not with the opening move, with the giving of the gift, but with the moment just after the gift has been received, when the obligation to make a return has arisen, the 'middle point' of the transaction.[8] The perspective is that of the recipient of the gift, upon whom the obligation now weighs. And what is crucial is the form in which the obligation presents itself. It presses upon the recipient

---

[6] Lerouxel 2014, 112. On the question of bronze, see also Zehnacker 1990, 310: 'Paleomonetary artefacts do not serve the same functions as money. They are neither payment for labour time nor the fruits of capital; they are not usually used for the acquisition of consumer goods. They are not subject to the law of supply and demand that orders relations in the sphere of the market. Rather, they serve to reproduce, or, in other words, to justify, perpetuate and eventually transform social structures. Their holding is the privilege of the ruling classes and the aristocracy; the more evolved the social hierarchy, the more complex and codified the functions performed by paleomoney.'
[7] Mauss 2012, 26: 'Quelle est la règle de droit et d'intérêt qui, dans les sociétés de type arriéré ou archaïque, fait que le présent reçu est obligatoirement rendu? Quelle force y a-t-il dans la chose qu'on donne qui fait que le donataire la rend?'
[8] Schüttpelz 2009.

not in the form of a juridical obligation – as an obligation upon a person to act in a particular way in relation to a thing – but in the form of a specific 'mixture' or 'fusion' of person and thing, as a thing imbued with a 'force'. What is required – by this emphatically non-juridical 'rule of law and interest' – is that the recipient respond in kind; not by transferring an inert object, and by comporting themselves as 'person' in relation to that object, but by returning a thing in which their own person is similarly staked or invested so as to be eclipsed in a specific mixture or fusion. Reciprocity implies 'meeting' the giver's fusion of person and thing with a prestation that hybridises person and thing in such a way as to exert a properly judged 'counter-force'.[9]

The Gift develops a critical relation of Euro-American society to its own past. As Mauss puts it, accounts of the form and reason of exchange in different 'ethnographic fields' tell us something about the making of our own society: 'Institutions of this type have really provided the transition towards our own forms of law and economy.'[10] But 'transition' here should not be understood in the sense of linear evolutionary process; for the institutions uncovered in the ethnographic and historical documents are also still at work in contemporary Euro-America: 'this morality and organisation still function in our own societies, in unchanging fashion and, so to speak, hidden, below the surface'.[11] Mauss does not have in mind only localised or peripheral survivals – in Provence, the gift of an egg or some other symbolic gift on the occasion of a birth,[12] or the old values that are honoured 'at certain times of the year or on certain occasions'[13] – but rather the latent or potential persistence of the logic of the gift as a total social phenomenon.

The Gift was addressed to a post-1918 Europe in which the welfare state – '*ce socialisme d'État*'[14] – was beginning to take shape,[15] and Mauss was particularly interested in the way that emerging forms of 'social insurance' drew on the deeper participatory sensibility of gift and counter-gift. The focus of his attention was on the situation of the worker, 'who keenly feels that he exchanges more than a product or labour time, that he gives something of himself, his time, his life'.[16] The collectivity and the bosses could not defray this contribution simply by paying a wage; the worker was owed 'a measure of security in life, against unemployment, against sickness, against old age, and death'.[17] The object of Mauss' sociological re-presentation of the laws of giving and receiving was to equip society with a

---

[9] In the Trobriand Islands, reciprocity cannot have a simple dyadic form because goods are given and returned in two directions at once.
[10] Mauss 2012, 47.
[11] Mauss 2012, 4.
[12] Mauss 2012, 214–15.
[13] Mauss 2012, 213.
[14] Mauss 2012, 216.
[15] In a further study I shall explore the resonances between Mauss' approach and Léon Bourgeois' notion of quasi-contract (see Tixier 2016).
[16] Mauss 2012, 232.
[17] Mauss 2012, 217.

vocabulary that would enable it to reconnect with, reactualise, and reflect on itself in terms of these deep moral principles: 'it is not enough to notice [the tendency towards collectivisation and solidarity], one has to deduce from it a practice, a moral precept ... We have to say that this revolution is good [*Il faut dire que cette revolution est bonne*].'[18] More precisely, and much though Mauss appreciated the 'anglo-saxon' ethos of patrician or bourgeois euergetism and social responsibility,[19] the point was that 'returns' made by the collectivity should not be construed as charity.

Why is law – and *nexum* in particular – the object and medium of this project? For Mauss, law was the social institution in which the distinction between persons and things was most effectively cultured or consecrated in European societies:

> We live in societies that draw a strict distinction [*qui distinguent fortement*] between real rights and personal rights, things and persons (the contrast is now criticised by jurists themselves). This division is fundamental: it constitutes the essential condition for a part of our system of property, transfer, and exchange ... Yet are not such distinctions fairly recent in the legal systems of our great civilisations? Did these not go through an earlier phase in which they did not display such a cold, calculating mentality?[20]

The legal distinction between persons and things, or between personal rights and real rights, is the servant of this 'cold, calculating mentality' because it hides from us the sense in which all exchange presupposes, participates in, and reproduces the social. It allows or compels us to participate in the social only in the manner of what Marx characterised as the 'emancipated' individual of civil society. But Mauss did not propose the eradication of the distinction between personal rights and real rights; in a footnote, he observes that 'the legal principles which govern the market, or market exchange [*l'achat et la vente*], and which are a necessary condition for the formation of capital, can and should subsist alongside newer principles and older principles'.[21] As the last chapter of *The Gift* makes plain, Mauss' particular brand of 'socialism' was predicated on the positive value of self-interest: '[The individual] has to be forced to count on himself rather than others ... He has to defend his interests, personally, and collectively.'[22] Of course, this was not the self-interest of the utilitarian economist.[23] The art of giving and receiving was that of holding together self-interest and social participation: 'the citizen has to have a keen sense of himself, but also of others, and of social reality. He has to act while taking account of himself, of subgroups, and of society.'[24]

---

[18] Mauss 2012, 218.
[19] See Dzimira 2007, 136–42.
[20] Mauss 2012, 47–8.
[21] Mauss 2012, 217.
[22] Mauss 2012, 219.
[23] Mauss 2012, 229: 'In [other] civilisations, people are interested, but otherwise than in our times.'
[24] Mauss 2012, 220.

The contemporary controversy over *nexum* might have led Mauss to believe that lawyers – or an advance guard of legal historians – could be induced to reimagine and recontextualise the distinction between real rights and personal rights. Here, in the archive of European law, was an institution that differentiated and recombined person and thing in ways that could not be explained by the Romanist distinction between real rights and personal rights. Although some historians, notably Henry Maine, saw in this institution only an original state of confusion from which this modern distinction had precipitated, others might have been able to see in it forms or artefacts that presented person and thing in an entirely different light. And the ethnographies of the gift compiled by Mauss revealed techniques and processes that animated person and thing in such a different way and to such different effect. If for Mauss the point of the analysis was 'to allow another juridical melody to be heard [*faire résonner une autre musique juridique*]',[25] then the relations revealed by the ethnographies served to 'reorchestrate' the technicalities of *nexum* so as to generate this '*autre musique juridique*'.

Nexum has a central role in *The Gift*, first, because it (re)connects archaic Roman law with the complex gift economy of so-called primitive societies. In *nexum* one could almost see a gift economy in microcosm; the institution articulated a number of different 'transactions' in one: 'there are many symmetrical acts of taking possession, of things and of persons, in the same operation'.[26] And this composite operation could be construed in terms of the 'principles' elicited from the ethnographic material compiled by Mauss. It is not implausible to suggest that Mauss found in the ethnographic material on gift an illustration or analogue of a 'rule of law and interest' that he had already elicited from archaic Roman law, and from *nexum* in particular.[27] But the point of the exercise was to 'historicise' the ethnographic material and, in return, to 'ethnographicise' the historical material. The splicing of past European societies into the contemporary 'primitive' societies studied by ethnographers was the essential move in the constitution of the spatially and temporally variegated dimension that Mauss calls the 'archaic'. So, along one axis, *nexum* combines Roman, Indo-European, and Pacific practices to form the archaic; the technicalities of *nexum* were taken apart and put back together again according to principles elicited from the ethnographic dimension of the archaic.

Along a second axis, *nexum* articulates a relation between this invented province of the archaic and modern European society. Roman law itself is divided between the poles of this second axis: in its 'prehistoric' forms, it belongs to the archaic; in its 'historical' forms, it is already modern. And *nexum* functions as the hinge between these two poles. It articulates a chiasmus between the principles

---

[25] Mauss 2012, 186.
[26] Mauss 2012, 185.
[27] Stephanie Frank suggests that the source of Mauss' figure of gift exchange is not the Maori sense of *hau* but 'a certain (historically questionable) construction of the Roman legal institution of *nexum*' (Frank 2016, 257).

of gift economies and the cold rationality of the modern distinction between personal rights and real rights, the better to dissolve the hold of the Romano-European distinction in the modern world. How does this chiasmus work?

For Mauss the essential point about the principles of exchange in Melanesia or the Trobriand Islands is that they do not work with the forms of 'person' and 'thing' as they are found in 'historical' Roman law. But he triggers a resonance between archaic and modern exchange by introducing the vocabulary of historical Roman law into the analysis of exchange in archaic societies. So, for example, the gift that one receives is characterised in the following terms: 'property and possession, a pledge and a thing hired, a thing that is sold and bought, and at the same time deposited, mandated, and entrusted [*déposée, mandatée et fidéocommise*]'.[28] This might seem to suggest that archaic modes of exchange confuse operations or transactions that are clearly differentiated in Roman law (along the lines of Maine's analysis of archaic law – see below).[29] But for Mauss the archaic jurisprudences of gift hold or yield the forms of modern 'Romanist' law in much the same way as one term of an analogy already inhabits the other. The comparative insight was that modern legal operations exist in a radically different form in the archaic gift economy, and the vital question, asked now, almost a century on from the publication of *The Gift*, is how we should understand this difference. So we need to turn to the specific form of the analogy, and to the position of the reader of *The Gift*, who, rather like the person to whom a gift has just been given, finds oneself at an intermediate point. We are invited to see the archaic Pacific in Europe, and/or Europe from the perspective of the archaic Pacific.

Schüttpelz observes that Mauss' 'Eurocentricity' involves a particular form of self-interpretation:

> It is true that Mauss develops a self-interpretation of European categories, which reproduces the dynamic and the romance of the gift: having started with Roman law (and an Indo-European text) it returns to Rome (and to the Indo-European). Between these two moments, however, one finds the obverse and the counterpart of any figure of self-interpretation: an alien interpretation of our own distinction between person and thing.[30]

As long as we recall that Rome or Roman law itself figures twice over, as the archaic and the modern, and that there are two axes in play at the same time, this very nicely describes the strategy of *The Gift*. And my hypothesis is that anthropological scholarship since Mauss has developed this criss-crossing of self-interpretation and other-interpretation into a mode of recursive comparativism: particular forms are seen from the perspective of an ethnographic other that is elicited by the categories and textual strategies of anthropology. In Mauss, this

---

[28] Mauss 2012, 108. In English, these last three terms would be more accurately translated in terms of bailment, gratuitous agency, and fideocommissary inheritance.
[29] Indeed, Mauss (2012, 108) suggests that the gift in the Trobriand islands 'participates in all kinds of legal principles that we, us moderns, have carefully separated from one another'.
[30] Schüttpelz 2009.

move is only implicit or latent; perhaps it can be made explicit only by treating *The Gift* as a work in progress, by honouring Mauss' characterisation of it as such.[31] And Roman law is not a bad place to begin with such a 'restoration' project, precisely because *nexum* functions as a hinge between modern European law and the archaic legality of the gift.

2.1. Nexum se dare

The controversy over *nexum* was sparked by Mitteis' critique of the theory proposed by Huschke in 1846, according to which the act *per aes et libram* had a dual effect: there was a conveyance of property (the bronze bullion) from the creditor to the debtor by way of mancipation, and, in the same ritual procedure, the formation of a contract of personal obligation by way of *nexum*. According to Huschke, the verbal formula (*nuncupatio*) of *nexum* recited a condemnation (*damnatio*) which had the same effect as a judicial pronouncement, and which allowed the creditor to proceed directly to execution of the debt. The form of words, uttered publicly before the five witnesses and the *libripens*, was sufficient in itself to establish the legal ground for the debtor's apprehension (by way of the *legis actio per manus injectionem pro judicato*) in case of failure to pay on time. Mitteis argued that there was nothing distinctive about the form or effect of the loan which ultimately led to the debtor becoming a *nexus*. The path to servitude began with a contract of debt called *nexum*, which was made *per aes et libram* and which was enforceable by *legis actio sacramento in personam*. The debtor who found himself unable to repay this loan would be faced with the prospect of becoming *judicatus*, in which case he would be 'addicted' to his creditor, and, according to the notorious terms of the Twelve Tables, he might be sold into slavery across the Tiber or have his body divided between his creditors. To avoid these consequences, the debtor would subject himself to his creditor by means of a self-mancipation, which was also called *nexum* and which was also effected *per aes et libram*. Mitteis refers to the annalistic sources in support of this interpretation: first, Livy's references to *nexum se dare* or *nexum inire* only make sense if the servitude of the debtor was the result of an additional transaction, rather than the enforcement of the first *nexum*; second, given that both *nexi* and *judicati* were subjected to the same treatment, the distinction made between them in the annalistic sources could have made sense only if it reflected a difference in the juridical basis of their condition.

Huschke's theory would already have held some interest for Mauss, for reasons that are brought out by Maine in his *Ancient Law*. Maine paraphrases Huschke's theory of *nexum* as follows: 'the same term described the conveyance by which the right of property was transmitted, and the personal obligation of the debtor for the unpaid purchase-money'.[32] Thus, according to Maine, *nexum* betrayed a

---

[31] See the final sub-chapter of *Le don*: 'Conclusion de sociologie générale et de morale.'
[32] Maine 1870, 310–11.

'primitive' mentality which confused categories that a 'mature jurisprudence' had learned to distinguish:

> Mancipation was a *conveyance*, and hence has arisen the difficulty, for the definition thus cited appears to confound Contracts and Conveyances, which in the philosophy of jurisprudence are not simply kept apart, but are actually opposed to each other. The *jus in re*, right *in rem*, right 'availing against all the world,' or Proprietary Right, is sharply distinguished by the analyst of mature jurisprudence from the *jus ad rem*, right *in personam*, right 'availing against a single individual or group,' or Obligation. Now Conveyances transfer Proprietary Rights, Contracts create Obligations – how then can the two be included under the same name or same general conception?[33]

For Maine, then, law consists in a set of 'conceptions' which hover over human history as quasi-transcendent forms, which are only fully realised in the world when they are properly apprehended. Consider another of his characterisations of *nexum*: 'We have indications not to be mistaken of a state of social affairs in which Conveyances and Contracts were practically confounded; nor did the discrepance of the conceptions become perceptible till men had begun to adopt a distinct practice in contracting and conveying.'[34] So the two 'discrepant' conceptions existed already, in potential, in the primitive institution of *nexum*, as elements waiting to be fractioned out of the aggregate in which they were confused. The confusion is accidental rather than substantial, so to speak; it arises only because people in archaic Rome lacked 'the faculty of distinguishing in speculation ideas which are blended in practice'.[35] Maine does not imagine that something radically different might be going on; a form of transaction that is neither contract nor conveyance, neither real right nor personal right, and which does not 'confuse' these terms because it understands the underlying terms – persons and things – very differently.

But the symptomatic point of 'confusion' that caught the attention of Mauss and his collaborators was the theme of self-mancipation that was emphasised by Mitteis' critique.[36] Although those who engaged in the controversy did not agree that there was a distinct contract of loan called *nexum*, there was general agreement on the point that the debtor transferred or subjected himself to his creditor. Writing in 1940, Pierre Noailles summarised the state of play in the following terms:

> Almost all [authors] came to admit that the *nexus* was a man who had given himself to his creditor by way of self-mancipation. We can say clearly and simply that he had placed himself *in causa mancipii* through a mancipation, or, more obscurely, that he gave his person as pledge or security for his debt, within the real bond [*lien réel*] that subjected him to his creditor.[37]

---

[33] Maine 1870, 315.
[34] Maine 1870, 316.
[35] Maine 1870, 315–16.
[36] In fact, the characterisation of *nexum* as a self-mancipation had been proposed by Niebuhr in 1853. Niehbuhr's argument was that a debtor sold or mancipated himself conditionally, so that he would not fall under the power of the creditor unless he defaulted on the loan.
[37] Noailles 1940, 213.

So, in his article on *nexum*, Huvelin was able straightforwardly to characterise *nexum* as a sale of the self: 'The term *nexum* or *nexus* is given to a free man who entered into a bond by making himself a slave by his debt [*qui s'est obligé en se rendant esclave par sa dette*]. *Se nexum dare* means to transfer to one's creditor property in one's own person.'[38] One can see why this would have engaged Mauss' interest. In the idea of a sale of the self one finds a more sociologically congenial expression of Maine's question about the difference between conveyance and contract, or real rights and personal rights: 'We start with sale as an ultimate conception, and we derive from it a transaction whose operation is *in personam* only because the person is treated as a thing.'[39] For de Zulueta, the theory of self-mancipation offered 'an intelligible transition from conveyance to contract',[40] but from Mauss' perspective what was interesting was not the emergence of the pure forms but the original 'confusion' – the state in which something could be 'personal' only if it was treated as a 'thing.'

One should notice the basic historical-anthropological point that the cultural horizon or scenography of archaic law was different in ways that Maine could not appreciate. From a modern perspective, the technique of making contractual obligations bind is essentially that of controlling time; or, more precisely, that of regulating the 'risk' inherent in any deferred exchange: 'How is [the person who divests himself of his property first] to be guaranteed against the danger of not receiving the counter-delivery?'[41] By contrast, Louis Gernet suggests that *nexum* belonged to a world in which legal techniques had no purchase on time. He construes *nexum* as an example of the archaic technique of binding or compelling persons in the present rather than seeking to bind them into the future. These techniques used 'effective symbols': 'Their effect, without explicit reference to the future and with no relation to the psychological notion of a future obligation or performance, was to produce a change in the state of the partner.'[42] So, in the case of *nexum*, which already presupposed a radical disparity in means and status between the parties, the obligation was made by subjecting the *nexus* to a further and more brutal reduction of status. For Gernet, *nexum* could not be a contract because it did not project itself into the future: 'its effect was immediate'.[43]

One might suggest that bonds were material, perhaps both figuratively and literally, because they effected such a change in state. Revisiting the rule of the Twelve Tables – *Cum nexum faciet mancipiumque, uti lingua nuncupassit, ita*

---

[38] Huvelin 1901, 80.
[39] De Zulueta 1913, 141.
[40] De Zulueta 1913, 141.
[41] Lévy-Bruhl 1944, 52.
[42] Gernet 1982, 141.
[43] Gernet 1982, 142.

ius esto[44] – Magdelain argues that in this formula *nexum* was a material operation: 'In this text, *nexum* is not, as is commonly supposed, the act in its totality, action and speech (*geste et parole*); rather, it is a simple material operation.'[45] So the *mancipium* with which *nexum* was associated was itself a material gesture. Etymologically, *mancipium* in archaic law should be broken down into *manum capere* rather than *manu capere*; the difference being that in the former case *manus* does not signify the instrument or means of taking hold but the thing of which one takes hold: 'The *manicipium* that is associated with *nexum* in the XII Tables has nothing to do with the conveyance of property, it is the gesture of the hand by which the debtor subjects himself to the creditor [*se place sous la dépendance du créancier*].'[46] Magdelain goes on to argue that the bond of *nexum* was neither the knot of chains emphasised by the annalists nor the abstract juridical obligation imagined by modern legal historians, but a material-symbolic bond made by attaching a symbolic ingot (the *aes nexum* or *rodusculum*) to the neck of the debtor by means of a necklace or cloth tie. Only later did the meaning of *nexum* expand to encompass any act carried out *per aes et libram*. And the discontinuity between the archaic and the newer meaning was disguised by the fact that both operations depended on a gesture of the hand: 'The etymology was only slightly disturbed by the shift from *manum capere* to *manu capere*.'[47] From that point on, it was assumed that *mancipium* had always signified *manu capere*, and *nexum* became identified with the act *per aes et libram* and hence with mancipation in general.

2.2. Complementary exchanges

Mauss' discussion of *nexum* is cued up by a brief discussion of the Germanic *wadium*, which, following Huvelin, he treats as an example of the agency of 'supplementary tokens [*gages supplémentaires*]'.[48] In 'Magie et droit individuel', Huvelin described *wadium* as a form of contract in which the creditor or person to whom the obligation was owed retained some personal item or token as 'security': a ring, a coin, a glove, or a knife. The object pledged was usually of little pecuniary value, so why would a creditor take it as security, and why would a debtor be so keen to redeem it? According to Huvelin, it was not sufficient to say that the object had some sentimental value, or that through it the debtor's honour was put in question; the quality of honour was itself constituted and enforced by the institution of *wadium* that it was supposed to

---

[44] 'When he shall perform *nexum* and mancipium, as his tongue has pronounced, so is there to be a source of rights ['*cum faciet nexum mancipiumque, uti lingua nuncupassit, ita ius esto*]': XII Tables, VI.1 (in Crawford 1996, 654).
[45] Magdelain 1990a, 136.
[46] Magdelain 1990a, 137.
[47] Magdelain 1990a, 140.
[48] Mauss 2012, 175.

explain.⁴⁹ Rather, the answer lay in the fact the object pledged was intimately associated with the body of the debtor, it was a bodily good [*un meuble corporel*], and it affected the debtor through the agencies of sympathetic magic:

> These objects were sometimes called life tokens [*gages de vie*], and any harm suffered by their master also affected them: if they perished, their master was in danger; on the other hand, by acting upon them one acted upon their master. Through them, one could bewitch him, take control of him, or possess him. To leave such an object in the hands of an enemy was to expose oneself to the deadliest enchantments [*les pires maléfices*].⁵⁰

The forces of sympathetic magic sufficed to make the verbal promise effective. Huvelin proposed that *nexum* could also be seen in these terms; it was 'a contract formed by staking the body of the debtor, combined with a conditional condemnation (*damnatio*) pronounced by the creditor'.⁵¹

According to Mauss, the resonances between Roman law in the period 'before it truly entered history' and Germanic law, and in particular the association made by Huvelin between *nexum* and *wadium*, suggested a new answer to 'one of the most controversial questions in legal history, the theory of *nexum*'.⁵² Given the part it plays in his story, it is interesting that Mauss relegates his discussion of *nexum* to an extended footnote. Perhaps that is because the action in *The Gift* was supposed to be in the text in 'larger font [*en gros caractères*]', with the footnotes being essential only for the 'specialist',⁵³ but I shall suggest that that were some strategic reasons for insisting on the significance of *nexum* while allowing it to be eclipsed in the text. In any case, Mauss presents *nexum* as a ritual in which one can still see the traces of the economy of reciprocal gift-giving; in *nexum*, 'the legal "bond" comes as much from things as from men'.⁵⁴ But what is essential is the notion that two kinds of 'currency' were in play: the bronze bullion that was the principal subject matter of the debt and a token ingot that functioned as a pledge, token, or symbol:

> I would suggest that the Romanists, Huvelin included, have generally not paid sufficient attention to a detail of the formalities of *nexum*: the vocation of the bronze ingot, the contentious *aes nexum* of Festus. This ingot, upon the formation of *nexum*, is given by the *tradens* [the creditor] to the *accipiens* [the debtor]. But I believe that when the latter gains his freedom, he not only performs the promised prestation or delivers up the thing or the price, he also, using the same balance and before the same witnesses, returns this very *aes* to the praetor, or to the creditor. And the latter buys it and receives it in his turn. This ritual for the *solutio* of *nexum* is clearly described by Gaius. In an

---

⁴⁹ Huvelin 1906, 30.
⁵⁰ Huvelin 1906, 31.
⁵¹ Huvelin 1906, 36. Huvelin speaks of a '*contrat formé par l'engagement du corps du débiteur*,' where '*engagement*' plays on the term *gage*: pledge, token, or stake.
⁵² Mauss 2012, 175.
⁵³ Mauss 2012, 66.
⁵⁴ Mauss 2012, 177.

outright sale, these two acts take place at the same time, so to speak, or at close intervals, the double symbol being less apparent than in the case of a deferred sale or a solemnly made loan; which is why this dual move [*double jeu*] has remained unnoticed. But it functioned nonetheless. If my interpretation is right, there is indeed, in addition to the *nexum* that comes from solemn form, in addition to the *nexum* that comes from the thing, another *nexum* that comes from this ingot which is alternately given and taken, and weighed with the same scales, *hanc tibi libram primam postremamque*, by the two contracting parties, who are thereby bound alternately.[55]

Mauss insists on this theory of *aes nexum* as a symbolic token; first, in order to take his distance from the theories of Huvelin and Davy, and, second, to set up an analogical relation between archaic and contemporary law.

The proposition that *aes nexum* was not the bronze bullion as such but the symbolic ingot (or *rodusculum*) is echoed in Magdelain's analysis of *nexum* (which largely ignores the old legal-historical debate).[56] Magdelain revisits the essential passage of Varro's *De Lingua Latina*, and finds in it a distinction between *pecunia quam debet* and *aes nexum*. After an extended critique of the annalists' (literary rather than juridical) interpretations of *nectere* and *obligare*, and after noticing the association of both terms with magical rites, Magdelain suggests that although *nexum* was absolutely not religious in character, it did have magical qualities and effects:

> The ingot remains the property of the creditor, who exercises a subtle hold over the debtor by means of it. When Varro writes '*ut ab aere obaeratus*,' he means that by virtue of a fiction, which is the essence of the act, the *nexus* is bound to repay less because of the loan than because he is the debtor of the magical ingot.[57]

So *nexum* binds both ingot and debtor, the *aes nexum* and the *nexus* – and indeed binds the ingot to the debtor: 'the bond that binds the ingot, the *aes nexum*, is the same as that which binds the debtor, who is also *nexus*. They are bound to one another.'[58] Magdelain interprets the concluding phrase of Varro's paragraph – *ab aere obaeratus* – in the following terms: 'the symbolic *aes* inscribes the person of the *nexus* not abstractly but materially: in the course of the ritual, the miniature ingot is tied around his neck.'[59] The *aes nexum* that is bound around the neck of the creditor actually represents or embodies the person of the creditor: 'In this figurative form, the person of the creditor holds on to the person of the creditor much as predator holds on to its prey.'[60] And the suggestion, which is as pictorial

---

[55] Mauss 2012, 177.
[56] On the essential point, Magdelain (1990b, 723) straightforwardly prefers the interpretation associated with Huschke: 'Le débiteur est nexus dès la conclusion de l'acte: *dum solveret (solvat), nexus vocatur*, dit Varron . . . Il est nexus avant l'échéance.'
[57] Magdelain 1990b, 734.
[58] Magdelain 1981, 132.
[59] Magdelain 1981,131–2.
[60] Magdelain 1981, 132 [*Sous cette forme figurée, c'est la personne du créancier qui s'attache comme à sa proie à celle du débiteur*].

as anything found in the annalistic accounts, is that the *nexus* might actually have worn the ingot around his neck; there was 'a necklace, bracelet, or bandanna to which the *rodusculum* might have been attached'.[61] For Mauss, the interesting thing about this interpretation would have been the sense in which the thing bound the person. But Magdelain's understanding of *nexum* as a material-magical bond actually recalls Huvelin's analysis of *wadium*: 'As has been suggested, the identification of a bodily good [*bien meuble*] with its owner is apt to explain how in the practice of gift and countergift . . . the person of the giver exercises upon the recipient through the interposition of an object a binding magical force that encourages reciprocity.'[62]

Besides the notion of sympathetic magic, one might also notice the notion of formulaic or 'mechanical' magic. For example, Davy proposed that 'primitive obligations' should be analysed in terms of their 'physiognomy';[63] their effects were attributable not to the 'force' of their semantic or conceptual contents alone, but to a combinatorial articulation of semantic, gestural, and material elements. And, with particular reference to *nexum*, Huvelin characterised the verbal formulae of archaic law as 'rythmic oral formulae (*concepta verba, nuncupationes, carmina*), which had to produce a given result mechanically, through the inherent force (*la vertu intrinsèque*) that they drew from their rythm, their obscure form, and the fatidical terms that were combined'.[64]

But for Mauss, there was more to *nexum* than magic, whether sympathetic or mechanical: 'There is a bond within things [*un lien dans les choses*] that supplements magical or religious bonds, or the bonds formed by the words and gestures of legal formalism.'[65] Indeed, he emphasised the role of the symbolic ingot precisely so as to distance himself from the analysis of archaic rituals in terms of an innate magical force, generated by the articulation of various ingredients. He speaks of 'supplementary exchanges [that] express by means of fiction this back and forth between souls and things that are confounded with one another'.[66] The notion of 'fiction' is crucial here: the *aes nexum* is fictional or symbolic in the sense that the translation of the *aes nexum* from creditor to debtor and then back again makes explicit a 'rule' that might otherwise remain invisible. Hence Mauss' suggestion that even in an immediate sale, in which the moment of obligation seems fleeting, there is nonetheless a 'symbolic' and an 'actual' transaction: 'both acts take place at the same time, so to speak, or at close intervals, the double symbol being less

---

[61] Magdelain 1990b, 735.
[62] Magdelain 1990b, 736.
[63] Davy 1921, 334. On the relations between Mauss and Davy, see Fournier 2007 and Besnard 1985.
[64] Huvelin 1901, 23. One might also see some affinities with Elizabeth Meyer's notion of the 'unitary act' in Roman law: 'When performed correctly, a unitary act irrevocably changed some aspect of the visible or invisible world; it did not need human enforcers, but drew its power and authority from the formal ritual of its own making' (2004, 118).
[65] Mauss 2012, 178.
[66] Mauss 2012, 176.

apparent than in the case of a deferred sale or a solemnly made loan'. Interestingly, Magdelain makes a similar observation, suggesting that all mancipations in archaic Roman law included a symbolic ingot or *as* that bound the person of the transferor. Mancipation could only give the buyer a conditional title, subject to any superior claim that might be held by a third party, and the seller would be obliged to repay double the purchase money if such a claim were asserted before it was extinguished by the operation of *usucapio*. The formulae for mancipation did not explicitly acknowledge this obligation, but Magdelain surmises that the first part of the phrase *hoc aere aeneaque libra* must have had as a felicity condition the symbolic weighing of a miniature ingot or *as* which expressed the continuing obligation of the vendor.[67]

Whatever its plausibility, Magdelain's theory nicely expresses the reason for Mauss' insistence on the symbolic or fictional logic of the *aes nexum*: even transactions that look like punctual exchanges imply bonds that attach persons, and that fuse or hybridise person and thing into a specific normative artefact. The 'mixing' that is proper to gift economies is present even in the simplest sale. From this perspective, the limitation of Huvelin's approach, with its emphasis on the 'inherent force' of mechanico-magical ritual, is that it deprives gifts or prestations of one of the elements that are hybridised in the making of a counter-gift. There is no sense that things themselves act, have a force, and do so precisely because they are more than or other than 'things' in the ordinary sense; and, crucially, there is no sense that 'the bond between things is a bond of souls, because the thing itself has a soul, is made of soul'.[68]

2.3. Pledge

Having drawn attention to the symbolism of the *aes nexum*, Mauss then turns to the example of *familia*, which seems at first sight to resonate much more closely with his ethnographic examples than either *nexum* or *wadium*. There is a sense in which the category of *familia* made things of people. In archaic Roman law, '*familia* included all together the people and the goods of a household: parents *in potestate*, slaves, land, buildings, and household capital (which roughly corresponded to the category of *res* that were called *mancipi*).'[69] When the heir took possession of the *familia* he took possession of the 'thing' that encompassed all these 'things'. By contrast, Mauss highlights the sense in which in *familia* things figured as persons. He identifies *familia* with patrimony, or with the 'permanent and essential goods of the household', as distinct from 'transitory things [*les choses qui passent*]'.[70] In the scholarship of the day, the antique formula *familia pecuniaque* was construed as

---

[67] Magdelain 1990a, 29–33. Magdelain suggests that the archaic practice is clearly manifested in the formula of the *mancipatio sestercio nummo uno*.
[68] Mauss 2012, 180.
[69] Thomas 1980, 421.
[70] Mauss 2012, 180.

the distinction between *res mancipi* and *res nec mancipi*; for Mauss the things that could only be transferred through the solemn act of mancipation were the more significant goods of the household, whereas *res nec mancipi* were such things as minor livestock or money (*pecunia*). Mauss suggests that these *res mancipi* would originally have been marked or stamped with the personal seal of the family. And, when they were sold, there would be a moment, however brief, in which they remained 'of' the family: 'they would remain bound to it, and they would bind the new possessor until he freed himself by executing the contract, that is, by the compensatory transfer [*la tradition compensatoire*] of the thing, price, or service that would in turn bind the transferor [*le premier contractant*]'.[71]

Why does Mauss not lead with *familia* rather than *nexum*, given the more obvious continuities between this past archaic figure and one reading of the mixtures or entanglements of his contemporaneous 'archaic' societies? And especially given the speculation on the historical-sociological etymology of the term *res* which immediately follows the discussion of *familia* leads to the proposition that in any transfer of a thing, 'the simple fact of *having the thing* places the *accipiens* [recipient] in an indeterminate state of quasi-culpability (*damnatus, nexus, aere obaeratus*), of spiritual inferiority, of moral inequality (*magister, minister*), with respect to the transferor (*tradens*)'.[72] After all, this condensed dossier of speculation seems to offer rich resources for the interweaving of archaic Rome and archaic Pacific. My hypothesis, again, is that the institution of *nexum* is so important to Mauss because it articulates a chiasmus between 'exchange' in modern European societies and 'gift' in archaic societies, between the pure legal forms of person and thing and the mixtures or entanglements that one finds on the side of the archaic. And the insistence on the *double jeu* of the symbolic ingot is important because the 'fiction' played out by the ingot turns the impersonal exchange of the modern economy inside out to reveal its archaic double. And again, strategically, the idea is that this confrontation of modern law with its double might help to relocate and confine the distinction between real rights and personal rights to its proper sphere. To develop that point we have to return to the analogy between *nexum* and *wadium*.

In a slightly more expansive discussion of *wadium* and its kinship with *nexum*, in the context of a discussion of Germanic contracts, Mauss again distinguishes his approach from that of Huvelin:

> Huvelin has already observed that the thing is of little value, and usually personal; he quite rightly construes this fact in terms of a '*gage de vie*' or 'life-token.' The thing transferred is indeed entirely occupied by the individuality of the giver [*toute chargée de l'individualité du donateur*]. The fact that it is in the hands of the recipient impels the debtor to perform the contract, to redeem himself by redeeming the thing [*à se racheter en rachetant la chose*]. So the *nexum* is within the thing, and not only in magical acts, or in the solemn forms of contract, the words used, the oaths given and rituals performed, the hands shaken.[73]

---

[71] Mauss 2012, 180–1.
[72] Mauss 2012, 184.
[73] Mauss 2012, 207.

But it is apparent from this analysis that the dynamic of redemption is very different from the dynamic of ongoing reciprocity. In the case of *wadium*, something of the 'person' of the debtor remains with the creditor. When the debt is repaid, this personal token returns to the debtor; what was of the self returns to the self. As the reflexive form of the phrase '*se racheter en rachetant la chose*' suggests, the relation that imbues the token with the personality or 'individuality' of the debtor is a relation of self to self. Of course, the debtor is obliged, and the obligation is 'felt', because the thing pledged represents his person. But the debtor is affected, so to speak, by his own person, by the fracture or exposure of his own person, and not by the overbearing person of the creditor. And although the fracture is made precisely because the token remains with the creditor, the token itself does not manifest the person of the creditor (notice that whereas the *aes nexum* moves from the creditor to the debtor, the token moves in the opposite direction). What impels the debtor to redeem the pledge – and himself – is the urge to reclaim or reintegrate his person.

Ignoring this difference, Mauss attempts to assimilate the pledge and the gift. In his presentation of *wadium*, he suggests that the creditor who retains the pledged token is as much bound as the debtor. The token is like a gauntlet thrown down to the creditor, who receives it as a challenge (here, the analogy is with the Trobriand Islanders who give a gift by throwing it at the feet of their rival or partner with a display of exaggerated modesty).[74] The gift has to be defied, disdained. The honour of the debtor is equally at stake; he 'remains in an inferior position so long as he has not freed himself from his wager-contract [*engagement-pari*]'.[75] It is true that for the duration of the loan the token is in the hands of the creditor, and in that sense the creditor holds the 'person' of the debtor. But the token exerts no obligatory force on the creditor, for whom there is no bond in the thing. More important, there is, as we shall see, no possibility of 'acquitting' oneself in the Melanesian or Polynesian contexts that are described in the ethnographic sections of *The Gift*. First, there is an emergent and renewed 'mixing' of persons and things into specific normative artefacts; and, second, gifting has a dimension of 'totality' that is less evident in the logic of the pledge.

2.4. Reciprocity[76]

In concluding his review of the ethnography of the Kwakiutl and other North American peoples, Mauss offers the following synthesis of the obligation to return:

> If we give and return things, it is because we give ourselves and return 'respects' – or as it is still said, courtesies – to one another. But it is also that in giving we give ourselves, and, if we give ourselves, it is that we owe ourselves – the self and its goods – to others.[77]

---

[74] Mauss 2012, 104.
[75] Mauss 2012, 207.
[76] It is interesting to notice how infrequently this term is used in *The Gift*.
[77] Mauss 2012, 171 [*Si on donne les choses et les rend, c'est parce qu'on se donne et se rend 'des respects' – nous disons encore 'des politesses.' Mais aussi c'est qu'on se donne en donnant, et, si on se donne, c'est qu'on se 'doit' – soi et son bien – aux autres*].

What does it mean to say that 'in giving one gives oneself', or that 'one owes oneself to others'? What is the nature of the obligation, and in what sense does it involve an exchange of both selves and things? Mauss suggests that the reciprocal gifting effects 'a synthesis of contingency and necessity';[78] there is a norm of reciprocity (necessity) but no fixed measure of what constitutes a proper return (contingency). The predicament of the recipient of a gift is that he or she has to judge how, with what, and when to fulfil the obligation to return; this is the strategic dimension of the gift that is so richly developed in the work of Pierre Bourdieu.

To form a sense of what would be an appropriate return one has to anticipate how one's self and one's countergift – 'soi et son bien' – will be perceived by the addressee of the countergift. Self and gift are entangled, in the sense that the qualities and prestige of the thing are modified by the qualities and prestige of the person, and vice versa: 'We understand clearly and logically that in this system of ideas one must return to the other what is in reality a parcel of his nature and substance [une parcelle de sa nature et substance]; for, to accept something from someone is to accept something of his spiritual essence, his soul.'[79] And it is the addressee who will fix that relation, who will judge whether or how the 'personality' invested in their gift is being 'met' by the countergift. So the person making a countergift has to anticipate how the 'entanglement' of the self and the gift (soi et bien) will be perceived and resolved by the addressee, and they have to style themselves in the light of this anticipation. So, for Mauss, the entanglement of person and thing in the form of the gift goes beyond the simple proposition that gifts are imbued with the personality of the giver (and beyond that with the persona of the group or collectivity). Things given and returned do not merely convey personality; they are nexuses in which the attributes of personality and thingness are constituted and exchanged, or constituted through exchange. Donor and recipient switch or exchange perspectives in the sense that they anticipate how their prestation will be seen by the other party; they 'owe' or 'give' themselves in the sense that they stake themselves on this anticipated perception. The recursive form of the exchange of perspectives is also significant for reasons which I shall get to later, but for now the point is that gifting is a process of reciprocal co-constitution in which the fusion or mixing of person and thing is performed within a logic of apprehending oneself being apprehended. This is the specific mode of 'confusion' that is absent from the pledge relation.

The second point is that this work of reciprocal mixing takes place within a much broader frame than the dyadic frame of the pledge relation: 'The circulation of these signs of wealth is unceasing and unfailing. One must not keep them too long, nor must one be too slow or too hard in parting with them; nor must one satisfy someone other than specific partners in a specific direction, the direction of bracelets, or the direction of necklaces.'[80] Trobriand Islands bracelets and

---

[78] Mauss 2012, 72.
[79] Mauss 2012, 82.
[80] Mauss 2012, 108.

necklaces travel in opposite directions, so the 'reciprocity' of the gift relation is an exchange within an exchange. Notice too that 'there is a force [*vertu*] which compels gifts to circulate, to be given, and to be returned'.[81] This intensifies the difficulty of presenting '*soi et son bien*', or of constituting oneself as a worthy recipient, and hence counter-giver.

So why does Mauss insist on the analogy between *nexum* and pledge? One can begin with Mauss' distinction between Roman law 'before it became truly historical',[82] and Roman law as it existed historically; or between 'prehistoric' and 'historical' Roman law:[83]

> The law and morality of the Latins must once have had [the forms of the gift], but they were forgotten when their institutions entered history. For it was the Romans and the Greeks, or perhaps the Semitic peoples of the North and the West, who invented the distinction between personal rights and real rights, who separated sale from gift and exchange, who distinguished moral obligation and contract, and who above all conceived the difference that now exists between rituals, rights, and interests. It was they who, through a true, great, and venerable revolution, overcame an outworn morality and a gift economy that was too uncertain, too ruinous and overly sumptuary, that was burdened with matters concerning persons, that was incompatible with the evolution of the market, commerce, and production, and, fundamentally, at the time, anti-economic.[84]

The legal-historical debate had identified *nexum* as an institution that was essentially archaic, and whose ordering principles were alien to classical Roman law, but the institution was so intriguing to historians because it offered a glimpse of classical law in its raw formative state. From within the archaic, legal-historical speculation retrieved prototypical forms of real and personal right. Mauss adapted this understanding of *nexum* as a specific historical laboratory to his own anthropological purposes. Although *nexum* plainly belongs to his 'prehistoric' phase of Roman law, one could already see in the articulation of its component operations a foreshadowing of the modern form of contractual exchange.

In particular, the 'complementary' exchange of the *aes nexum* between *tradens* and *accipiens* seemed to be at once archaic and modern, or to unite these two dimensions disjunctively, so to speak. In its archaic dimension, the exchange of the *aes nexum* metonymically stood for the richness of a gift economy; the symbolism of the miniature ingot highlighted the fact that, in the complex of ritualised gestures and verbal formulae that composed *nexum*, normative force was an effect of the hybridisation of person and thing. On the other hand, seen from the perspective of the modern division between real rights and personal rights, and given Mauss' insistence on the analogy between the *aes nexum* and a pledge, the

---

[81] Mauss 2012, 153.
[82] Mauss 2012, 175.
[83] Mauss 2012, 187.
[84] Mauss 2012, 187–8.

transaction in which the *aes nexum* was exchanged looked something like a modern contract. The very aspects of the pledge that Mauss had to overlook in order to characterise *wadium* as an expression of the archaic gift economy – the strictly dyadic form of the pledge relation and possibility of redeeming or 'acquitting' oneself – facilitated the resemblance. Thus, *nexum* was foregrounded as the institution in which the analogy between gift exchange and modern contract – and, perhaps, the possibility of recovering what was lost in the 'venerable' revolution of Roman law – appeared most clearly.

2.5. Recursive Anachronism

Schüttpelz's characterisation of *The Gift* as a *lettre persane* written 'from Europe and to Europe' is suggestive.[85] In Montesquieu's eighteenth-century originals, epistolary form fashioned an exchange of perspectives between a fictionalised land and 'home' as construed from this fictionalised counterpart. *The Gift* develops a more complex relation between Europe and its others, in which Mauss shows us the legal-economic form of contract from the perspective of a culture – which one might provisionally call 'the archaic' – that is fictional in a more subtle and disruptive sense. Of course, Mauss took the mass of ethnographic detail compiled in his dossier entirely seriously; ethnographic documents had their own particular flavour,[86] it mattered that they were written by people who lived on the spot,[87] and the method of *The Gift* was inductive in the sense that the 'rule of reason and interest' was elicited from the facts rather than imposed upon them.[88] Nonetheless, Mauss' ethnographies, both his original monographic sources and his synthesis of them, were 'controlled fictions',[89] and these fictions were mobilised in an immanent critique of contemporary European law. This operation of fiction is clearly articulated in recent anthropological scholarship, and my hypothesis is that it was already at work in *The Gift*, and indeed that the technique of fiction is analogous to the 'rule of reason and interest' that Mauss elicited from his archaic societies. The form or sense of the gift is not only the object of the analysis, it is also the method of the analysis.

A recent collection of (largely) anthropological scholarship addresses the theme of 'Comparative relativism. Reflections on an impossibility'.[90] The relation of comparison and relativism is here presented as a paradox: how can one engage in a comparison between self and other if one denies the possibility of a 'ground' for such a comparative exercise? Any comparative analysis has to address (or repress) a fundamental question: what is the meta-perspective from which

---

[85] Schüttpelz 2009.
[86] Mauss 2012, 66.
[87] Mauss 2012, 92, referring to the Dutch anthropologist van Ossenbruggen.
[88] Karsenti 1997, 305–6.
[89] Strathern 1985, 6.
[90] See Jensen 2011.

one can say that 'this is (not) like that'? A particular take on the paradox emerges from an observation made in a classic text by Marilyn Strathern on the theme of nature, culture, and gender:

> In selecting from our own repertoire of overlapping notions certain concepts envisaged in a dichotomous or oppositional relationship (nature vs. culture), we are at best making prior assumptions about the logic of the system under study, and at worst using symbols of our own as though they were signs; as though through them we could read other people's messages, and not just feedback from our own input.[91]

In making comparisons between cultures or between Euro-America and other cultures, anthropologists posited the distinction between nature and culture, and used it to differentiate the 'fields' under consideration. If, for example, we say that people cultivate nature in different ways, we start with nature as a common premise or backdrop, and then differentiate cultures according to the ways that they apprehend, organise, or domesticate this transcultural resource. Differences between ethnographic fields therefore appear as variations on an a priori relation between culture and nature, as different ways of 'acculturing' nature. Hence the notion of 'feedback from our own input'. We can only see what our cognitive schemata – in this case the distinction between nature and culture – allow us to see, and the 'information' that we elicit from the field necessarily returns to us with this 'input' still attached to it as a kind of heuristic felicity condition.

One could indeed reduce this to the problem of relativism: so the paradox is that what we can see and say of others is a function of our own indigenous conceptual frames. But instead of giving in to the movement of infinite regress that this invites – the reflexive movement of trying to take account of one's conceptual frames – it is more interesting to turn the paradox to productive effect. Feedback is input in a transformed or enriched state. In the language of cybernetics, feedback yields both redundancy and variety: the original schema and what it retrieves from the world. What if, instead of trying to fraction variety out from redundancy, or trying to immunise variety from the effects of redundancy, one were to privilege redundancy – 'our own input' – and pay attention to how it 'reappears' against the horizon of variety? What do our own concepts look like when they are returned to us within an ethnographic relation? This may be part of what is implied in the proposition, made with respect to the anthropology of Marilyn Strathern, that the art of the Melanesianist is that of 'redescribing Euro-American concepts from the perspective of "Melanesian" realities'.[92] The point about Melanesia, or 'Melanesian reality', is that it is itself an artefact of the Euro-American conceptual forms that are being 'redescribed'. In other words, we see ourselves being seen from a perspective that is located in a 'field' that we have generated or 'fictionalised' for ourselves. My hypothesis is that the political and epistemic

---

[91] Strathern 1980, 179.
[92] Viveiros de Castro and Goldman 2009.

strategy of *The Gift* articulates just such a relation.[93] And law, and more especially *nexum*, is the 'machine' that articulates this relation through the encounter between the modern form of real rights and personal rights, and the archaic entanglements of person and thing.

As Florence Weber observes, the text of *The Gift* itself has a recursive ('spiral') structure, which recapitulates a particular set of ethnographic data several times over, from the introduction through to the conclusion.[94] In the course of these moves, a phenomenon first identified in Polynesia is then found to be generalised across the span of the Pacific, from the Trobriand Islanders to the Kwakiutl; then, having gained in complexity and extension, the phenomenon is rediscovered in archaic Indo-European societies; finally, this common substrate (Mauss speaks of '*un des rocs humains sur lesquels sont bâties nos sociétés*')[95] is held up against contemporary European law and society. At the risk of overworking the theme of circulation, one might say that this strategy itself reprises the logic of the gift. The ethnographic material circulates and is transformed through a number of encounters, in each of which there is an exchange of perspectives between each of the cultures that compose the archaic and then, 'finally,' at the end and the beginning, between the archaic and contemporary Europe.

The relation to the past that is constructed by *The Gift* is very different from that which structured the legal-historical treatment of *nexum*. For some participants in the historians' debate, *nexum* was intriguing because it was still sufficiently 'of' the present to engage the distinctions and categories of contemporary law. And this effect of intrigue is precisely what made *nexum* so interesting to Mauss. Nonetheless, although not all legal historians assumed the reductive distinction between primitive and modern law that one finds in Maine, they shared his sense that *nexum* manifested a state of 'confusion' that modern law had resolved. And they would certainly not have recognised the move through which Mauss constructed the 'archaic' as a counterpart to contemporary Europe. Mauss collapsed the distinction between 'the societies which immediately preceded us and which still surround us',[96] thereby splicing historical or temporal distance into comparative or spatial distance. There was an obvious 'material' context for this synthesis. Mauss never actually carried out ethnography in the field. One imagines that, in his library, documents describing archaic European contexts quite readily combined with documents relating ethnographies of contemporary 'primitive' societies. Mauss' technique might at some points appear philological, but it is the basis of an original epistemic and political project of making ethnography fungible with history, of accommodating twentieth-century Polynesia and archaic Rome on the same plane.

Mauss had an ethical and methodological aversion to evolutionary understandings of society and to the use of the term 'primitive' to characterise any

---

[93] Karsenti 1997, 308. See also (at 312) the idea of a 'unconscious structural dispositif'.
[94] See Weber 2012.
[95] Mauss 2012, 65–6.
[96] Mauss 2012, 238.

living society; societies currently studied by ethnographers should more properly be called 'archaic', because 'their institutions and social life have aspects that are at least equal in quality to those that were manifested by the societies from which our own societies descended'.[97] And these 'archaic' societies, whether past or present, are not mere precursors to the contemporary but fields with their own inherent sense and dignity. So what then is the relation of modern society to the archaic if it is not evolutionary? Reflecting on the 'unconscious sociology' that informs legal and economic history, which assume 'a priori notions of evolution', Mauss observes that 'the point of departure is elsewhere [*le point de départ est ailleurs*]'.[98] Instead of a linear shift from barter to sale, there is a diversification of gift into barter and different modalities of sale and exchange. Karsenti observes that the method is not evolutionary but 'archaeological', in the sense that it involves a 'subterranean search for a foundation that has been forgotten but which is nonetheless essential for understanding the present'.[99] There is indeed a sense in which the reference to archaeology – and, perhaps, to the notion of a past that is still materially effective in the present[100] – helps to clarify the peculiar anachronism of *The Gift*. The collapse of many temporalities into one, and the indeterminate locations of archaic Roman law, which in some places figures as a system that has 'already collapsed', and in others as a repository of a legality that is still vital, might be explicable in these terms. But if there is an archaeological substrate in *The Gift*, a stratum that can be traced through different periods and locations, then it is produced not simply by uncovering the past but by Mauss' strategy of turning historical distance into comparative distance.

3. CONCLUSION: THE FUTURE OF *NEXUM*

Although violence is omnipresent in the ethnographic record compiled by Mauss, his anthropology of *nexum* rather overlooks the particular violence that is expressed in Magdelain's image of the predator sinking its claws into its prey, or in Esposito's reference to Livy's characterisation of debt as 'an ulcer that, after consuming the debtor's property, penetrates his very body until it too is consumed'.[101] For those seeking resonances or continuities between *nexum* and debt in the contemporary world, Esposito's account of *nexum* as an illustration of a historically persistent '*dispositif* of the person', forged from an amalgam of theological, political, and legal elements, might seem to offer greater critical purchase. For Esposito, the category of the thing (*res corporalis*) 'is not a dimension in opposition to the person, but one of its internal modes';[102] and, because freedom was defined negatively, as the

---

[97] Cited in Karsenti 1997, 308.
[98] Mauss 2012, 133–4.
[99] Karsenti 1997, 309.
[100] See Olivier 2008.
[101] Esposito 2015, 138–9.
[102] Esposito 2015, 92.

condition of not being in servitude, this dimension was also implicitly an 'internal mode' of the free man. The figure of the *nexus* – the free person who submits themselves to servitude – reveals the operation of this *dispositif*. By treating the debtor's body as property of last resort, and by subjecting it to the power of the creditor, *nexum* turned the latent internal mode into the defining condition of the person: '[s]eparated in principle, from the living body, the person was sucked into the body when the latter lost its autonomy'.[103] Although it treats them as elements of a combinatory, Esposito's '*dispositif* of the person' still retrenches the classical Roman law terms of person and thing, granting them sweeping historical agency. Mauss' anthropology of *nexum* points towards a different way of understanding the fabrication of the categories of person, thing, and body.

Noailles suggests that *nexum* was neither contract nor mancipation: '*Nexum* is not a material bond but a legal bond. But this bond does not have the personal quality of an obligation; it creates a relation of dependence or real subjection.'[104] So the bond of *nexum* is created by a unilateral act by which the *nexus* subjects himself to the *potestas* of the creditor. Or rather, given that the *liber nexus* remains a free man, what is subjected or placed in servitude is not the person of the *nexus*, nor even his body, but rather his *operae*, or the products of his labour. Referring to Quintilian's analysis of the condition of the *addictus* as one '*qui servitutem servit*', Noailles suggests that there was in Roman law a genus of which the *nexus* was just one species:

> To the extent that the expression *servitutem servire* is counterposed to *servus esse*, it emphasizes that the services rather than the juridical person are in servitude. The person who believes himself to be a slave and the *addictus* both retain their condition of free men, but their faculties of labour are enslaved. That is exactly the definition Varro gives of the *liber nexus*: '*Liber qui suas operas in servitutem pro pecunia quam debetat, donec solveret.*' The *addictus*, the *nexus*, and the *liber homo bona fides serviens* all belong to the category of those whose *operae*, rather than their person, are in servitude.[105]

Instead of asking whether *nexum* was a contract or a mancipation, or whether the *nexus* was a person or a thing, Noailles directs our attention to *operae* as a legal form or artefact that was 'of' the person or body while being juridically distinguishable from it. The figure of *operae* is interesting because it suggests an interpretation of *nexum* in which person and thing are not the only units of accounting.

The construction of the legal category of *operae* is examined in Yan Thomas' study of contracts of *locatio operarum*. Although Thomas focuses on contracts

---

[103] Esposito 2015, 139.
[104] Noailles, 1940, 233. See also 234: 'The ritual that is performed by the person who creates the *nexum* at the same time as he weighs the *aes* and remits it to the *liber nexus* is a ritual of seizure [*mainmise*] similar to the analogous ritual performed by the recipient in a mancipation. The unilateral declaration which accompanies these gestures is a declaration of power; it is not a contract.'
[105] Noailles 1940, 236. De Zulueta (1913, 143) denies any technical meaning here; the formula *dabat operas* in Varro 'is a conjecture, [and] we have no right to deduce from this phrase a technical *datio* in the sense of a conveyance. The man "rendered his services" that is all.'

belonging to what Mauss called the 'historical' phase of Roman law – the period covered is roughly 100 BCE to 300 CE[106] – the point is that even in this period one finds legal artefacts or transactional forms that are not predicated on a division between person and thing. Because it was so closely associated with the condition of servitude,[107] labour was not generally perceived as a 'thing' that could be abstracted from the body of the slave or *mercenarius* by whom it was rendered. But Thomas shows how in legal thought and practice labour was reified as a distinct commodity.

It was not uncommon for a bequest to divide the ownership of a slave between a bare owner and a usufructuary owner. The usufructuary owner did not own the person or body of the slave; he had a right only to the use (*usus*) or profits (*fructus*) of the slave. If the bequest specified that the usufructuary owner was to enjoy only the use of the slave – perhaps in the form of some personal service (*usus ministerii*) – then the owner had a right only to the slave's labour as such (even if the slave was employed in the production of a commodity which was then sold for a profit). But if the usufructuary owner had a right to the fruits of the slave's labour, then he could hire that labour out under a contract of *locatio operarum*:

> The two alternatives [of *usus* and *fructus*] yielded a categorical distinction between two ways of exploiting labour. The first was a service, the second was a profit. The labour to which the *usuarius* was entitled was indistinguishable from his personal or domestic enjoyment of the slave – a use that excluded any commercial profit. By contrast, the labour to which the *fructuarius* was entitled could be sold in the marketplace for a price. In both cases, the use or the usufruct of the slave, the slave actually worked. But his activity, which in ordinary language would be called his labour, did not have the same significance in law.[108]

A contract for the hire of a usufructuary right necessarily precipitated 'labour', or 'labour time', out from the body or person of the slave as a 'thing' in its own right. First, and by virtue of the distinction between bare ownership and usufructuary ownership, the labour time of the slave had to be construed as something distinct from the person or the body. Although the usufructuary owner necessarily had physical custody of the slave, his ability to control or discipline the slave was limited by the fact that he had ultimately to restore the slave to the bare owner undamaged and undiminished. Second, the subject matter of the contract was labour time: 'a homogenous, divisible, and numerically measurable period of time',[109] and hence a commodity whose price was calculated in terms of time – *temporis merces*.

---

[106] In fact, Thomas observes that there is evidence of such contracts from the Hellenistic period, and that references to contracts of *locatio operarum* would have been intelligible to theatre-goers at the turn of the third and second centuries (Thomas 1999, 8).

[107] 'Labour was so closely identified with the body of the slave, with the body as an object of property, that "mercenaries" who hired out their *operae* appeared to submit themselves to a state of quasi-servitude' (Thomas 1999, 5).

[108] Thomas 1999, 12.

[109] Thomas 1999, 14.

The abstraction of labour from the body in the form of *operae* did not reduce the body (and person) to a thing. The construction of labour as a commodity did not, as the early twentieth-century legal historians assumed, require that the *nexus* or the slave be categorised as either person or thing. Of course, a contract relating to a usufructuary right in a slave was made against the background of a bequest affirming that the slave was property. But Thomas' point is that within this particular transaction labour was apprehended as a *res* in its own right, and not as an element or incident of the body. More broadly, the point is that the techniques that Roman law used to abstract, fabricate, or fictionalise its categories were not controlled by a fundamental division between the real and the personal. Legal artefacts owed their existence to the immanent capacities of legal technique, which construed the personal and the real in their own terms.[110] There is an evident divergence between Thomas' vision of Roman law and Mauss' anthropological project; first, the construction of categories such as *familia* is referable not to a total social idiom such as 'gift', but to the specific articulation of legal language and technique.[111] Second, the division between persons and things does not function in contemporary law in the way that Mauss supposed. But what both approaches have in common is a sense that critical engagement with Roman law has to begin within the medium of specific forms or artefacts; both invite us to rethink the nature of the techniques or operations that constitute and articulate these forms, and each offers a radically different vision of the evolution of contemporary private law. Almost a century on, Mauss' anthropology of *nexum* remains a lively resource for reflection on these fundamental questions.

Works Cited

Audren, F, 2001. 'Paul Huvelin (1873–1924): juriste et durkheimien.' *Revue d'Histoire des Sciences Humaines* 1:117–30.

Besnard, P, 1985. 'Un conflit au sein du groupe durkheimien. La polémique autour de La Foi jurée.' *Revue française de sociologie* 26:247–55.

Crawford, M, 1996. *Roman Statutes*, vol. 2. London: Institute of Classical Studies.

Davy, G, 1917. 'Pourquoi vaut la foi jurée?' *Revue de métaphysique et de morale* 24:327–53.

Dzimira, S, 2007. *Marcel Mauss. Savant et politique*. Paris: La Découverte.

Esposito, R, 2015. *Two. The Machine of Political Theology and the Place of Thought*. Translated by Z Hanafi. New York: Fordham University Press.

Fournier, M, 2007. 'Bouglé, Fauconnet, Davy: trois professeurs chez les durkheimiens.' *Anamnèse* 3:19–39.

Frank, S, 2016. 'The Force in the Thing. Mauss' Nonauthoritarian Sociality in *The Gift*.' *HAU: Journal of Ethnographic Theory* 6:255–77.

---

[110] See Pottage 2014.
[111] See Thomas 1980.

Huvelin, P, 1901. 'Les tablettes magiques et le droit romain.' *Congrès International d'histoire comparée. Annales internationales d'histoire* 4:15–81.
——, 1904, 'Nexum.' In *Dictionnaire des Antiquités grecques et romaines*, edited by C V Daremberg and E Saglio, vol. 4: 77–93. Paris: Hachette.
——, 1907. 'Magie et droit individual.' *L'Année sociologique* 10:1–47.
Gernet, L, 1982. 'Le temps dans les formes archaïques du droit.' In *Droit et institutions en Grèce antique*, 121–56. Paris: Flammarion.
Jensen, C B, 2011. 'Comparative Relativism. Symposium on an Impossibility.' *Common Knowledge* 17:1–163.
Karsenti, B, 1997. *L'homme total. Sociologie, anthropologie et philosophie chez Marcel Mauss*. Paris: Presses Universitaires de France.
Lévy-Bruhl, L, 1944. 'The Act *per aes et libram.*' *Law Quarterly Review* 60:51–62.
Lerouxel, F, 2015. 'Bronze pesé, dette et travail contraint (*nexum*) dans la Rome archaïque (VIe s.–IVe s. avant J.-C.).' In *La main d'œuvre agricole en Méditerranée archaïque. Statuts et dynamiques économiques*, edited by J Zurbach, 109–52. Bordeaux: Ausonius.
Magdelain, A, 1981. 'L'acte per aes et libram et auctoritas.' *Revue Internationale des Droits de l'Antiquité* 28:127–61.
——, 1990a. 'Le Ius archaïque.' In A. Magdelain, *Jus imperium auctoritas. Études de droit romain*, 3–93. Collection de l'École française de Rome 133. Rome: École française de Rome.
——, 1990b. 'L'Acte juridique au cours de l'ancien droit romain.' In A. Magdelain, *Jus imperium auctoritas. Études de droit romain*, 713–52. Collection de l'École française de Rome 133. Rome: École française de Rome.
Maine, H, 1870. *Ancient Law. Its Connection with the Early History of Society, and Its relation to Modern Ideas*. 4th edn. London: John Murray.
Mauss, M, 2012. *Essai sur le don. Forme et raison de l'échange dans les sociétés archaïques*. Paris: Presses Universitaires de France.
Meyer, E A, 2004. *Legitimacy and Law in the Roman World. Tabulae in Roman Belief and Practice*. Cambridge: Cambridge University Press.
Noailles, P, 1940. 'Nexum.' *RHDFE* 39:205–74.
Olivier, L, 2008. *Le sombre abîme du temps. Mémoire et archéologie*. Paris: Seuil.
Pottage, A, 2014. 'Law after Anthropology. Object and Technique in Roman Law.' *Theory, Culture, Society* 31:147–66.
Schüttpelz, E, 2009. 'Gift-gift.' *Trivium*. https://journals.openedition.org/trivium/4873.
Strathern, M, 1980. 'No Nature, No Culture: The Hagen Case.' In *Nature, Culture and Gender*, edited by C MacCormack and M Strathern, 174–22. Cambridge: Cambridge University Press.
——, 1987. 'The Limits of Auto-anthropology.' In *Anthropology at Home*, edited by A Jackson, 59–67. London: Tavistock.
Thomas, Y, 1980. 'Res, chose et patrimoine (Note sur le rapport sujet-objet en droit romain).' *Archives de philosophie du droit* 25:413–26.
——, 1999. 'L'usage et les fruits de l'esclave. Opérations juridiques romaines sur le travail.' *Enquête* 7:203–30.

Tixier, C, 2016. 'La théorie du quasi-contrat social chez Léon Bourgeois. De l'état-association au principe de mutualisation.' *Jus Publicum* 15:1–21.

Viveiros de Castro, E and M Goldman, 2009. 'Slow Motions: Comments on a Few Texts by Marilyn Strathern.' *Cambridge Anthropology* 28:23–42.

Weber, F, 2012. 'Presentation.' In M Mauss, *Essai sur le don. Forme et raison de l'échange dans les sociétés archaïques*, 1–36. 2nd edn. Paris: Presses Universitaires de France.

De Zulueta, F, 1913. 'The Recent Controversy about Nexum.' *Law Quarterly Review* 64:137–53.

Zehnacker, H, 1990. 'Rome: une société archaïque au contact de la monnaie (VIe –IVe siècle).' In *Crise et transformation des sociétés archaïques de l'Italie antique au Ve siècle av. JC. Actes de la table ronde de Rome (19–21 novembre 1987)*, 307–26. Publications de l'École française de Rome 137. Rome: École française de Rome.

Index

addictus, 194
ager Romanus Antiquus, 139–40, 147
Agnone Tablet (Teruentum 34), 13
agrarian laws, 90–1, 142, 146
agriculture, 157–8
Alba, Albans, 80–1
  deportation, and citizenship, 91–2
  recruited to the army, 88–9
ancestor worship, 28, 36, 120
Ancus Marcius, 81, 92
Andromadas, 62, 65
Annalists, 85
anthropology, 114, 165–7, 171, 177
Appius Claudius (*decemvir*), 61, 70
arbitration, 124
arboriculture, 64–5
archaeology
  and *nexum*, 193
  settlement-level, 30–1
archaic societies/gift economies, 190, 193
aristocracy
  and the *comitia tributa*, 148
  see also elites; *gentes*
army, armies, 30, 80, 81–2, 88–9
Augustus, Emperor, 81, 85, 91
Aveia 1, 10–11, 13

Bachofen, Jakob, 160–7
barter, 193

Big Gods, 119–21
Blume, F, 159
Boni, Giacomo, 58
boundary markers, 15
boustrophedon order, 18–19
bronze legal texts
  Greek, 11
  Italy, 10, 12–14, 19–20
bureaucracy, 114
burial exclusion, 35–7, 116–17
burial markers/goods, 13, 29, 32–4, 36, 62
Buxentum 1, 14, 19

Caere, 17, 19
calendar, Romulan, 70–1
Capogrossi Colognesi, Luigi, 78
Capua Tile, 16, 17, 18–19
Carthage, 63, 123
causa liberalis, 70
cavalry centuries, 88–9
censorship, and the *comitia tributa*, 142
census, 66, 84, 87, 135
centuriae/centuriate assembly, 61, 66, 69, 84, 87, 89
Charondas, 65
children, control of, *leges* for, 141
Cicero, 31, 62, 80, 83, 84, 91
  De republica, 85
  eclipse reference, 134
  on regal laws, 138
cippus, 58
  Etruscan, 18
  see also Lapis Niger
Cippus Abellinus (Abella 1), 14

cities *see* urbanisation
citizenship, Roman, 84, 88, 91
civitas, basic institutions, 82–6
cohesion/coercion argument,
    113–16, 121
coins, coinage, 134
Comitia, 68
    comitia centuriata, 142, 148
    comitia curiata see *curiae*
    comitia tributa, 142–8
Comitium, and community, 118
commercium, rules, 123
community, 15, 18
    and the *comitia tributa*, 144
    and the *Pomerium*, 143–4,
        146–7
concordia, 91
concubines, 102–8
consilium, 82
consuls, 58, 70, 84, 142, 144–6
contract, institution of, 171–3
conveyance, 179
Cortona Tablet, 17, 19
Crete, 26, 62
crime, 124
Curia Hostilia, 65
curiae/curiate assembly, 59–61,
    66, 82, 121, 140, 143–4,
    146
    and *leges regiae*, 78
    rules on how to constitute, 69
custom, 2–3, 4, 57–8, 120
    House society, 36–7
    inability to self-reform, 59
    see also oral traditions

debt, debt bondage, 172–3,
    178–94
decemviri, 61, 70, 71, 144, 149
deities, temples to, 118
Dionysius, 68, 70, 80
    on agrarian laws, 90
    on Servius Tullius, 84–5, 138
    see also Lapis Niger

Dionysius of Halicarnassus, 79,
    98–100
Draco, 62, 67
Drogula, Fred, 135, 140
Durkheim, E, 113

economy *see* markets
egalitarianism, 150
elections
    of tribunes, 144
    see also consuls
elites, 49, 114
    and the *comitia tributa*, 146, 148
    curiate constraint on, 121
    and power-sharing, 143
    see also gentes
empire, *imperium*, 142, 144–6
epigraphs and epigraphic analysis,
    30, 31, 47, 104, 133
ethnography, 187, 188–9,
    192–3
Etruria, Etruscan, 65
    commands, 20–1
    Greek influence on commerce, 63
    House society, 29–30
    legal texts, 15–18, 18, 19
    see also Poggio Colla (monument)
etymologies, 9–10, 88, 93, 103, 139,
    181, 186
Euboea, 63
Euro-America, exchange in, 174–5
exchange, form and reason of,
    174–7

familia, 185–6; *see also paterfamilias*
Festus, Pompeius, 101, 103,
    105–6, 107
Fetiales, 80–1
Fiesole, 47–8, 49
fines, 124
Flaccus, Granius, 68, 101, 102–3
foedus, with Alba, 80–1
Forum, 68, 69, 116–17
Forum Boarium, 118–19, 147

funerary monuments, 44; *see also* burial markers/goods; Vicchio stele
funerary texts, 13, 15–16; *see also* burial markers/goods
Fustel de Coulanges, Numa Denis, 36, 166–7

Gabii, 28, 32–4, 37, 117
Gaius (jurist), 1
Gellius, Aulus, 103, 104, 105, 124
gens, 31–2, 33
gentes, 33, 59, 137, 143–4, 147–8
Gibbon, Edward, 1
gift economies, 176–7
giving, reciprocal *see* Mauss, Marcel
González-Ruibal, A, 29
Granius Flaccus, 68, 69, 101
grave goods *see* burial markers/goods
graveyards, ban on, 35–7
Greece, influence on early Rome, 62–4, 65
Greek documents, boustrophedon, 19
Greek language, legal terms, 10
Greek law/lawgivers, 9
  and extension of political rights, 62
  mythical/divine status, 67, 70
Greek practices, 11, 17, 19
group commitment, 120

hairstyles, and the *paelex*, 102–7
Hammurabi, 67
heirlooms, 28, 32
Hermodorus, 61
Hersilia (wife of Romulus), 91
Histonum, 2 and 3, 14
historical writing, 133–4
Hölkeskamp, K-J, 122
Hoplitism, 62
House society model, 4, 26–37, 30
Huschke, 172, 178
Huvelin, Paul, 171, 181–3, 184, 185, 186
hydrography, 118

Iguvine Tables, 12–13, 17–18
imperium see empire
incensis, lex de, 87–8
Indo-European languages, 9–10, 20
infant burials, 32, 35
inheritance, 31–2
inheritance/area diffusion theory, 11
international law/relations, 67, 86
  and religious regulations, 80, 82
Italian documents, boustrophedon, 19
Italic languages, 10, 11–12
ius commercii, 123
ius Papirianum, 97–102

Juno, 102–5, 107–8
Justinian's Digest, 1, 2

Karsenti, B, 193
kings, government under, 2
kings of Rome *see* Regal period
kinship
  familia, 185–6
  House society, 28
  and inheritance, 31–2

labour
  agricultural, 172
  commodification of, 194–6
land, landscape, 163–4
  laws on landed property, 139
  and 'Roman territory', 135, 139
  see also agrarian law
land surveyors, Roman, 158, 159–60
land use, and distribution, 156–8, 164
Lanfranchi, Thibaud, 78–9
language groups, 12–18
Lapis Niger, 12, 18, 19, 58, 118
lapis satricanus, 69
Latin, 10–11, 13, 20–1
Latium, 26, 29, 31–3
Lavinium, 10, 12

legal documents, language and structure of, 19–21
legal systems, evolutionary model of, 5
leges curiatae, 140–1
leges regiae, 77–92
　local, 139
　and the *paelex*, 102–8
leges sacrae, 10–11, 13–14
legislative authority, Rome, 136–48
　the *reges*, 138–48
Lerouxal, F, 172–3
Lévi-Strauss, Claude, 26, 27
lex de incensis, 87–8
lex sacra, 10–11
liber linteus, 16
lictores, 140, 147
literacy, 49, 64, 133–4
Livy (Titus Livius), 31, 70, 77–92, 108, 178
　Ab Urbe Condita, 78–9
　on agrarian laws, 90–1
　and Augustus, 85
　characterisations of kings, 93
　on citizenship, granting of, 91–2
　on the *civitas*' basic institutions, 82–6
　on religious life *leges*, 80–2
　on Romulus, 82–3
　on Servius Tullius, 84–5
loan, contract of see *nexum*
Lucretia, 70

Magdelain, A, 138, 181, 193
magic ritual, 182, 184
magistrates, power of *imperium*, 142, 144–6
Magna Graecia, 62–3
Maine, Henry, 5, 166–7, 176, 178–80, 192
mancipation, 123, 178–9
Mantovani, Dario, 78, 79, 102

Marcus Aurelius, 1
markets, embedded, 115–16, 121; see also *nexum*
marriage, 70, 106, 141; see also *paelex*
matriarchy, 161, 165
Mauss, Marcel, *The Gift*, 171–96
McLennan, John F, 166–7
Melanesia, 177, 187, 191
Mesopotamia, 67, 114, 116
Messapic, 18
military strategies, foot soldiers' political participation, 62
Mitteis, Ludwig, 171, 172, 178
modern law, and primitive law, 192
Momigliano, A, 166–7
Mommsen, T, 138, 165
Murlo, 29–30
myths and symbols, 164

natural law, 112
Navius, Attus, 66, 68, 89
nexum, 171–96
Niebuhr, Barthold Georg, 155–60, 163–4, 172
Noailles, Pierre, 70, 179, 194
Nora stela, Sardinia, 19
Norenzayan, Ara, 119–21
Numa Pompilius, 61, 66, 67, 71, 98–9, 102–3, 133
　edict on spoils, 139
　and the *Fetiales*, 80

oral traditions, 28, 134; see also custom
Oscan, 19
　sacred laws, 11, 13–14
　Tabula Bantina, 12
Osteria dell'Osa, 32–3

paelex, 102–8
pagi, 146
Panzano stele, 47–8

Papirius, Gaius, 98–100
Papirius, Publius, 100
Papirius, Sextus, 68, 69, 78, 99–100
parricidium, 66
paterfamilias, 136, 141, 142, 144, 147
patriarchal society, debate on, 166
patricians, 70, 172–3
Paulus (jurist), 68, 101, 102
Perugia Cippus, 17
philology, 155, 159, 163
Phoenicians, 9, 19, 64
plebeians, 70, 172–3
pledge, and *nexum*, 185, 188–90
Plutarch, 79
Poggio Colla (monument), 41–51
  destruction of, 46, 49
  reuse and display of temple parts, 46–7
  as sanctuary, 41–4
Polanyi, Karl, 115
Polynesia, 187, 192
Pomerium, as a legal division, 140–1, 146
Pomponius, 71, 140
  Enchiridion (Manual), 1, 68, 100
  on the *ius Papirianum*, 98–100
Pospisil, Leopold, 114, 122
pottery, 63, 64, 65
priesthood, 80–1
primitive law, and modern law, 192
property
  and inheritance, 31–2
  right of, 178–9
Proto-Indo-European, 9, 11, 12
provinciae, 135
public construction projects, 60, 65–6, 68–9
public institutions, 58
  custom and rationality of, 59–61
punishment, 124

Rapino Bronze, 13, 20
rationality, 165

reciprocal giving, 187–90
Regal period, 91–2, 138–48
  comitia curiata, 140
  creation of public institutions and legislation, 58–61, 66–9
  expulsion of the kings, 84, 99
  leges regiae, 77–110
regulation, concepts of, 121
religious practices, 119–21
  elite rites and inscriptions, 46–7, 50
  regulation of, 80–2
  see also myths and symbols; sacrifice
Republican Period, Republic
  early organisation of, 60
  House society, 31
res publica, 143
rights
  personal and real, 175–6, 177, 189
  political, 62
rogationes, 143, 146
  rogatio Terentilia of, 462, 144, 146
Roman law, 'origin narratives' of, 3
Roman territory, and Roman law, 139
Rome, Roman
  expansion, 133–4, 149
  identity and culture, 134
  size of, 116
  see also legislative authority, Rome
Romulus, 31, 58, 59–61, 66–7
  creation of cavalry centuries, 88
  laws, 69
  Livy on, 82–3
  use of *concordia*, 91
Roselaar, S T, 123
Ruiz-Gálvez, M, 29
rural tribes, Roman, 145

Sabellian, 12–15
Sabines, 13, 60, 82–3, 87, 91

sacred laws *see leges sacrae*
sacrifice/sacrificial texts, 13–14, 16–17, 102–8
sale
　modalities of, 184–5, 193
　see also nexum
sanctuaries, 41–4, 139
Savigny, 155, 160, 162–3
Schüttpelz, E, 177, 190
Scott, James, 114
secular laws, 70–1
Senate, 60, 68, 69, 141, 142
senators, 66, 83
servitude, 194–5
Servius Tullius, 58, 60–1, 66, 67, 69, 138
　agrarian reform, 90–1
　and the *comitia tributa*, 142
　depicted as ideal sovereign, 84–5, 87–8
　leges regiae, 83–4
　'Servian Constitution', 139
　strengthening of the army, 89
Sicily, 18, 123
signature, 19
slaves, slavery, 10, 172, 178, 180, 194–6
social relations, and markets, 115
South Picene, inscriptions, 15
state(s)
　formation theory, 113–14
　and market practices, 115–16
stone stelae, 10–11, 13–19, 21, 62; *see also* Vicchio stele
Strabo, 139
Sulla, 84

Tabula Bantina (Bantia 1), 14
Tadinum, 13, 19
Tarquinius Priscus (Tarquin the Elder), 58, 60, 69, 83
　Livy depicts as ambitious, 89–90
　opposed by Navius, 66, 68, 89

Tarquinius Superbus (Tarquin the Proud), 66, 68, 83
　leges regiae, 138
　strengthening of the army, 90
　tyrannical tendencies, 100
temples, forum area, 118
theft, law of, 14
title, regulation of, 123
Titus Tatius, 88
tomb markers *see* burial markers/goods
topography, 160
Tortora stela, 14–15, 18
trade, right to, 123
tribal assembly *see comitia tributa*; *tribus*
tribes *see comitia tributa*
tribunician law, 99, 100
tribus, 147–8, 150; *see also comitia tributa*
triumph, institution of, 147
Trobriand Islanders, 177, 187, 188–9
Tullus Hostilius, 58, 80, 85, 88–9, 92, 139
Twelve Tables, 2, 70–1, 124
　Greek influence, 61–2
　and Latium, 31–2
　and *nexum*, 178
Tyrrhenian area/peoples, 64, 65

Umbrian, 11
　rituals and regulations, 12–13
　Tabulae Iguvinae, 12
urbanisation, 25–6, 65, 113–14, 121
　archaeological evidence, 34–5
　and burial exclusion, 35–7

Varro, 107, 183
Veii, 63, 116–17, 119, 133
Velitrae bronze, 13

Verginia, 70
Vestal virgins, 106
Vibo 2, 11, 13–14, 19
Vicchio stele, 42–51
'villas', rise of, 143
voting rights, 84

wadium, 181–2, 186–7, 190
Weber, Max, 113
welfare state, European, 174

women, 14
  and *concordia*, 91
  House society, 29
  maternal line, 31
  matriarchy, 161, 165
  paelex, 102–8
  Poggio Colla, female agency at, 47
  Sabine, 60, 87, 91

Zaleucus, 65

EU representative:
Easy Access System Europe
Mustamäe tee 50, 10621 Tallinn, Estonia
Gpsr.requests@easproject.com

www.ingramcontent.com/pod-product-compliance
Lightning Source LLC
Chambersburg PA
CBHW070355240426
43671CB00013BA/2516